Fay Taylour
Queen of Speedway

Brian Belton

With an Introduction by Reg Fearman

Panther Publishing

Published by Panther Publishing Ltd in 2006

Panther Publishing Ltd
10 Lime Avenue
High Wycombe
Buckinghamshire HP11 1DP
UK

The rights of the author have been asserted in accordance with the Copyright, Designs and Patents Act 1988.

Acknowledgements

What follows would not have been possible without the assistance and interest of Ninette Gray. Reg and Eileen Fearman (cockney Knight and Scouse Angel) started it all and continued to give hard labour and dedication to the cause above and beyond the call of duty. And then there is Rosy, who insisted I complete this book and Christian, who also kept reminding me that I 'should finish it'.

I thank these people for helping make a record of Fay Taylour's deserved place in motorcycle and feminist history.

Illustrations and photographs
Many of the photographs included in this book are of unknown origin and whilst every effort has been made to trace the copyright holders, the passage of time has made this extremely difficult.

ISBN 09547912 4 X

CONTENTS

Dedication

To 'Fearless' Reg Fearman, rider with the West Ham Speedway team and 'East End boy dun good'; Zorro of the Cinders, entrepreneurial hero, loyal, protective and convivial raconteur; Plaistowian Cavalier, Golf Warrior, Duke of Henley, Ace of Diamond Geezer, Field Marshall Promoter, Doyen of the Grape.

A True Gentleman

One of the Last of the Few

Ruthlessly Honourable

Old Guard Dependable

Kind

Resolute last line of defence - Determinedly first into attack.

Uncommon weaver of words, insight, experience, wisdom and wit.

Intrepid adventurer, latter day Drake, who in spite all temptations to belong to other nations, remains an English man. A soul of rare integrity, generosity and implicit dignity.

Immortal, Independent, Irreplaceable, Inimitable, Irrepressible, Inspirational Iconoclastic.

Individual of many incarnations: soldier, husband, father, teacher, philosopher, metal guru, racer, poet, prize fighter, pioneer, businessman, historian, mate.

Famous, Major International Authority of the Track (quoted in various magazines). Giant Spirit of the Speedways; Architect and Creator of the modern manifestation of the 'Jet Age Sport'. Legend in Legendary Times. Brave Hearted. Honest as sure as the longest day. Holder of the past, giver of futures...My Friend.

Brian Belton

February 2006

Forward

This book on Fay Taylour comes about by an almost unbelievable coincidence. As a young boy I used to read much history of speedway racing and, after getting Fay Taylour's autograph at West Ham Speedway in 1947 she captured my interest. In later years I was to learn of her amazing feats of speedway racing, motor cycling and many different disciplines of car racing. Although there were several other lady speedway riders during those early years of 1928 to1932, it was always Fay who captured the headlines. Thousands of words and many articles were written, in many countries, of her exploits around the world, right up to her death in Dorset in 1983 at the age of 75.

Then in 1973 John S. Hoskins, known across the speedway world as Johnnie Hoskins, invited Fay as a guest to the Veteran Speedway Riders' Association Dinner at The Rembrandt in London. Her audience included many old-time and pre-war speedway riders and ere enthralled as she related some of her racing experiences over the years.

Fay was a prolific writer who wrote tens of thousands of words covering her life story. In 1998 when I was doing a little research on Fay Taylour, I wrote to Ian Hoskins (son of the legendary Johnnie Hoskins) at his home in Harare, Zimbabwe asking him for his recollections of Fay. He wrote back to say that only the week before he had had lunch with a group of friends, one of whom had a visitor from England, a lady by the name of Ninette Gray. During the conversation, Ian told her that he had promoted speedway racing in the UK and South Africa, whereupon she replied that she had been left all of Fay Taylour's papers by her mother in her Will as apparently her mother and Fay had been great friends. I contacted Ninette Gray and waded through the many boxes of papers and manuscripts. Finding it all absolutely fascinating, I introduced her to Dr Brian Belton, author of several books on speedway racing, football and London's East End's history. I know that Brian's expertise will bring to life the many thousands of words that Fay wrote during her lifetime but were never published. When I was trawling through the manuscripts, I found it extremely difficult to put them down and I know this book will do the same for you - captivating as it is.

Fay Taylour, born into a privileged family in Southern Ireland
Fay Taylour, the speedway racer
Fay Taylour, the motor cycle racer
Fay Taylour, the midget car racer
Fay Taylour, the Brooklands racer
Fay Taylor, the Endurance car racer
Fay Taylour, the woman

It is all here.

Reg Fearman, January 2006

Former British Speedway Promoters' Association Chairman; England and Great Britain Test Team Manager; England World Team Cup and World Pairs Team Manager; VSRA President 1992 and International Speedway Rider.

Fay Taylour broadsides in spectacular style on her publicity photo.

1. Introduction

Fay Taylour is a part of that 'foreign land' where, as the late L.P. Hartley pointed out 'they do things differently'. Some years ago in Stanley, in the Falkland Islands, when going through a collection of books and magazines on a shelf in the house where I was staying, I found a copy of Speedway News. It was the 26 December, 1946 edition. As I turned the brittle pages my eyes fell on this headline: *Woman Held The Wembley Lap Record!* Written by L.F.G. Anthony named as 'One of the Earliest Speedway Correspondents'. Anthony wrote:

> Physically she was as sound as the average male and in addition she was a highly skilled mechanic. I have seen her dismantle an engine in ten minutes and there was nothing she did not know about them.

The piece went on to tell how Fay had her first ride on the speedway at the age of 24 and that she,

> ...took to the cinders like a duck taking to water. She rode all the tracks, Wembley, West Ham, High Beech, Crystal Palace, etc. and it was not long before she astounded everyone by beating such crack riders of that day as Tiger Stevenson and Harry Whitfield.

I had been an amateur speedway historian for many years by the time I read that article summarising Fay's dirt-track career, and since then I have lectured around the world and written a couple of books about the sport. Throughout that time, I have gathered information about Taylour's life and times, but around five years ago, my good friend Reg Fearman, made a huge haul of Fay's memoirs available to me. This massive collection of letters and her own writing was indeed a treasure trove of memories - the personal musings of a woman who has always been an enigma and a fascination to those of us who have become the holders of the history of speedway. However, it was also a gigantic mish-mash of material that included intended novels, letters written but never sent, sent but never read, autobiographies and film scripts. One of the first items I picked out from one of the several good sized cardboard boxes that held the collection, was a press cutting from the *Speedway Star* (29 October 1955), entitled 'Speedway's Strangest Stories No.2 Queen of the Speedways', in which Graham Payne argued:

> Fay Taylour was a daring young woman who was born to be a speedway star. She had a pair of man sized wrists *(Fay underlined this note and in her distinctive hand, had written: 'I often wished I had when the tracks were bumpy')* strong enough to withstand the violent bucking of a speedway machine. In her brief career, she defeated many male 'aces'.

In January 1929, a young, attractive girl walked down the gangplank from the big white liner and stepped on to Australian soil for the first time. Her auburn hair tossed in the warm sea breeze and her bright Irish eyes scanned the quayside expectantly. In her small case were a few cosmetics, a pair of stout leather gloves, a pair of goggles and a crash helmet! Fay Taylour had arrived.

In the ship's hold was her silver motor bike. She had come to Australia to do battle against the Kingpins of Aussie speedways - and she was the first Briton to go out and ride 'Down Under'. It was just another bit of history she had created, but she cared little for that. To have an oil smudge on her nose and a bucking machine beneath her was her only love.

Like so much of the published material on Fay, this cutting was chocker-block full of patronising palliatives and told me what I already knew, with the exception of Taylour's note. It was these few words that were my original motivation and that started me delving into those boxes for what now feels like a career. The material therein is tinged with great dollops of poetic licence, plagued by a diverse and confused chronology and prone to flights of fantasy, vague attempts at covering personal identities and massive repetition with myriad, often microscopic, variations. In short, this was going to be an enterprise the likes of which I had never faced before – not in the writing of over a dozen books or even in six years of Doctrinal studies.

For all this, Fay Taylour, in terms of her personality and experience, was a hard person to leave alone. Amongst all the millions of words that portrayed her life, she left some tantalising, beautiful, if fleeting insights into her own motivations for the sport of speedway racing. In one moment of such clarity, she wrote:

I raced less gloriously to prove to others that I could do it! And in the proving was the satisfaction of having created something my own way and of being applauded. Racing is an art, and a fight.

Fay was also able to express her understanding of the aesthetics of the dirt-track. The following is one of the most eloquent explanations of the sport's allure and the art of the speedway that I have read (and I've read a lot!):

The art of drawing curves to an advantageous pattern, knowing where to dab in or ease throttle, where to use brakes on a powerslide, how to play a gearbox, and above all how to match your equipment to the surface, for whether the course is fast, slow, loose or slick you are going as fast as possible under given conditions. And because you are on that limit line shooting to win it is also a fight, a fight for mastery. Over that line is no demilitarised zone, if you cross it the others keep shooting.

One of the enduring frustrations of Fay's life was that, in her own words: 'my pioneering and never-equalled efforts are not recorded in the Guinness Book of Records'.

She came to believe that this publication was more concerned to cater for those interested in such statistics as the 'slimmest waist, the largest toe or the champion consumer of hot-dogs'. This sounds a little pompous but one can understand this complaint about her own anonymity from the woman who, during the years when the new sport of speedway was only rivalled as a spectator sport by football, was known as the *Queen of the Speedway*, and the *World's Wonder Lady*. Fay was proud of those epithets, but privately thought of herself as a 'vagabond racer' and a loner. As one reads through her experiences, confusions and complexities, amongst all the obvious glory, and there was a good deal of that, in the end one does see a profound sadness and loneliness that perhaps could only be banished through speed.

As speedway grew other women took to the track, but few were as dedicated as Fay. How good she was is a matter of debate. The question is somewhat perfunctory as what is remarkable about Fay Taylour was not so much her relative ability as a racer, but the fact that, in her time, she actually managed to become a speedway rider and make any kind of mark at all! For all this, it is probably true to say that when she came into the sport she would have been used as a 'bit of a turn', a novelty presence, playing a part on the periphery of the sport. However, she did grow in confidence and skill and by 1930 was certainly a capable competitor, not in the class of the likes of Vic Huxley (Australian Captain and multiple record holder), but better perhaps than her mentor and sometime *beau*, the good amateur racer Lionel Wills.

The difficulty of assessing Fay's ability as a rider is not helped by the fact that much of her racing was undertaken under handicap conditions. In the first instance she would be given substantial starts, mostly measured in a number of seconds (5 seconds being a significant lead in a race of four laps that might be completed in less than 90 seconds). There was no real standardised handicapping system in the early days of speedway. Formulae did exist to take past results and the type of machine a rider brought to a meeting into consideration, but they changed over time in no consistent pattern and there could also be differences between countries, regions, promotions and individual tracks. Circuits were different shapes - it is probably true to say that no two tracks were similar in terms of profile or contour - turns were more, or less tight, straights were long or short. Whilst most tracks had four bends, at least one major Australian track had only three. Circuits had different surfaces, although even with like surfaces there were differences; two tracks might both be covered with cinders but one could be laid to a depth of four inches whilst the other might have barely two inches of coverage. Cinders could also have varying constituencies and the way tracks were prepared and maintained could also cause variations in performance. That some tracks were fast whilst others were slower and that weather conditions could change things round completely, further added to the lottery of handicapping.

While for the most part handicaps were set by officials, the 'informal' views of the promoter might sometimes influence handicaps, as would negotiations between individual riders although these arbitrations would hardly ever be overt or admitted. As a rule of thumb, handicaps were usually calculated to produce an entertaining race. In the first instance this might mean that Fay was little more than a hare for the likes of Ron Johnson, acting as the 'bait' to draw out a fast time, working on the premise that a male rider might up his usual risk taking in the face of the 'humiliation' of being beaten by a woman. However, Taylour developed, taking on and beating fine riders such as Sig Schlam on an equal basis from scratch.

Whilst Taylour was never dismissive of her rivals, male or female, she separated herself from the women in terms of her skill:

> I learned how to broadside properly, I was the only one, the others didn't really slide their bikes round the bends like the men.

John Addison, the Sports Editor of *The People* newspaper just after the Second World War, remembered Fay and the other women racers very well at the outset of speedway racing in England. He recalled:

> Because of the dangers, it was with some concern that I received the news that women were to compete on the cinders…Promoter A.J. Hunting had already banned women from appearing at his International Speedway tracks. He gave his reasons … 'I know of no woman who could start scratch against even an ordinarily good man. And to match her against one of the 12 best men in Britain would be to stage a procession. While I may admit for a moment their skill, yet I cannot convince myself of their strength to wrench a machine round a corner, nor of their robustness to take a spill without incurring a worse shock than a man.'
>
> Soon after that, I saw my first woman speedway rider in action at the Salford track. She was Fay Taylour; and she was good. She won a heat in which Hunting's 'ordinarily good men' were competing and when I talked to her after the racing, she was happy and confident. Fay was an exceptional woman, popular with everybody and well above the average ability of men.

Unlike the world of trials, the sport from which speedway developed, there was no tradition of female participation in this new and very masculine sport. Trials at least had some association with equine pursuits, but the dirt-track, being a contest fought out on the mystical oval, was more akin to the chariot racing of ancient times, and for most, no place for a woman.

For all this in June 1928, in the absence of her then immediate line-manager, Rudge competitions manager Graham Walker who was preoccupied with the Isle of Mann TT, Fay made her way down London with every intention of sampling the novel and attention grabbing dirt-track. Although women were racing at Brooklands, the very pinnacle of British motor sport, the promoters of the new sport were not sympathetic to Fay's ambitions.

In exasperation, she made up her mind to present herself unannounced at the Crystal Palace track in full racing gear, on an open practice night. This was the end to her career as a trialist and the start of an extraordinary infatuation with notoriety and the almost life long pursuit of fame. She swiftly picked up the leg-trailing cornering style that was an essential skill of the sport at that time.

Once more becoming restless Fay looked north, taking up with the legendary Australian promoter Johnnie Hoskins. Towards the end of the season she switched from Rudge to one of the newly introduced, Freddie Dixon designed Douglas machines derived from his TT model. The long, low speedway Duggie looked the part and it suited broadsliding. This bike was probably one of the main factors in the rise of the young sport of speedway.

By the conclusion of a successful season on the Douglas, Fay made the bold decision to follow the Australians back across the sea to challenge them on their own tracks during the winter season. She was the only British speedway rider, male or female, to do so at that time, and the Australian crowds welcomed and adored her because of it.

In Perth, her first port of call, she defeated West Australian champion, Sig Schlam, the man thought to be 'unbeatable' on his home track. In Melbourne, she got the better of local champion, Reg West.

On her return to Britain after her triumphant tour of Australia and New Zealand, in front of a 30,000 Wembley crowd she won the coveted Cinders Trophy for the fastest lap in an international contest, previously held by Ray Tauser of the USA. Perhaps more incredibly at Southampton she finished ahead of the mighty Sprouts Elder, the top American rider renowned for his dramatic performances on the long-wheelbase Duggie.

At the end of the 1929 season Fay again returned to Australia for the winter, and once again excited the appreciative spectators 'down-under'. However, on her return to the Northern Hemisphere the following spring she was shocked to find that women riders had been banished from the speedways of Britain. It was long thought that the ban was not the work of the promoters but had been imposed on the insistence of insurers, fearing media reaction to a woman becoming injured or being killed on the track. However, the story of the ousting of females from the sport of speedway went much deeper than that.

Denied access to the speedways, Fay turned to racing cars, again achieving a high standard of performance, and became one of the few people to find success on both two wheels and four.

During the Second World War Taylour was interned for her pro-German sympathies. She had shown little sign of having any definite political affiliations before the very late 1930s (long after she had ceased to be a participant in motorcycle sport) but her position with regard to what she seemed to understand as the needless British hostility to Germany was something she never denied and refused to recant. However, her position would make life after the War almost unbearable for her as she looked to return to racing.

Against all the odds, she overcame the obstacles once more and was able to re-establish herself in motor-sport. As such, in her life Taylour was both heroine and villain: onlookers find themselves admiring her qualities as well as being repulsed by many of her attitudes and personal weaknesses. For all this, her life was like that lived by any one of us, with light and shade, except that for Fay, the times of radiance were perhaps more dazzling, while the darker moments were probably more profound. That is possibly the key to Taylour's intrigue. In her, we can see the infinite potential of what it is to be human as well as the great frailties to which we are all more or less prone. For many of us, existence is a string of small successes and big mistakes; we do not, as the adage tells us, learn from our mistakes, but have a tendency to make the same mistakes over and over again. Perhaps the greatest moment in our personal growth comes when we admit this – Fay's tragedy might be related to her inability to acknowledge this irony.

This book is concerned with Taylour's motorcycle career (see the Appendix for an overview of her achievements), maybe the most captivating episode in her often-spectacular sporting life, and the start of her relationship with fame. The work provides the reader with the root of her character – the means through which she achieved much. It is based on press reports, the memories of those who knew her and her own letters and memoirs. This cocktail of sources provides the reader with something much more fascinating than the bald facts or Fay's eloquent if ambling prose. It is clear that she encompassed a number of personas in the late 1920s and early 1930s; not least Taylour as an inspirational figure to women, but her life was many faceted and full of incident and poignant lessons. How keen we are to learn from them is a measure of our similarity to Fay, a woman of alacrity, who rode the winds of change as if she were born to it as a purpose. It is easy to judge her and pass on, but she meant more than that. The driven pioneer alters the world; those who wish to be made whole by their need to overcome lead us into new territories, usually at great personal cost. Fay Taylour was one such soul, incomplete and intoxicated with the desire to become whole. Her journey, undertaken at speed, helped by example others to make pathways to become all they might be. Fay Taylour never really got where she wanted to go – speedway took her round and round in circles (tracks, countries, the globe) for the most part, but her passage was never boring and one, in the end, cannot but respect how much she wanted to live.

2. A Taste for Speed

It was a rainy day on 5 March, 1927. Surveying the muddy scene shortly before the start of Camberley Club's renowned Southern Scott scramble, garage owner Carlton Harmon turned to the novice trials rider he had mentored to take part in the event and said "Never mind, there are pushers on the bad hills and it will be fine for the afternoon circuit".

Carlton and his nervous apprentice were at the starting line. The teacher tried to give advice and encouragement to his student, but the neophyte was far too focused to really take-in any of the good advice. She was a member of Reading Motor Club's second team. She turned her head to watch the other riders lining up with her. Marjorie Cottle, Edyth Foley and Louise McLean were the only women looking to battle it out in the atrocious conditions. These three were the English Ladies team that took part in the 1927 International Six Days Trial held in the Lake District.

The International Six Days' Enduro is the oldest motorcycle competition in Europe. Organised by Federation Internationale de Motorcyclisme (FIM) the International Six Days' Trial (the event's original official name) was the biggest event of the motorcycling calendar and attracted a large number of competitors.

The current name, 'Enduro' was adopted in 1981. It was previously known as 'The Six Days Reliability Trial', however the first trial, 'The International Road Trial', was held in, and won by England in 1913. The event was a test of both the riders and machines for reliability and also endurance over six days, covering a distance of about 2500 km with a speed test on the last day. Today the distance must be at least 1200 km and a maximum of 1600 km. The rules of the first years stated that 'the route must consist of roads that are practicable in all weathers for every type of motor-cycle'.

The three English women had lost a mere five marks in the Six Days Trial of 1927 and won the International Silver Vase Trophy; they had dropped fewer marks than the all-male Trophy team. Each of these powerful women would be awarded a Gold Medal in the same event the following year. This being the case, to call this trio tough opponents was something of an understatement. Cottle in particular was a seasoned campaigner. Marjorie (or Marjory) Cottle was one of Britain's best known motorcyclists in the 1920s. She competed regularly in races and reliability trials, and was considered to be amongst the most talented motorcycle riders in the country – male or female. Once, in the mid-1920s, after competing in the Scott Trials, *The Motor Cycle* told its readers how she had successfully finished the grueling course, 'while burly men had given up from sheer exhaustion.'

Cottle won prizes for the best performance by a 'lady rider' in the 1927 and 1928 Scott Trials. In 1928 she would be the only woman to complete the course. In August, 1927, the *News of the World* carried a picture of Cottle, McLean, Foley and two other leading female motorcyclists, Mrs. M. Grenfell (who rode from London to Edinburgh under Auto Cycle Union (ACU) observation using a 1.5hp engine with a petrol consumption of 214mpg) and the appropriately named Mrs. Spokes. The five were described as, 'The British ladies who triumphed in the International Trials' on 20 August (presumably the Six Days' Trial of 1927).

As the downpour continued, the Camberley competitors were flagged-off at half-minute intervals. The course was damp and difficult. The first 24 miles was especially demanding, but the sun was drying the surface all the time and the hills had dried by the second (another 24 miles) stage of the race. The rookie rider passed several competitors as she roared up the awesome-looking 'Red Road' hill. This was followed by another climb nicknamed 'Kilimanjaro' (where her father watched, waited and worried) that offered a climb resembling the side of a house. She appeared to be at one with her bucking machine, taking little notice of the numbers she was passing. She was determined to take 'the Venus' home, the ladies trophy that would be awarded to the best woman on the day. The hills were strewn with spectators and she heard their cheers as she conquered the twin peaks of 'Wild and Woolly' unaided. The crowd were beginning to recognise her and the odd hat she wore; it was a man's cap, with a very large peak bent backwards.

Harmon was waiting at the finish with all the times and positions. After his pupil made it home she stayed close to him until the last competitor was clocked in. As they walked back towards where the motorcycles were parked, the young woman was afraid to ask the question that was tormenting her. However, her trainer's "Well done" was a strong clue to the standard of her performance. Finally, she could contain herself no longer and asked, "Did I win the Ladies Trophy?"

"The Ladies Trophy!?" Harmon smiled broadly, as he told her, "You won it all right. You also won the Men's class cup, and your performance gives us the team prize...you were the only competitor on the first round to climb 'Wild and Woolly' without assistance."

This was the first serious race the youthful rider had competed in and she gloried in the course. Finishing with two firsts, the Venus Cup for Ladies and the Class Cup for 350cc engines, and defeating Marjorie Cottle, probably the best female trials rider around at the time, would have been a fantastic achievement for any competitor, but for a young woman in her early twenties, fresh to a contest of such a high standard, her victories were phenomenal. Fay Taylour's competitive motorcycle career had begun with a bang.

Two months later E.O. Spence (who later became the manager of the legendary Belle Vue Speedway in Manchester) organised a dirt track meeting, staged on a course laid out over an area on Camberley Heath in Surrey, on behalf of the Camberley Motor Cycle Club. The CMCC hoped the event would attract interest in the club and the paying public.

The track was a quarter-mile sandy circuit and the races that made up the meeting were conducted over four laps, with three riders taking part in each race. A large crowd turned up to see the new sport. This event, staged on 7 May 1927, is understood by some as the first dirt-track competition in Britain. However, because the Camberley track was marked out with posts at the end of the straights, had a sand surface and the riders rode turns to the right (so competitors raced in a clockwise direction) it is more widely accepted that the venue for the first British Speedway meeting was at High Beech, next to the Kings Oak Inn in Epping Forest, Essex, on the 19 February, 1928, nearly a full year after the Camberley event.

However, at Camberley Fay defeated all the male competitors except one: she could not better Charles Harman in the 350cc event and had to be content with second place in that contest. Fay had her revenge when she won the Unlimited cc Trophy on her 348cc AJS, beating the men on bigger machines (W.H.C. Shearing - 497 Ariel and G.Beard - 493 Sunbeam).

The 350cc event was a close run thing. Harman (349 O.K.), Fay (348 AJS) and M.Martin (348 Velocette) lined up for the final, which took place after the solo heats had all been completed. Taylour got away fast, but too fast, before the starter's flag fell. Following a successful second attempt to get the final underway, all three contenders nearly touched handlebars at the first corner, which was, at that stage in the meeting, badly cut up. At the end of the first lap Harman was just ahead with the Fay's AJS close on his heels. Both Harman and Taylour were using middle gears for the straights and bottom for the corners, but Martin was relying on bottom gear all the way round and on the second lap went out with his gear-box protesting in its final throes.

The O.K. had gained about 20 yards on Taylour who was making frantic efforts to catch up, but Harman did not intend to lose his lead. Fay's brilliant riding and determined footwork failed to bring her first to the winning post.

In the second semi-final of the Unlimited Cup the two stars, Harman and Fay Taylour met again. Neither was spectacular but each rounded the corners exceptionally quickly and this time Taylour was the faster. She gained a lead right at the start and Harman finished 25 yards behind her.

In the final G. Beard (493 Sunbeam), Fay (348 AJS) and W.H.C. Shearing (497 Ariel) were pitted against each other. Not for the first time that day, Fay arrived at the initial corner in front by a few yards. On the second bend she increased the gap. Then Beard and Shearing just touched handlebars causing Beard to falter momentarily. Shearing drew up to second place, chasing the woman's AJS. However, he did not manage to make up the distance he had lost and finished with a smoking clutch about 20 yards behind the leader. Fay was a winner! From then on she locked on to the idea, the means and purpose of victory. She had found something that touched an internal chord, a challenge that resonated deeply within her very being. This activity scared her, but its rewards and content lit a fire that sent a flame through her consciousness. She felt born to this lust, welded and wedded to the dirt, grease, oil and speed and most of all, finishing at the front of a roaring pack, hogging the light and fame gifted by glory. Fay seemed to be magnified by the racing oval and she relished that intensification of life, and the enlargement of self that it brought.

The King's County Comet

Francis Helen Taylour was born in Birr, King's County (which later became Offaly), Southern Ireland in 1904[1] (although some have claimed she first saw light in 1908) to Helen Allardice and Herbert Fetherstonhaugh Taylour.

The Taylour family, at the time Fay came into the world, lived at Oxmanton Mall, in the centre of Birr, and were well off by the standards of the period. Fay seemed to have very contradictory memories of her initial years. In her own words, 'I was brought up in the sheltered atmosphere of nannies and governesses in the old Ireland' but, 'to the sounds of Ireland fighting for independence'. At one point, when she was home on holiday from college, whilst the family were stationed in East Galway, she played a small role in resisting the 'rebellion' when she 'took charge when we were raided one school holiday, my father, Herbert, being at Dublin Castle at the time'.

Herbert Taylour, the man Fay would always refer to as 'Dordy', was a district inspector in the Royal Irish Constabulary (RIC), Ireland's armed, country-wide, colonial police force. He came from the 'long-settled' Anglo-Irish families of Wolseley and Fetherstonhaugh, the matured seed of Tudor sackings from Elizabethan times and the Cromwellian scourging of Ireland. He had risen to the rank of colonel in the British Army before taking up his position in the RIC. Herbert Taylour's father was the Marquis of Headford, and that Irish Marquis family name being Taylour, this would be the name that Herbert was to inherit. Herbert's father deserted Fay's grandmother, a shocking and scandalous act of a diabolical 'cad' in their class context and the straightened Victorian times, leaving her to bring up young Herbert and his two sisters without a penny. It seems this part of the family history, in the puritan traditions of the British 'respectable society', was hardly ever mentioned in the Taylour household.

Fay's maternal grandmother had married a cousin to Lord Wolseley, Commander-in-Chief British Forces and favourite of Queen Victoria. Fay's mother, Helen Webb[2] had been born in Dresden while her parent's had been holidaying there. Helen Webb was of Scottish and English inheritance. She had spent her early youth in Gibraltar, where her father Randolph Webb was stationed. He was a Surgeon General in the Royal Army Medical Corps, who had served in the Crimean War and been awarded medals for his bravery.

According to Fay, her mother Helen had been the belle of many Castle balls in Dublin after Randolph was transferred to Dublin Castle. She had attended a finishing school in Paris, and along with her two sisters, had been presented at court as a 'debutante'. The 'Webb' girls were an odd trio. One of Helen's sisters was a suffragette who Fay, as a child, was taken to visit in Holloway Gaol. The other was to become a lecturer at Alexandra College in Dublin. The girls had a brother, George, who became a Professor and Fellow at Dublin's Trinity College. His wife, Dr Ella Webb was a much revered character. It was through her mother's family that Fay claimed Lord Riddell of Walton Heath as an uncle (he was married to a cousin of her mother). She was to constantly reiterate this connection with the British aristocracy throughout her career in motor sport.

Fay remembered her mother as appearing to be created out of 'Dresden China…because of her dainty waist and delicacy' and described her father, the young officer Herbert, as something of a flirt, using his upright figure and square shoulders, together with his blue eyes, dark hair and good features, to charm the young women of the Dublin Anglo-Irish community. However, Fay claimed that from the moment he set eyes on his 'Nellie' as he was to call Helen, he knew that she would be his only real love.

This portrait of the early days of her mother and father's relationships is typical of the way in which Fay Taylour projected her background and experience to the world. It has all the trappings of the popular romanticism of 1930s England. Sweetness and light, the pale, genteel woman and the raffish boy-man come together within a social environment underpinned by controlled desire that emerged as establishment decency. It is just one of many aspects of Fay Taylour which show her to have been a very English woman in temperament, accent, attitude, class and genealogy (or as she might put it 'pedigree'). However throughout her life she would claim to be Irish, English or British (and later she would become an American citizen) according to what suited the situation and/or her temperament at any given time.

Taylour's essentially English character is further illustrated by one of her first memories that captured Fay sitting in a pony trap with her governess on the outskirts of an Irish country town. The trap was backed against the high kerb outside a dressmaker's house. The street was on a steep slope and she recalled seeing a small boy flying past the trap in a soap box on wheels. In that time and place such a conveyance was known as a 'boggie car'. From that moment on she claimed that toys on wheels consumed her childhood fascination and she recalled telling Miss Orr, her governess, how she wished she could ride in such a chariot as piloted by the young lad who had caught her imagination that day. But little Fay was quickly informed that such pastimes were for boys and that 'girls are made of sugar and spice and all things nice…' This is the instant that Fay portrayed as the start of her rebellion against her social position and the gender roles ascribed to her. It is the canvas on which she developed an image of herself as a sort of female buccaneer and a person of many differing hues of personality. However, she was of her class and could not help but demonstrate the values and flaws of this background throughout her life. Yes, she was born in Ireland, but of a family 'of the Pale', hailing from and allied to the earliest days of England's primal colonial ravages. Her father was a commander in an occupying force and her mother the child of Empire and the military that held it under the sway of the British aristocracy to which Taylour unashamedly claimed relation. As such Fay was more an 'expat' than a part 'of the old sod'.

Fay spent the first part of her life in various Irish country towns where her father was stationed, moving every few years. Consequently, from her earliest days she was somewhat rootless, having no definite sense of belonging. What was referred to as 'home' (England) amongst the family was a land Fay did not know and she was never in one place long enough to begin to become familiar with any part of Ireland to the extent that she might associate her identity with a place. This instability in terms of location was aggravated by her position in the family. At the age of eight Fay, a shy and reserved little girl, recalled asking why she could not have a new dress like her older sister, Hilda. This question followed her sibling's emergence from the dress-maker's house, pirouetting down the foot path, showing off her new attire. The answer is not recorded but it must have been a bit sharp as all Fay got into was a sulk. She claimed that she too appreciated pretty things, but saw her position as a middle child working against her desires. To Fay it seemed Hilda got the new dresses, and Enid, her younger sister, with her big eyes and turned up nose, got the petting. Fay seemed to see herself as being in an awkward position, finding it hard to develop a role or an identity within the family. She was to always insist that her parents wanted their second child to be a boy. However, there was some help provided when following the incident of Hilda's dress, her governess handed her the reins of the trap, feeling sorry for her 'middle-child' sufferings. Fay was allowed to drive home and from that time on her orchestrated prayers (supplications mediated through and marinated in her family's Anglican affinities) were followed by secret supplications to the deity for a pony of her own.

The day after the visit to the dressmaker, Fay recalled watching her two sisters dancing to entertain the adults in the family drawing-room where her grandfather's medals were laid out on the table. Hilda was wearing her new dress. Fay looked on, feeling certain that she was able to dance just as well as her sisters, but was prevented from taking part by what she thought of as her natural shyness. However, it may have been more to do with her feelings of psychological awkwardness manifesting themselves physically. She was aware that the pretty blonde locks of her sisters grabbed adult attention more than her own straight reddish brown hair. She wanted to be the centre of attention, but claimed even then she knew that she would need to look to her own instincts to take the limelight. What seems clear is that growing up in this atmosphere Fay developed a competitive streak, fed by low-level sibling rivalry for adult attention. However, as those of us who carry this trait may know, it is often born out of feelings of inadequacy. She would never be petite, in fact for most of her life Fay might best be described as 'robust'. Her physical qualities, a sturdy frame and muscular strength would stand her in good stead in her adult years, but in a time when femininity was associated with the diametric opposite of the 'strapping gal' Fay undoubtedly was, her identity confusion was further heightened by her bodily make-up. Despite her protestations, she had not inherited the frame or the feet of a 'dainty dancer'.

It seems that Fay, early on, became acutely aware of what she felt to be her personal inadequacies. This appears to have caused her to magnify the talents of others, thus creating a vicious circle. Gender/class expectations together with identity and role confusion would have both inspired and confirmed this cycle of doubt, probably provoking guilt and the concomitant partner of that sentiment, resentment, in the Taylour's second born.

Fay compensates with a story that depicts her persecution and isolation, but interestingly it also presents her as having the capacity to save herself. She tells of how, unnoticed, she wandered away from the dancing performance to the harness-room where the house groom and gardener, Gallagher, known as 'Gally', was busying himself. She writes of telling him about the boy on the coaster and asking Gally if he could make her such a vehicle. He agreed and out of an old toboggan, salvaged from the attic, produced a customised 'boggie car'. Fay the racer was born, sitting, with an air of nobility, in her newly wrought four wheeled steed at the top of a steep garden path. From this start she created a 'whacky races' scenario that involved her ploughing through her father's prized flower beds at the foot of the slope.

The steward's enquiry took place in her father's study. Fay claimed that he was a believer in firm discipline, but he handed his middle-child nothing more than a stern scolding. According to Fay, she never doubted her father's love and regretted butchering his beloved chrysanthemums, but remorse and a good telling off were not enough to dampen her fledgling appetite for speed. However it did motivate her to become a more skilful pilot. Her next descent was attended by her younger sister Enid, who, having grown intent on becoming a doctor, was hoping to put her medical skills to the test on Fay. "Daddy'll kill you if you ride over his flowers again," Enid warned. Fay told her sister that she intended to "slide round the turn". With little faith in Fay but the enthusiasm of one with a vocation Enid, bandages in hand, started running hopefully to the bottom of the drive. Fay gave herself up to gravity and came hurtling down the incline. Just short of the flowers she threw her conveyance into a skid that brought the coaster to a violent and shuddering standstill. Fay had devised a means of spinning around the wide gritty path at the foot of the slope to avoid the flowers. It was not unlike the technique she would, in years to come, deploy many times when careering round the bends of loose-surfaced race tracks. Enid, yet to get to the foot of the slope, watched the decent as she ran, but in her surprise at the safe landing she fell and Fay was obliged to use Enid's bandages to dress her sister's grazed knees.

This story is one of identity acquisition. Enid, the medical doctor of the future, is depicted by Fay as having all the essential qualities already 'in' her. At the same time Taylour portrays herself as also having a 'natural' drive, seemingly born within her. Hence, for Fay the future is predetermined, it is just a case of personal qualities 'emerging' and we become what we innately are. This gives us potential, but along a definite line of predisposition, corralled by our inherent limitations. For Fay Taylour, one had 'natural' gifts, which might be honed and sharpened by experience, but in the last analysis she saw individuals carrying telling, almost inescapable propensities. However, if you can be 'born' with something you can also be born without it. From Fay's point of view, the lack of qualities in some was as inevitable as their presence in others. (This is confirmed by some of her later writing appertaining to race and gender). This mode of thinking about the self and others was being adopted in all sorts of spheres as Fay moved towards adulthood. It had seductive explanatory power and of course was one of the main-stays of German National Socialism, a political and social system that Taylour would become enamoured with as a young woman.

The following afternoon, Miss Orr witnessed yet another descent, as she was tranquilly picking flowers in the garden. Enid was again waiting in anticipation that her medical services might be necessary. As Fay ascended to the summit Enid called to her, "Bet you this silver sixpence that you can't slide the turn like you did yesterday", producing the coin from her first aid box, she held it aloft, looking like a juvenal hybrid of Nurse Cavell and the Statue of Liberty.

Miss Orr was quick in her response, "Children! You know your mother doesn't allow you to bet".

"Daddy does", Enid retorted, even at her young age knowing her father's 'sporting' predilections, and continued, "Quick, come to the turn and watch Fay".

Enid dragged Miss Orr close to the spot where Fay had made her decisive manoeuvre the day before, yelling, "She slid all the way round yesterday.... now watch!"

As Fay approached at a frightening lick, Miss Orr, could only let out a terrorised shriek as she froze in terror. The governess was pebble-dashed as the boggie car went into a spectacular spin, whilst little Enid squealed in astonishment and delight. Fay had shocked and thrilled her first 'crowd'!

The budding speedster was to also become interested in two wheeled transport. The spokes in wheels of bicycles had fascinated her before she was tall enough to ride her older sister's bicycle. When her mother gave up cycling, having been advised to desist from such exertions because of her 'weak heart', Fay commandeered the 'bone-shaker'. She had several crashes whilst teaching herself to ride, one particularly bad incident occurred when she attempted to 'do a wheelie' while, because of her lack of inches, still having to stand on the pedals. However, after that she became something of an expert at that particular stunt and could be seen racing at breakneck pace, forcing the old nag of a pushbike into a stallion stance.

Her father taught Fay to shoot, fish and ride horses. She became something of a sharpshooter, and took to 'borrowing' the landlord's pony and galloping round the fields without saddle or bridle. But as Fay matured what she saw as her life's dual preoccupations began to form; speed and the 'opposite sex'. The human element of her initial love objects was Billy, one of the young boys who came to the frequent parties at the house in Fay's early childhood years. They would climb trees together and often sit, hand in hand, at the top of her favourite leafy pinnacle, her secret hide-out. When Billy returned to boarding school after the holidays Fay would scale the barky tower once more and up amongst the branches she would write the boy long letters, which she persuaded Bridget, the household cook, to mail.

On a visit home Billy asked Fay to stop coasting down the garden path and come with him to their tree. There he told her that he wanted to marry her one day but that he would not want his wife to be involved in racing of any sort. For the first time, although by no means the last, Fay's future was premised on romanticised experience and the confrontation between expectations that she would take up accepted female roles and her own instincts for adventure and risk.

Hilda and Enid did not share their sister's interest in 'boggie car trials'. Hilda played with gargantuan dolls and their clothes whilst Enid, in the open summer house at the top of the garden, spent more time bandaging her dolls than actually playing with them. At the same time as Fay's driving ability was blooming, her father became mechanized. Although she cried bitterly when the family horse, 'Laddie', was sold, her pleas to steer the car were heard. She quickly became acclimatized to the big Buick that replaced the white horse - her former grief was swiftly consoled. Fay could, from the first days of her family's adoption of motoring, be relied on to accompany her Father when he went driving. She constantly begged to be allowed to drive and when she reached the age of ten, although her relatively gangly legs were barely able to reach the pedals with pointed toes, her father let her park the car in the garage. By the age of twelve she was able to drive with some confidence.

Unfortunately a brick wall was careless enough to collide with the Buick while she was at the wheel and added to Fay's long list of shunts that included many rolls in the potato patch before the coaster had reached the bottom of the garden.

Overall, Fay's portrayal of her life before school depicts her as being something of a 'loose canon' within a kind of semi-aristocratic family environment. However, this might be an idealised picture of events. Her family's relatively transient life-style during her childhood meant that it was unlikely that she would have experienced the kind of domestic continuity suggested by the picture she provides of her first years. At the same time, her father was an officer in a colonial police force during what was for all intents and purposes, a war. The ever present danger of being in the 'front-line' would not have been conducive to 'familial stability'. Any pretence of this was ended when Herbert and Helen sent their girls to Miss Fletcher's boarding school in Fitzwilliam Square, Dublin. Here Fay forgot, for a while at least, about her passion for velocity. But, apparently her taste for adventure and excitement persisted. She described herself as sociable young woman, making friends easily and becoming accomplished at tennis and hockey. Her school days bore some resemblance to those of young heroines lionised in girl's comic books of the time. Taylour's memoirs of her full-time education are punctuated by tales of escapades, midnight feasts and 'japes', such as climbing the hazardous fire escape of the school tower. The consequence of this 'high jinx' involved dealing with punishments like being obliged to take her lunch break in the class room for a term, which, in the best St Trinian's traditions, she foiled as her friends smuggled 'tuck' and 'cookies' to sustain her. She told of how she was a leader in mischief and made life-long friends as she 'pirated' her way through formal education on a seeming tide of jaunts, larks and jolly antics, encoded in the genre-language that those familiar with 'Famous Five' and 'Just William' would immediately recognise.

The single-sex environment also seemed to have an effect on Fay. She recalled how college girls lived in the same boarding house as schoolgirls. No boy friends were permitted. Perhaps as a consequence of dealing with sexual maturation within this somewhat insular community, in many ways cut-off from everyday realities (according to Fay, the shooting outside was less important than school life to her), Fay tells of girls who kissed and held hands, which she scorned as 'mushy'. However, she did develop 'crushes' on teachers and older girls. Although to Fay these seemed all-important, the serious and deep feelings she had were, according to her, too private to permit of anything more than secretly wandering around the cloakroom and putting chocolate bars in coat pockets of those who were the focus of her ardour.

Fay saw herself, contradictorily, as being both shy and brazen, again demonstrating her confusion in terms of her personal identity. However, her lust for speed was not totally erased during her school career. The institutional gymkhana included bicycle races in which she proved to be invincible. In fact she was so accomplished that according to Fay bicycle races were dropped from the programme due to the lack of competition for the Taylour girl.

Changing worlds

In 1919, at the age of fifteen, Fay's education continued at Alexandra College, then situated in Earlsfort Terrace where the Conrad Hotel now stands. Up to relatively recent times, librarian Jean Hazlett kept files of cuttings relating to well known past pupils and Fay Taylour was one of them. She merited a sizeable collection.

At this point, her mother, who had suffered from ill health for some time took a turn for the worse. It seemed to everyone expedient for Fay to take a year-long course in Housecraft in addition to the usual subjects as she completed her education. It was thought that this would be useful as it would allow her to take-on domestic responsibilities in her father's household and perhaps dull her taste for more 'masculine pursuits'.

Independence for Ireland came when Fay was still at college. During the final term of her training, she received a letter from her father, who had retired after the disbandment of the RIC in 1922 and moved to England. It summoned her, on the conclusion of her course to join him at Burghfield Bridge Lodge, the new family home in Berkshire. Her mother had now been diagnosed with cancer of the liver, and was too ill to run the family home. Fay's elder sister Hilda had married a young British officer turned farmer whilst Fay was still at school, and there were plans for Enid, the youngest of the Taylour children, to go to Cheltenham Ladies College and later study medicine at University College London.

During her education, Fay had no thoughts of or ambitions relating to motor sport, she won the college tennis championship and, inspired by her gym mistress, she wanted to train to be a sports teacher, but instead the Housecraft Course dominated her last year in college. Fay was not really interested in the 'disciplines of the home', but she did well in her final examinations in cooking, laundry, sewing and housekeeping, and finished her education on a relatively high note. In her last term at Alexandra, in 1922 she won one of the two scholarships awarded, making her a 'champion housekeeper'! With the scrolls and the honour, she was given a cash prize of fifty pounds for her Post Office Savings Book, a sizable sum in those days.

For Fay her school and college days were all too brief. She was to remember this time as the happiest of her life. Even as a young woman she was a complex character: although living in Ireland, she was a 'daughter of Albion', the offspring of English parents with aristocratic pretensions. The old social order was now eroding as financial power was redistributed, status and position were questioned and formerly taken-for-granted hierarchies of respect dissipated. As the values of Empire retreated, the likes of Herbert Taylour and his family were left teetering on the boundary between the British 19th century lower-upper and 1900s upper-middle class strata.

In many ways, as Fay left college she saw herself still as a sentimental tomboy, who enjoyed 'pranks' and school picnics when she would wander off alone to pick wild flowers for her favourite teacher. She was also an incorrigible romantic and later in life, she often thought that had she been at a coeducational school and college, large parts of her school days might have been spent with a boy like Billy. However, for a girl of that time and of her class origins, within the 'givens' of her social position, such an experience would not have been an option. For all this, Fay's own telling of her life story is filled with repetitions of starry-eyed yet essentially platonic encounters with men. This idealised and sanitised catalougue of sickly sweet interludes is made up of yearning prose, strewn with yarns of male infatuation with Fay's none too obvious charms. Without exception, all the tales reach a climax with Fay having to choose between marital status together with the routines that went with the female 'place' within the society of her time and a vague future promise of uncertain excitements. Almost inevitably the stories end in Fay's loss or casting off of love, letting it fall through her fingers as a diamond into a rushing river of fate. Taking pause between the lines the reader cannot help but think of the breathless writer, 'methinks thou protesteth too much'.

At the age of eighteen, Fay returned to her ancestral and her family's spiritual homeland. She was, by her own description, a sporty and lively young woman and had made a host of good friends. She was more excited than sad as she waved goodbye to her school pals on the pier at Kingston (now Dun Laoghaire) from the rails of the ship that would take her to Britain, carrying the tennis trophy she had won at school. Although she had visited London as a child, in her mind she saw herself living in 'great big wonderful England' for the first time, the centre of the 'civilised' world and the focal point of the shared consciousness of her kith and kin. She looked forward to tennis parties, dances, and an 'all-round wonderful time'. However, what she found in Britain was disillusionment and loneliness in the large country house her family now occupied. With Hilda living the life of a well-off farmer' spouse, Enid at college in Cheltenham and her mother close to death, Fay's fate seemed sealed. Existence at Burghfield Bridge Lodge in the small village of Burghfield in Berkshire, nestled anonymously in the south of England, and without the company of young people of her age and background, was dull and slow in comparison to college life in Dublin.

Fay's mother worried about her future and just before her death, told what she might well have seen as her dangerously unconventional daughter, "you ought to be meeting men". On the death of her mother, Fay's isolation seemed to be complete. Looking at Helen's stunning red hair, which still shone as she lay on her deathbed, life felt particularly empty for Fay. The lifeless woman she stared at had been a beautiful, popular and happy person. She had been a friend of the famous actress Lady Constance Benson, the wife of Sir Frank, whose 'Bensonian Company' (the precursor of the Royal Shakespeare Company) played Shakespeare all over the world, including the Gaiety Theatre in Dublin, where Helen had thrown kisses from the stalls.

At Helen's funeral, with all the grim enthusiasm for mourning that could be churned from what was left of the Victorian predilection for the celebration of death, Lady Benson took time off from her Shakespearian school in London to deliver a sombre elegy over her devotee's grave in Burghfield village churchyard. The recitation had all the melancholic quality of an impassioned dirge that caused the very birds in the trees to sob in lament. Ceremonials of interment tend to provoke feelings about the inconsequential nature of life, but by the conclusion of Lady Benson's dramatic expression of grief, even the most optimistic of souls would have been ready to cast themselves down into the pit with the lowered coffin.

After the funeral, Fay returned to the big house with her father. The only real company she had after her move to England had been the nurses who had attended her mother in the last year of her illness. With the passing of Helen even they had left. Understandably, Fay became restless and unhappy. She needed the company of young people and missed her school friends. She began to envy the family's young housemaid who had a 'beau' and went to the village dances. Although her father received invitations to the local Hunt Balls, Fay was, for the most part, unable to attend without a partner. When she was able to be present at such functions alone, she told how others, 'mocked me as they stood by the mantelpiece'. This may have been an early manifestation of her later tendency towards slight paranoia, but it is probable that she looked out of place, not having the frame of a 'flapper' or the social reference points of maturity. Possibly confirming this discomfort with her own persona, Taylour tells how she was asked to go driving with a group of younger people one evening. She recalled:

> I go with them, but, unlike the other two girls in the party, I do not come home with silk stockings. I don't fit in there either, and never go again. It seems as if the melody and fragrance of life will never be mine.

Her father held tennis parties from time to time, but older people mostly populated these and Fay was still a very young woman, she had no social life and no prospect of any kind of future outside domestication.

The immediate period after her mother's funeral was a drab nightmare for Fay. She recollected that a maiden aunt came to stay at the family home. She draped her niece's large bosom with scarves. Fay had, from her early teens, in her own words 'a well-developed bust', which she saw as 'more mature than her mind'. She recalled feeling ashamed of this, and she understood the incongruity between her physical and emotional self. She recollected:

> I nearly died with shame when a hired hospital nurse discovered it and laughed. I was in bed with measles, and she insisted on washing me. For three years, since then, I'd been trying to hide it, wearing tight flat bodices, and hoping that this might stop it growing. But it grew and grew, and now the aunt's attention embarrasses me. I buy still tighter bodices. It seems so unfair to be inflicted with such an encumbrance.

Breaking out

Fay had driven the family car regularly since she had been in England, but only really enjoying its potential for speed when travelling alone. She joined a hockey club in Reading, the nearest town to her home, making the journey by bus or driving her father's car. She became good enough to play for the county, but quickly found this pursuit did not compensate for the dullness of her life. 'The hockey players' according to Fay, 'were sophisticated county women with husbands and expensive cars; they spoke a language I didn't understand, and hurried away after the game.' Her father was not a good driver although he was a keen sportsman, possessing many cups for shooting, fishing, sailing, golf and other activities. No one in her family had been in the motor trade or interested in cars, but Fay enjoyed the freedom speed gave her.

On one occasion when Fay was using her father's car to drive to hockey, someone had backed into the vehicle (she also, in another version of events claims the car merely broke down) and the Buick had to be taken to the local garage for repair. When the telephone call came to confirm details of the repair it was Fay who went to the garage to monitor progress. It was on her initial visit that she first set on eyes on Fred, the good-looking young mechanic who worked at the garage. After a lengthy conversation in which Fred's passion for all things mechanical became apparent, the pair agreed to meet one evening after work to go for a ride on his motorcycle. In one version of this courtship Taylour tells of how her infatuation with Fred was motivated by his big, throbbing, powerful bike, and the prospect of a tutorial in the riding of the same. However, in another account she claims at first to have had no interest in the bike, being attracted originally by Fred's 'manly charms'. For all this, after her third visit to the garage Fred suggested that she ride his machine.

When Fred had fixed the damaged car and Fay lost her excuse to visit the garage, she found herself wishing that the repair had taken longer. However, she had agreed to him teaching her to control his bike as it would mean seeing him again, but again Taylour provides other reports that cite the lessons as the prime motivator for her liaisons with Fred. Whatever the case, they were soon meeting regularly and twice a week she would tell her father that she was going to the village sewing class, but ride her bicycle franticly for the thirteen miles to the couple's secret meeting place at a cross-roads (it is something of a mystery why Fred could not have met her at least half-way). In her own words, Fay, as yet, did 'not know what she carried below her waist' and 'knew nothing of sex', but she did feel, after a while, that she had become enamoured with Fred having succumbed, 'with all the frustrated pent-up love in her heart'. However, in another version of more or less the same story, Fred's role is taken by 'Bradshaw', a chauffeur called to take her to hospital after a hockey accident. In this account of events she was not allowed to drive her father's car and was seduced by the 'beautiful, big Mercedes Benz' Bradshaw drove (but at least he rode 25 miles on his motorcycle to see her!).

For all this, with romance in her life Fay felt that her existence was once more worthwhile. Different accounts provide contradictory versions of the motorcycle lessons, one has it that they did not materialise, while others portray the lessons and riding with Fred as the start of her passion for two wheeled adventure. Indeed, her feelings for motorcycling and Fred seem to merge into a symbolic unity at points, where even Fay seems to be unable to distinguish between them. But apparently the company, comradeship and conversation Fred offered her was at the root of the love she felt for him. He was older than Fay and was, according to her, always a gentleman, and characteristically of all Taylour's accounts about her associations with men, he respected the innocence of his young love, although she did claim that with Fred she experienced, 'the full awakening and awareness of sex' though she did not recognise it as such at the time.

But the relationship was never to blossom. For Fay it was because Fred saw the great social gap between them that he eventually told her that their meetings had to cease. He had promised to marry a girl in the village. He instructed her to forget him, as she put it, 'before gently placing a farewell kiss' the best of many in one account, the first and last they would have in another, on her lips 'in the moonlight of a late summer's evening'. Apparently as they had finished kissing Fred suggested she should buy a motor bike (which must have killed the moment a bit) in order get away from the lonely house. Fay rode home with swimming eyes, hardly able to see where she was going. She had found a great happiness in her relationship with Fred but she seemed left with little more than practical advice on the therapeutic possibilities of motorised travel and despair.

When Fay got home she felt that her father could sense something was wrong, but could only guess at what the problem was. She believed he worried about what her sadness might be about as he listened to her sobbing herself to sleep, but Fay recognised that he too was lonely. She also understood that it was likely that he wished for a way through the traditional barriers of reserve between fathers and daughters, which her family had inherited from the English upper-classes, to allow him to make the move to comfort his maturing child. As it was, they each suffered their sadness alone.

In an interview that took place in 1980 Fay claimed to have returned to the cross-roads that she and Fred had made their meeting place, on a Tuesday evening, a week after her split with Fred. She waited for 'what seemed like an eternity' before accepting he was not going to turn up. Not wanting to leave and without hope she returned home reluctantly, feeling that she belonged to that isolated cross-roads where, sitting on the wooden gate onto the heath, she had felt she had found everything she had missed, 'just talking to someone who respected the innocence I didn't understand'. The prospect of existence at home without these meetings felt unbearable to her. The ride back was desolate, and she recalled once more crying herself to sleep.

However, in an earlier version of events Taylour tells that the morning after Fred removed himself from her life her distress had remarkably transformed itself into rebellion. According to Fay's reflection on the moment, 'rebellion comes from desperation'. This seeming dramatic change of mood was a trait Fay would exhibit regularly in later years. She had a propensity to move from apparently being distraught to, in a short space of time, a belligerent defiance. She invariably adopted the label of 'rebel', perhaps at some level looking to identify with the nationalist insurgents that her father had been employed to put down in Ireland. To this extent she seemed to be in almost a constant state of pubescent turmoil against the basic values that defined her father's role in the world and the very character of her broader family heritage. Her life was to provide a catalogue of such confused affiliation. Later, she would seem to find no contradiction in supporting the 'German system' before and during the Second World War. She also claimed Irish citizenship and applauded the fruits of the Irish revolution against the Crown, whilst pointing out her 'blood connections' with the English aristocracy as well as asserting herself as a British subject, annexing the rights afforded to British nationals!

In the mist of this particular adolescent storm seemingly brought on by Fred's rejection of her love, Fay decided that she was unable to live out the lot she had drawn in life. Following an uncomfortable breakfast she took her Post Office Savings Book from the roll top desk in her father's study and bicycled to Reading. She returned with her feet planted firmly on the foot-rests of a new motorcycle. This was the prize she awarded herself from the money won for her achievements in housecraft, as a consolation for the loss of Fred. "Buy a modern cooking stove with the money" her teacher had suggested. Well, now she was 'cooking with gas'. Herbert regarded the new purchase with resignation. "I hope you'll get some fun out of it dear" was the best response he could muster.

She had acquired a modest two-stroke Levis motorcycle. The little machine would have been enough to mark Fay out as something of a tearaway at that time. However, her father's acquiescence was transformed to concern three days later when Fay, having found her original purchase somewhat easy to control ('too easy' was her assessment) exchanged her unpretentious bike for a more 'peppy' Levis - a bigger, heavier, and more potent vehicle. But this was also a short lived acquisition and within three months it was replaced by 'something with a bit more guts!' as Taylor put it later - a nifty, second hand, valve-in-head (OHV), 348cc AJS, the same make ridden by the eponymous Fred.

As often seems to be the case with Fay, she supplied an alternative version of events. In an interview with 'Patric' published in *The Motor Cycle* (25 September, 1930) Taylour had said that her first purchase was financed by a nest-egg bestowed on her by a kind grandfather. It seems that the second bike might also have come courtesy of her family connections, as in the same interview she told how she had bombarded

> ... a trustee uncle with news cuttings about the conquests of a famous
> woman trials rider, and wouldn't the uncle be proud if his niece was like

that, and she was sure she could if she had a bigger, better motor cycle...Uncle fell.

For all this, Fay found roaring around the countryside helpful in her efforts to get over Fred. It was certainly more exciting than going to tennis parties with her father, where most of the men were retired majors or colonels, and where the smell of freshly-cut English lawns, the ping of tennis balls against tightly-sprung racquets, and the aroma of china tea from the steaming cups under the beech trees made her sad because she had no one, no Fred, to share it with.

With not much else in her life Taylour found she had the time to explore the works of her new motorbike but, according to her, mostly all she did was to get dirtier than any mechanic. Fay took her machine to a garage in Reading for any major adjustments or repairs.

She had not been riding very long when the repair shop owner and motorcycle enthusiast, Carlton Harmon, who had been watching her motorcycle buying with keen interest, told her that she rode well and suggested that Fay should compete in an important 'scramble' race not too far from where she was living and described the famous Camberley Club's renowned 'Southern Scott Scramble'. This event was organised by the Camberley Club in response to a northern trial with a similar name said to demonstrate the toughness of northern riders. However the northern version became a speed event while the southern version continued to put emphasis upon both time and observation and as such remained a combined test of both rider and machine reliability. In general Trials are a slow speed motorcycle sport but they are none the less a tremendously spectacular sport where rider and machine appear to defy the basic laws of gravity. The range of events is extremely varied in both the level of competency required as well as the length of course, number of competitors and so on.

At that time scrambling was a new sport in Britain, but had grown alongside the development of the post World War One motorcycle market, when machines became available comparatively cheaply. Motorcycle sport, such as hill climbs, grass track racing and cross-country events attracted thousands of enthusiasts, and among them a few women. These females neither asked for, nor were given, any favours. They rode against the best on equal terms and they progressed, according to their skill, with their male opponents.

The Southern Scott was ranked as the supreme event in the minds of rough riders. It was held on Camberley Heath, near Reading, over a circuit of some 24-miles, being covered once in the morning and once in the afternoon. The 'Venus Cup' was the women's competition, alluding to which Harmon told Fay, "You could easily beat the three top women trials riders who compete each year", and he added that crack trials riders and TT racing men from Coventry also competed.

A month before the Camberley event, on a whim, Taylour had competed in a women's race organised by the North London Cycle Club. She had failed to impress, sacrificing her clutch on the final hill climbing contest, having used unnecessary acceleration in her ignorance of technique and tactics. But this was not a concern for Harmon. Indeed, for Harmon when she exhibited her penchant for speed, it indicated something about her character as a rider. Harmon did not see that type of contest as her forte, such competition being about the ability to ride up a hill slowly, and making timed arrivals at given points. He told her,

> "You are a fast rider. You must compete where the fastest up the hills wins; where you go hard all the time, and do not have to bother with watches.' He informed her that 'The three factory women...are professional riders, but except for this event they compete in trials, like the event where you burnt your clutch. They are not racers."

He educated her about the course, explaining that it was contested by the best racers from all the major motorcycle factories in Coventry (then the 'motor-city' of the UK) including their best TT riders.

Fay was taken by his description of the course with its steep, stony hills and other frightening looking surfaces, including awkward sandy stretches and mud. The following day she made a trip to look at the circuit for herself. Taylour felt humbled by what she saw. It did not seem possible that any motorcycle could climb 'Red Road', the first hill she gazed at.

The next Sunday she travelled with Harmon to Camberley and the starting point of the event. It was the cold January of 1927, two months before the race, but the Reading Club members were already practicing. Fay watched them climb the almost perpendicular slopes. It seemed unthinkable that the machines did not fall backwards, but the riders got up the hills and raced across the narrow goat paths and heath land, towards the treacherous sandy stretch. She was relieved to see the riders spread all over 'Red Road' many of them reaching the top, but nearly half the competitors failed to complete the course. As a girl, Fay, hidden in her favourite tree, would read stories of the cowboys and rough riders of the days of the American 'Wild-West'. She was always taken with the thrill and adventure of these tales and as she watched the roaring bikes fight the challenging terrain she saw it as the nearest thing she might get to riding across the landscape as depicted in those books that filled her child's imagination.

Harmon began to tutor Fay in technique. He advised her to stay in middle gear for the steepest hills. "Rush at them" he told her, "The faster you go, the less likely it is that you'll come adrift. And that goes for the sandy stretch as well. We'll try you on a shorter hill first", Harmon said, and he took his pupil to 'Kilimanjaro'. It was shorter, but even steeper than Red Road. "Take it flat out", he instructed, "keep revving and you'll reach the top, but shut off on the crest or you'll fall down the other side". She tried an assault and was pleased to reach the top of the dam face-like crag, but she forgot to shut-off the throttle. Her motorcycle leapt forward and she was sent flying into the heather, part way down the other side of the incline. Luckily she avoided injury.

Harmon took Fay over the rest of the course, and she began to get a realistic grasp of the level of skill and courage needed to conquer it. However, her attraction to the challenge of Camberley was undiminished. Day after day Fay practiced riding the course alone. She managed to overcome most of the problems the circuit had to offer but there was one section that persistently defeated her, the double summit known as 'Wild and Woolly'. She decided that she would endeavour to descend 'Wild' very fast to take the gutter at the bottom at speed in order to reach the top of 'Woolly'. However, the obstacle had been, and would be the bane of many a contestant. On failure it was the tradition for spectators to push riders to the top, but the racer who made the climb unaided would have the edge in terms of speed. Fay filled a rucksack with apples, nuts and chocolate bars and spent a full day fighting Wild and Wooly, determined to overcome its physics.

Persistent rain did not help Fay in her struggle, but the sun eventually broke though the clouds and made the task a little more pleasant. She had given herself a demanding task having to re-mount, descend, and return to her starting point after each failure. An army padre from the nearby military barracks, who had been watching her work from a distance, rode up on his horse whilst she was resting following several failures. He was surprised to find that it was a girl attacking the hill.

"I thought it was a lad trying to kill himself" he told her. Fay explained that she wanted to conquer the double climb, and would if she could build the confidence to make the descent at a greater speed than she had so far achieved.

"If I get down Wild fast enough, I'll reach the top of Woolly" she told him.

The padre smiled and with the patronising tone that often seems to be the specialist province of the church he said, "Pardon me if I say that I think *you* are a little wild and woolly!" At that point he withdrew to a safe distance, wishing her luck (yet another expertise oft practiced in the realms of organised religion).

Fay took several deep breaths before resuming. The sun had improved the ground and she roared down one side and up the other – right to the top. 'More tea vicar?' she smiled to herself.

Official practice day arrived and Jimmy Simpson, who set numerous records on the Isle of Man in the 1920s and 1930s, and George Rowley, another TT ace, both factory riders for AJS, were at the course. The arrows that traditionally marked the circuit for such events were not in place at that point, so spotting a figure on an AJS that seemed familiar with the route the two factory men decided to follow 'him' round. However, the fellow in the peculiar cap proved to be too swift for the AJS chaps. Later, at the local race headquarters, George and Jimmy recognised the enigmatic AJS rider they had tried to shadow (it was the hat that gave it away) and were amazed to find out that the mystery jockey had been a girl.

The practice paid off of course and Fay, to the collective amazement of trials enthusiasts not only claimed the Novice Cup, but also the coveted Venus Trophy. The next day her picture appeared in many of the London Sunday newspapers.

At the Camberley meetings Fay had noticed that one or two of the other women competitors were sponsored, riding for factories (Marjorie Cottle rode for BSA). Inspired by this, she wrote to AJS in Coventry and the company, persuaded by her notable achievement, offered to tune her machine and enter her for trials as a member of their representative team. She turned out for the AJS factory in the National Cotswold and Kickham Cup Trials. The latter involved hill trials wherein speed was not a factor, but Fay gained good marks for climbing the heights without losing balance and the consequent 'footing'. The ascents were muddy and some had deep ruts. Fay was faced with a rough furrowed hill for the first trial. Many professionals decided that it would be next to impossible to climb it without putting a foot on the ground here and there. But Fay saw only one way to make the effort. She charged at it like a shot from a gun. Just when it looked as if her boldness had paid-off she had to drop a foot at the last moment on a bad, slimy, rutted stretch. But she reached the summit and her meteoric clamber was applauded by the many spectators. Later, at the official hotel she was reprimanded and mocked by some of the AJS factory men including Rowley and Simpson. She was told that, "You can't ride like that in a trial. A trial isn't a race. You started the wrong way." Rubin Harveyson, a renown journalist of the sport, was listening and defended the lone woman, "Let her ride her own way" he told them "and in case you've forgotten", turning directly to George, "she got further up that hill before dropping a foot than you or any of the others!"

Fay was to meet Cottle, Foley and another prominent female rider, Eva Askquith, in some of the big hill climbs of the trials circuit, such as the famous Post Hill at Leeds, which has a one-in-one gradient and Dalton Bank at Huddersfield. Meetings at these venues drew crowds of about 8,000 to 15,000 spectators several times a year and the women riders were tremendous attractions. In her relatively short time as part of the scrambling world, Taylour sampled club events, grass-track, sand, and cross country races. She achieved four premier Awards and three fastest times.

One of Taylour's earliest glories was a first-class (special gold) award (ranking next to the various class winners) in the Leeds £200 Trial. Out of a huge field only 47 individual riders managed to finish within the time allowed for the course - just six of the 32 sidecars finished within the time limit. The only woman entrant to finish the trial was Fay. She lost only 219 marks. The media viewed her endurance as remarkable as many of the male riders were exhausted during, and on the completion of the trial. One even had to receive medical attention.

Fay won Gold Medals in the National Alan and Travers Trophy Trials and Silver in the Colmore Cotswold and Victory Trophy Trials (in which there were 218 participants). She took a Bronze Medal place in the Bemrose Trial, the Wood Green M.C.Ladies' Trial and won a Gold Medal in the Auto Cycle Union's Six Days Trial, run over a 750 mile route (ACU Motorcycling GB was the governing body of motorcycle sport throughout Britain). She only lost three marks in that event.

She completed the Demonstration Climb on Hepolite Scar, becoming the only woman to scale the Rodeo course. At the Alms Hill club meeting Fay had been the only rider (man or woman) to successfully ascend the hill. She had only taken part in one other event of speed work, and this was the only event which brought no result, an accident putting a stop to any further racing.

Taylour revelled in competing against England's most famous riders. It was said of her, the more 'sporting' the course the better she liked it and her tactics usually relied on 'opening the taps and hanging on'.

For four months Fay's trials work was a path of glory and she become a prominent figure in the works team as well as in the trials world in general. Taylour had made an indelible mark on motorcycle sport almost from the word go. For all her contradictions and complexities (perhaps because of them) there was no doubting she was a rider of consummate skill with a striking determination and a courageous spirit. She was, by any reckoning, a phenomenon.

1927– both as regards the rider and the gallantry of those who helped Miss Fay Taylour over a nasty piece of road in the " Southern Scott Scramble " at Camberley yesterday.

Fay receiving some assistance at the Southern Scott Scramble at Camberley

3. The Big Bang of Speedway

The height of Fay's love affair with motorbikes coincided with the initial boom in British speedway racing, the daring and ruggedly glamorous motorcycle sport that had already become established in America and Australia. When plans for a new speedway racing promotion in the city of Coventry were mooted in the local newspapers, there was much discussion by the local trials riders. Fay was inspired to such an extent that she spent a weekend attempting to skid her motorcycle round a friend's sand tennis court, using the newspaper pictures of speedway riders as a model for her practice. After wrecking the tennis court she decided it was too small to really get a feel for the technique she needed to perfect, so she entered the pioneering 'oval-race' event at Camberley. Her success and experience there only stoked the fire of her ambition.

Intent on finding out more about the new sport, Fay made her way to London. it was there she experienced her first 'real' live speedway event.

The worker's racing

Speedway can be understood as a product of, or a response to road racing, although even when controlled and administrated by a common governing body a dichotomy is evident. Road racing was largely pioneered in Europe. The first generation of race drivers were, in the main, from the higher echelons of society: they were professionals and/or members of the gentry. The development of the internal combustion engine for transport in Europe took place on a relatively advanced system of roads, so it was logical to use the existing road networks for place-to-place races, and city-to-city contests became extremely popular as the 20th century dawned. This type of competition became firmly established in the mind of the general public as the preserve of amateur gentlemen, the only group that had the time and the money that the sport demanded.

In the early days, France was generally regarded as the home of the motorcar and as such Paris became the starting point for many of the long distance events. Paris to Berlin, Paris to Amsterdam and Paris to Vienna were all among the early road marathons. These contests were often dangerous affairs, and after the terrible events and near carnage of the Paris to Madrid race of 1903, open road racing was effectively abandoned and replaced by closed road circuit competitions. This started the sport on the evolutionary path that has given rise to the contemporary Grand Prix circuit and its association with massive development and staging costs.

Motorcycles have been a feature of organized oval track events for over a hundred years all over the world. There are references (although confirmation as to their authenticity is not available) to forms of motorcycle short-track racing on a circuit with a loose dirt surface, at Pietermaritzburg, Natal in South Africa in the spring of 1907, but, geographically speaking, the sport has three main strands of development.

The American dream

Speedway, as a generic discipline, is a product of the USA. It was there, just after World War I, that the sounds and smells of motorcycle oval racing first hit the atmosphere in any meaningful and consistent way. The expression 'speedway' was first used in the American context in 1902. As early as 1906 motorbikes were racing on the American fairground circuits under the auspices of the Federation of American Motorcyclists. By the early 1920s these events had evolved into racing on huge dirt tracks (thus the term 'dirt-track racing' came into existence) originally laid down for horse racing. Many of the tracks were a mile or even more to the lap, but the majority were half-milers. It was the very size of these circuits that discouraged any attempts to surface them. The spectacle was a big public draw and highly dangerous, with racers using giant 1,000cc machines. These high-powered bikes needed superb riders, and the Americans certainly rose to the occasion. These bulky hulks, with 'vertical' handlebars and massive power plants, did not allow for any measure of controlled broadsiding. The technique of cornering was to roll around the bend, with a little throttle and the wheels in line, similar to the road-racing style.

There was very keen competition between manufacturers such as the Harley-Davidson, Excelsior, Indian, Peerless and Cleveland companies. These and other producers retained professional riders to regularly race on the improvised, loose surfaced tracks, which, despite precautions such as the spraying of light oil or calcium chloride on the surface, threw up great, voluminous clouds of dust. This, together with dangerous fences, inevitably caused numerous fatalities that eventually obliged organizers to limit competition machines to 500cc.

The introduction of smaller capacity motors permitted a more spectacular method of cornering. It was called the 'pendulum skid', a kind of powerslide, which came to be known as broadsiding. This enabled a rider to negotiate a 180-degree turn on a powerful machine in a controlled skid in which the rear of the bike swung out - like a pendulum - and then back into line as the turn was completed.

The credit for the innovation of broadsiding in 1922, has been given to a man by the name of Maldwyn Jones, an Excelsior and Harley-Davidson rider. Jones was a well-known racer and racing motorcycle builder of the first third of the Twentieth Century. During the first decade of the 1900s, Jones was perhaps the best dirt track racer in the Midwestern America. During 1922 other 500cc aces had mastered the new style too. One of these was Eddie Brinck, who was an AMA Class A racing champion of the 1920s. Brink won AMA national titles in 1925 and again in 1927 riding a Harley-Davidson. He was killed while racing at Springfield in August 1927. In spite of this within a couple of years the smaller engine machines (500cc) were being raced everywhere in the United States, and broadsiding was recognized as the swiftest way of rounding the dirt-track bends. It would become the basic art of speedway racing.

Towards the end of 1925, 350cc racing machines made their debut on the Milwaukee dirt-track, including the Harley-Davidson and Indian 350cc road models modified for racing purposes. These events caused a great sensation. In the Harley range, the 21 cubic-inch 'Peashooters' as they were named, averaged over 69mph in five-mile races. They were just two seconds slower than the famous 500cc.

Advance Australia fair

An early form of motorcycle track racing in Australia dates back to 1909, around a quarter-mile slightly banked asphalt track at Maitland, in the Hunter River Valley, New South Wales. That track was closed in 1917, however, the same year grass track racing was held at the nearby Newcastle Show Ground. During 1918 Sydney based and interstate riders turned up to do battle with the locals on the one mile race-course at Wallsend, New South Wales.

For all this, while the development of dirt-track technology and style was going on in the USA, it was in rural New South Wales, back in the Hunter River Valley under floodlights at West Maitland Agricultural Showground on the 15 December, 1923 that the first incarnation of modern short-track, solo motorcycle racing, shortly to become accepted as speedway, took place. The person behind the event was a New Zealander, one John S. Hoskins, better known as 'Johnnie'. This restless and energetic man was to become the acknowledged father of speedway and his life story charts the sport's history. It was Hoskins who organised the *West Maitland 'Electric Light Carnival'* that took place that evening, celebrating the then recent installation of electricity in West Maitland. He decided to add interest to the event by including short-track motorcycle racing on a ¼ mile dirt surface. Few rules would encumber the adventurous spirit and ingenious spontaneity of speedway's first contestants, although riders were instructed that they could not put their foot down to help their stripped down road machines round corners. Australians always called their dirt-tracking 'speedway'. The title was not officially adopted in Britain until 1930, although because of the number of Aussie riders on the scene before that year the informal epithet was widely used.

The success of that Maitland meeting led Hoskins to conclude that he could make what started out as something of a gimmick, into a new and exciting form of racing. More meetings were organised at West Maitland, and it came to be recognized as the birthplace of speedway with Hoskins acting as its midwife. It is probably more realistic to see speedway as the product of the frontier context that demanded the use of durable, simple, rough and ready forms of light transport for everyday use as well as the sport of motorcycle racing.

As the sport reached out across New South Wales to Newcastle and more importantly, Sydney, the organization of events became more stylish and sophisticated. The Australian riders of the time, including the now-legendary figures of Vic Huxley, Billy Lamont[3], and Frank Arthur, were reinforced by some American pioneers notably the gigantic (in height as well as talent) Lloyd 'Sprouts' Elder.[4]

Speedway's origins are therefore set in the working culture of the US and Australia a far cry from the origins of road racing. Speedway, like other forms of oval tracking, is essentially the product of the 'new world', rural areas colonized by Britain and other European powers. North America and Australia were as enthusiastic as Europe about automotive competition, but their circumstances were very different. They were countries built on a continental scale. At the start of the 20th Century, their road networks were at best sketchy. Those highways that did exist were often little more than rutted tracks, unsuited to the type of racing that developed in Europe. Land, however, was not in short supply and not, as say in Britain, mainly in the hands of a landed aristocracy or gentry. Early enthusiasts in America and Australia found it a simple matter to mark out basic dirt courses on which anyone who wished could race. Motor races were very often associated with carnivals and local fairs, and most fairgrounds had show rings or dirt horse racing ovals. Car and bike racing on these tracks was a natural development and became tremendously popular. Thus motor sport was centred on a modest local circuit that was contested by riders who honed their skills within the transport requirements of the rural and agricultural work environment.

The geographical character of the frontier countries placed ordinary workers at the forefront of motor sport to a much greater extent than their European counterparts, but the nature of the social hierarchy also had an impact. The entrepreneur, not the landed gentry, topped the social strata. This social group was more focused on the development of business than the sporting pursuits associated with the European 'leisured classes'.

One result of all this is that Speedway has often been associated with rowdy fairground activity and projected as a slightly seedy, down market pastime. Historically it has often been considered to be rather less than respectable by sections of the motorcycle racing establishment. This was not helped in the British context by the establishment of tracks in greyhound racing arenas, that themselves had a less than savoury reputation (although this was more a product of class snobbery than anything else). However, this has meant that speedway has never lost its working class roots: more than any other sport, perhaps it has remained true to itself.

The British experience

If America was the mind of speedway and Australia the soul, Britain has been where the body of the sport was established and where it found a home. There are reports of a form of speedway racing being held in England at Portman Road football ground, Ipswich, in 1904. But it was only when the news of the new Australian daredevil sport filtered through the veins of Empire, that England (in particular) started to become the seed bed of speedway in Europe. Just how the sport arrived in Britain remains a controversial question. The Speedway Control Board had it that a license was granted by the Auto-Cycle Union (ACU) for the meeting at Camberley Heath in Surrey on 7 May, 1927 (the local club claimed credit for many new events, including scrambles and even football on motorcycles). They staged the event subsequently described in *Motor Cycling* as 'the first British Dirt Track Meeting'. However, as the day's races were run the 'wrong way round' on a track of loose sand, it would appear to have had more of a resemblance to modern grass-track racing than speedway. There was even a race with pillion passengers!

Northern followers claim the first British speedway meeting took place at Dodds Farm, Droylsden, near Manchester, on 25 June, 1927. This meeting, organised by the enterprising South Manchester Motor Club, took place on a 550-yard cinder trotting track (trotting is a form of horse racing). It is said that the riders raced in a clockwise direction and that the meeting bore little resemblance to a modern speedway meeting.

High Beech

Speedway is generally understood to have its British roots in the East London/West Essex area when a race meeting was organized at the King's Oak track (an abandoned running/cycle track) at High Beach in Epping Forest, Essex on 19 February, 1928. The track was situated behind the Kings Oak Public House, which still stands in its original location to this day. A Conservation Centre has been built on the approximate site of the track, but the visitor can still walk round what remains of the dirt mound from where spectators watched that first speedway racing in Britain. Of all the dirt-track type events that took place in the 1920s, the Kings Oak contest came closest to the look and feel of what was to become modern speedway.

Jack Hill-Bailey, the Secretary of the Ilford Motor Cycle Club was the person behind this historic meeting, however the Kings Oak track was by no means his first choice of venue. In 1928 the newly opened Custom House Stadium, the edifice that was to become the home of West Ham Speedway, was initially chosen to stage the event. However, the stadium (like the venues of most speedway competitions during the history of the sport in Britain) was built primarily for greyhound racing and the owners of the arena were loath to open their new stadium with anything other than a greyhound meeting. This somewhat defensive attitude prevented the impressive stadium from providing an inspiring stage for the first ever speedway meeting in Britain.

Hill-Bailey, in talks with Lionel Wills and Keith MacKay[5], had also attempted to stage races at Parsloes Park, a half-mile trotting track near his home, in Barking, Essex, about five miles east of Custom House. He was not able to pull this off, however if this idea had been successful High Beech would never have gained its distinction as the birthplace of speedway in Britain, but then neither would Parsloes Park as the track would have been too long!

So, Hill-Bailey moved on to his third choice. Initially he had planned an open permit event at High Beech for 9 November, 1927 but the ACU would not grant permission for racing on a Sunday. A long list of entrants were disappointed, to the extent that many would-be competitors were ready to go ahead and stage a meeting in defiance of authority. Eventually Hill-Bailey, working with the Colchester Motor Cycle Club, obtained a permit from the ACU for the meeting, which was issued to the Ilford Motorcycle Club. The inaugural High Beech meeting became the first to be staged after the new ACU sub-committee responsible for licensing tracks had come into being. The application list was opened once more, and the response was immediate. First-rate riders from far and near applied to take part.

Hill-Bailey was expecting about 3,000 spectators to turn up, so 2,000 tickets and 500 programmes had been printed. When he arrived at 8am, a crowd of 2,000 had already gathered in front of the Kings Oak. Hill-Bailey was amazed, given that there were still two-and-a-half hours to go before the start of the day's racing.

The crowds kept coming. With an hour to go, all the tickets had been sold, as had the last of the programmes. The cash booth had been swept aside and eager spectators were pouring in, some equipped with pliers and metal cutters to be used to breach the barbed wire surrounding the arena. It became clear that the collection of further admission fees was unrealistic. With thirty-minutes left before the event was due to start 15,000 people surrounded the track and thousands more were streaming along the lanes approaching the Kings Oak track. Every police station within a radius of ten miles was alerted for reinforcements as the crowds jammed the roads out of East London.

Hill-Bailey had considered that the event would be of little interest outside London's East End and West Essex, but his expectations with regard to the number of potential spectators turned out to be an underestimate in the order of a 1,000 percent! More than 30,000 people turned up to watch the day's proceedings. It is surprising that the expectation of attendance was so low. Just five years earlier West Ham United, a football club nicknamed 'The Hammers' with its root support in the East London/West Essex area, had attracted close to a quarter-of-a-million spectators to the initial Wembley Cup Final and the Hammers first FA Cup Final appearance against Bolton Wanderers (the White Horse Final).

The ACU had insisted that all spectators should be confined behind a rope barrier on the inside of the track, but such was the crush that the rule was unenforceable with spectators swarming around the inside and outside of the track.

The initial races were described as 'hell on wheels'. Many competitors were trials riders and considered it unethical to allow their feet to touch the ground. Several Australian riders, including Billy Galloway and Keith MacKay, were present at High Beech that day and might be regarded as the vanguard of the invasion that was to come. They demonstrated the art of leg-trailing or broadsiding, by then the accepted form of cornering in Australia. For some reason Hill-Bailey had not advertised their appearance, had he done so the crowd may well have reached 60,000. One of the British riders at this historic meeting was Phil Bishop[6] who was to become a bit of a legend in speedway.

The morning following the High Beech meeting The Daily Mirror, which became one of the most consistent sponsors of speedway, covered the very first British speedway contest. Pictures of the action and the crowd were accompanied by a report that included the following:

> Dirt-track motorcycle racing, the sport popular in Australia, where it rivals greyhound racing, was seen in England for the first time yesterday at Kings Oak Speedway, High Beech near Loughton. The size of the crowd was a surprise.

The event pushed *Bluebird* and Sir Malcolm Campbell's (at the time Captain Campbell) new world land speed record of 206.596mph into second place on the front page.

The results of the races at High Beech were:

Event 1: Novice (5 laps):

1st	Fred Ralph	(344 Coventry-Eagle)	Time: 2min. 20s.
2nd	Ivor Creek[7]	(490 Norton)	
3rd	H.M.Smyth	(493 Sunbeam)	

Event 2: Solo (5 laps):

1st	Alf Foulds	(493 Sunbeam)	Time: 2min. 2s.
2nd	Billy Galloway	(494 Douglas).	

Event 3: Sidecars (5 laps):

C.M.Harley	(488 Zenith sc.).	Time: 2min. 29s.

Event 4: Novices (3 laps):

1st	Ivor Creek	(490 Norton)	Time: 1min. 25s.
2nd	Alan Day	(493 Sunbeam)	
3rd	G.Fletcher	(557 Ariel).	

Event 5: Solo (3 laps):
1st   Reg Pointer[8]   (497 Ariel)   Time: 1min. 17s.
2nd   A.Duce   (343 Sunbeam)
3rd   P.R.Bradbrook   (344 Coventry-Eagle).

Event 6: Sidecars (3 laps):
1st   Arthur Noterman (498 Triumph sc.)Time: 1min. 23.2s
2nd   Alf Foulds   (493 Sunbeam sc.)
3rd   H.Lock   (498 AJS sc.).

Event 7: cancelled owing to lack of time.

Event 8: Fastest Lap from Standing Start:
Solos
1st   W.Medcalf   (348 Douglas)   Time: 26.8s
2nd   A.Foulds   (493 Sunbeam),   27s
3rd   F.R.Pointer   (497 Ariel)   27.2s.

Sidecars
1st   A.Noterman   (498 Sunbeam sc) Time   30s
2nd   L.J.Pellat   (344 O.K.Supreme sc.)   30.6s
3rd   A.Foulds   (493 Sunbeam sc.)   31.6s

Also at High Beech that day was Jack Parker on behalf of manufactures BSA. Both he and his brother Norman were 'works' supported trials riders, Jack for BSA, Norman for 'New Hudson'. Jack had won the Colmore Cup in 1928 on a BSA and also represented Great Britain in the International Six Day Trial. Within weeks of Kings Oak both Jack and Norman commenced speedway careers that would last over twenty years and would see them form one of the most formidable partnerships ever fielded in an England team.

The High Beech track continued for some years after its first event. The 1929 High Beech Champion was Jack Barnett who, not long after this meeting won the Golden Gauntlet at West Ham, beating Sprouts Elder and Roger Frogley in the Final, despite being last on the first lap.

Frogley had made his Speedway debut in June 1928 at High Beech. He rode a 1927 Rudge-Whitworth 500 and straight away thrilled the large crowds who attended that venue. Frogley moved to the Crystal Palace and came into prominence early in 1928, when riding at Stamford Bridge where some marvellous performances enabled him to win many prestigious handicap and trophy races. Frogley was one of the finest English riders of the pre-1930 era and was the top scoring rider for England (with six points) in the first England v Australia Test Match at Plough Lane in 1930.

The early days of dirt-track riding were dominated by a number of riders that started at High Beech including Ron Howes, who started out at Wimbledon as a mechanic and later worked with Vic Huxley before taking up riding. One of his most treasured possessions was a set of leathers that once were worn by the great Vic Huxley. Ron was to move to West Ham and then to Rayleigh when the Weir Stadium opened.

Speedway crowds were large! This photo was taken at Odsal Stadium some years later.

The Aussie Invasion

Following the massive popularity of the High Beech event, there were moves to establish speedway in the British context. Crowds of 15,000 had been attracted to 'path racing', racing along a narrow tortuous circuit at Crystal Palace as early as 1927, so there was a clear niche for a new form of motorcycle sport - one that could be easily viewed by mass audiences in venues convenient to major centres of population.

In 1928 it was feared that the greyhound racing boom of 1927, another recent import from the USA had burnt itself out. Greyhound promoters were therefore keenly interested in the rent which speedway could provide. Thus it can be understood that in the latter part of the 1920s the time was ripe for the introduction of speedway racing in Britain, but it needed racers who could pull in the crowds and provide models for the development of British riders.

Almost from the start of speedway in the UK, Australian riders graced the tracks. This influx was facilitated by two Australian companies. International Speedways headed by A.J. Hunting and another headed by Johnnie Hoskins, organized the transportation of parties of Australian and American riders to establish speedway as a commercial venture in Britain. The champion riders brought a new persona to popular sport and their demonstrations of this novel and exciting racing drew spectators in their tens of thousands.

This is illustrated by the following extracts from a letter written in Britain by Johnnie Hoskins to his Australian colleagues in July1928.

> Charlie Datson, Sig Schlam and Ron Johnson are doing well. They are still racing at the Crystal Palace, London. Charlie has a wonderful motor and last Saturday he put up what was described as a 'most lurid ride.' He holds the track record: in fact, I think it is the fastest time yet recorded on a small track here. He is quite an idol. Sig was in a scratch race last week and he was going so slowly round a corner that he fell off and his opponent passed him with one lap to go. Sig jumped on again and you know he goes when anyone is in front. He simply flew down the straight and just passed his man at the gun. The crowd of 20,000 went crazy. Ron has been having a lot of trouble with chains, but is riding wonderfully well. There were about 70,000 people at the Palace at a big sports gathering and Ron gave a wonderful exhibition of cinder throwing. The crowd gave him a great hearing. The boys are at present in Brighton among the local lads waiting for the opening of our first track on June 23. As all of the tracks were held up pending my arrival we have been slow getting under way, but it is all for the best as we are profiting by the advertising and the mistakes of those earlier in the field.
>
> By the way, Ron Johnson raced Miss Fay Taylour last Saturday night at the Palace. The racing starts at 7 o'clock and finishes at nine in the day light. Ron's motor 'packed up' and he rode Lionel Wills's Rudge. He gave her three-quarters of a lap start and gained about 50 yards in the four laps. Miss Taylour is not only the greatest woman motor-cyclist in England, she is one of the greatest motor-cyclists. She broadsided round the corners and was winning easily when, through being over-cautious at the last bend, fell off, turned a couple of somersaults, jumped up, grappled with the motor and with the help of Charlie Datson jumped on again and rode in over the line to the cheering of twenty thousand people.
>
> The exhibition was very fine. Charlie holds the track record and went out in an endeavour to break it but missed by one second. Sig gave an exhibition of painting the fence with cinders and thrilled the crowd with the best show I have seen him put up yet. Some of the English riders have come

along wonderfully well, and though they are not yet, in my opinion, up to the Australians, they are not far from it: in fact, we have to keep the motors in the very best condition to stand them off. On other tracks English riders have been beating Australians in some events. No doubt the English motors are good and now that the T.T. is over we expect the manufacturers to put something specially good under our boys.

I went to the Isle of Man to see the T.T. races and the excursion trains were absolutely packed. Over 12,000 people went over on Thursday night and stayed till Friday night as I did. The Isle of Man is one of the prettiest places I have seen. We had to walk four miles away up into the hills before we could get a sight of the course. Every vantage point at the different corners was crowded with people. I am glad of this as we finally found ourselves well up in the hills with a good view of Caution Corner and a couple of other bends. Gradually, just as we heard the big boom of the starting rocket, the fog began to come down the mountain, and before half a dozen riders had passed our corner, the fog was so thick that it was impossible to see more than the width of the street. I believe the fog was even thicker higher up, and yet the riders drove through the fog at 60 miles per hour. You could hear the roaring of some speedy machine, sometimes two or three almost together. Gradually it would come closer and closer and still nothing was visible through the fog. Then a ghostlike apparition would emerge and in the twinkling of an eye it would be abreast and one had just time to see the numbers when it was lost in the fog again. There were 15 spills in the first lap.

I was hoping that we had some West Australian representatives over again. The course is such a difficult one that a first year man has practically no chance against the old hands who know the course so well. I was pleased to hear the old hands speak so well of the boys who came over last year. Aubrey Melrose came in for quite a lot of praise and they still remembered some of his tall stories about the West. Dirt track racing seemed to be almost as much talked about on the train as the T.T. races but there was nothing but motors talked all the way there and back again.

As a spectacle, however, I must say that at the risk of being thought prejudiced, the T.T. is not in it with the dirt tracks. Of course, one realises that he is watching the world's great motorcycling classic, one knows something of the trade importance of a win in this great event, one feels with all those fine fellows who have spent months of preparation for this one event, and this all helps to make the visit worth while.

What was called the 'Australian Invasion' started in the spring of 1928. Johnnie Hoskins (then the managing director of W.A. Speedways Ltd) led his men aboard the Oronsay on Tuesday night, 10 April. These men were understood to be Perth's leading dirt track riders. Hoskins was under contract with the Crystal Palace Co. to appear on 12 May (the opening meeting at Crystal Palace was originally scheduled for that date, but the first meeting at that track actually took place a week later). There was no guarantee of anything beyond this, only the possibility of further contracts if all went well. The riders were to be paid appearance money. On the night they would compete in match races to the value of £100, and have the possibility of winning other prizes. Hoskins was to act as adviser to the promoters.

A letter from Hoskins arrived in Perth on 1 May 1928 from Colombo during the Oronsay's stopover. It told of how the dirt-track party were in good spirits and that in all there were 13 riders on board including Sig Schlam, Ron Johnson, Charlie Datson and Spencer Stratton. Nine men from Queensland included Vic Huxley, Frank Arthur and Frank C Pearce[9]. Charlie Spinks, Hilary Buchanan[10], Ben Unwin[11] and Noel Johnson[12] were also part of the team. Of these Huxley and 'Wizard' Frank Arthur[13] would become perhaps become the most famous and influential of the early dirt-track migrants. Whilst in the tropics Hoskins had worked out regular exercise routines for his charges, starting at 6am and then again at 4pm. Later, the exercise was doubled.

By the spring of 1928 there were twenty applications before the Auto Cycle Union for permission to open tracks. The representatives of greyhound racing felt uneasy about the ACU's wish to keep the sport free of betting but had no qualms about the insistence on the provision of safe tracks. The eagerness to establish the sport was probably a direct result of the first High Beech meeting in 1928. Hoskins was offered the management of the 10 or 12 greyhound tracks controlled by the largest combine in Britain.

This was the start of the enduring link between speedway and greyhound racing (a representative of the National Greyhound Racing Association was on the board of International Speedways).

Most speedway meetings were held at greyhound tracks, with the rest at tracks being situated where other sports were played. Only a tiny number of speedway stadia were purpose-built before 1939 and none of these could be regarded as among the major venues of the sport. Nine of the ten tracks of the speedway National League in 1933 also staged dog racing. Without the availability of greyhound stadia there may well have been no speedway.

The oval dirt tracks that would stage this new sport fitted into the huge greyhound stadiums well. The circuits were loose-surfaced, about a quarter of a mile long, with two straights and sweeping curves at each end, but no standard measurement or shape, so some turns were much sharper than others while straights also varied in terms of length.

In the first instance, speedway was an individual sport, team racing would follow, but in those initial years riders competed against each other in scratch events. Right from the start the sport produced frequent crashes and the occasional death. But the crowds were as likely to cheer for the rider who picked himself, or in the case of Fay Taylour herself, up from the track or waved from the first-aid stretcher as they were for a winning racer. There was a great appreciation for the skill, bravery and sportsmanship of the competitors.

All the tracks had practice days and English riders new to the game spent these sessions nerving themselves to plunge into the bends without 'cutting' (shutting off the engine). Even if they got their wheels angled into the professional broadside, many did not have the experience to hold the slide all the way round. The technique had to be perfected by degree and much 'biting the dirt' would have to be endured. Professional American and Australian riders were paid fantastic sums in 'appearance money', sometimes for just a few exhibition laps. But the racing was the spectacle that attracted the watching thousands. Often the professional riders took the curves with such abandon that it would seem impossible that they could prevent themselves from ploughing into the retaining fence. Many, like Australian Billy Lamont, rode with what seemed like utter recklessness, but riders of his ilk and apparent wildness were great favourites with the crowds.

Speedway held all the hope and optimism of the mechanized age. Its prospect was as exciting as its enactment and this was perhaps the kernel of its appeal to the likes of Fay Taylour.

The legacy

Although Australia was the birthplace of the sport, after the huge success of speedway meetings in England in the 1930's and 1940's, Britain was to become the place where short, oval, loose-surfaced track motorbike racing grew to international status.

The appeal of speedway is that it really is about racing. When spectators paid their money at the turnstiles they got to see all the action, not just a fleeting glimpse of competitors as they flashed past a particular vantage point. The concept and experience might be basic, but its immediacy and raw excitement was hard to match. That is what made it such an attraction and why, over the years, millions flocked to their local tracks week after week. Although the sport has, in many ways been very fragmented, speedway people the whole world over have much in common. They are united in their love of the race, the romance of speed and the thrill and power that the combination of human, machine and an oval cinder track brings into being.

Speedway has trod a difficult if exciting path over its seventy or so years. Like most minority sports, it has always had to fight for survival. It has had the advantage of being reasonably well organised under the auspices of a single international sanctioning body, but it seems likely that in the future the sport will have to survive the same trials and tribulations that have plagued it since its first days in the frontier environments of Australia and America.

The oval of alacrity

Every night of the week somewhere in Britain, the high, covered stands were packed, often with crowds in excess of fifty thousand, to view the new 'gladiators of speed'. They thrilled the spectators with their power and daring and with the audacious but graceful skidding turns they made as each corner of the track was reached at full throttle.

A huge, buzzing crowd encircled the floodlit oval, a quarter mile band of dirt lit up in the night time city-scape, a true theatre of speed. The tension grew as the time ticked towards the first race. At the pit gate, the dark knights adorned in leather sat astride their revving chargers, shrouded in exhaust smoke. Last adjustments to helmets and gauntlets were made, as much to placate nerves as anything else. Then the signal for a push start.

The bikes circled cautiously towards the starting line. The floodlights flickered across the riders' race jackets as they crossed the line. Engines snarled in response, propelling the metal steeds into a hail of dirt and shale created by the madly spinning rear wheels.

The thundering monsters hurtled into the initial bend; the bikes leant horrendously sideways into almost surreal broadsides. The helmeted pilots were involved in a fight to hold the mechanical hurricanes, but there was not a thought for giving quarter. Wheels were forced in to a wavering approximation of a line as the contestants hammered into the back straight. Four laps eaten at an average speed of over forty miles an hour. The war to outrace and out-think was compressed into something little more than 90 seconds by the chequered flag. The smallest slice of a second could make a rider a Champion or a loser, a somebody or a has-been. Every individual in the crowd had filled their eyes with the brief, uncomplicated, all-action spectacle which seemed to ignite reality into the fantastic, metallic metaphor that was speedway.

Of bikes and men

The Speedway machines of the early era of the sport did not look so very different from those that were ridden half a century later. They were different, of course, but the changes that were made were subtle, taking place over many years and gradually incorporating modern technology. They were more adaptations of the original model to changing tracks rather than radical innovations. The men that built them didn't change much either.

In the late 1920s and early 1930s, the most exciting years in the history of speedway, there was no such thing as a production speedway motorcycle in Britain. Riders followed the Australian pattern of stripping down and modifying their ordinary road machines for dirt-track meetings. But it soon became plain that specialised machinery was necessary for such a specific type of racing. Initially Norton, BSA., and Velocette started offering 'speedway models'. Although there was some weight reduction achieved by precluding fittings such as chain-cases and mudguards, these machines were road bikes with some modifications. For example, they had no brakes. In fact, a bike with brakes violated the rules of the speedway. It was imperative to take away the temptation to 'put the anchors on' and so prevent the kind of incident that could take place if four riders were charging into a bend at break-neck speed and suddenly the leading rider applied the brakes.

By the end of 1928, seventeen well-known manufacturers were displaying speedway machinery at the London Motorcycle Show. At first the Harley 'Peashooter' proved the most popular bike, but already several leading Australian riders had adopted modified Douglas machines. Douglas were the first concern to set about making a pure speedway motorcycle, and despite the efforts of well-known names such as AJS, BSA, Cotton, New Imperial, Scott, and Triumph, their creation was selected by most of the star speedway riders. This horizontal twin-cylinder bike is still held in great affection by those who rode it or saw it raced, although it lasted only a short time as a top machine. It was supplanted by the Rudge, but this bike too, was destined for a short career.

As the speedway motorcycle evolved the gearbox was maintained, but intermediate gear pinions were removed resulting in the option of only one gear. The countershaft, as it was known, carried a sprocket, which, like the engine sprocket and rear wheel sprocket was made so that it could be changed either between races or between meetings. Most riders did not change the countershaft sprocket in order to get a different gear ratio; they usually changed either the rear wheel sprocket or the engine sprocket. They changed gears because the larger tracks needed higher gears to allow the bike to move faster. Smaller tracks required lower gears in order that the bike could accelerate more quickly. The gear ratio was sometimes changed between races in order to suit the track surface better. In broad principle it can be said that a deep or heavy surface needed a lower gearing than a 'slick' or fine surface. Since the track covering might change according to weather conditions, a rider, even on their 'home' track, did not always know what to expect and could sometimes arrive at a meeting with the incorrect gear ratio fitted to their machine.

The riders identified the gear ratio by a number, and this number was calculated by finding out the number of times the engine revolved to give one revolution of the rear wheel. Thus a 'low' gear would be say 9.1 and a high gear would be for example 8.0. This means that the engine revolved 9.1 times to turn the rear wheel once in the case of the 'low' gear, but only 8 times in the case of the 'high' gear. The lower the number of times the engine revolved to get one turn of the rear wheel, the higher the gearing. To save time in calculations, each rider had a chart[14] showing them which sprockets were needed to get the desired gearing. At West Ham for example, a fairly big track, a rider would have fitted about 8.1 or 8.2, whilst at Oxford, a much smaller oval, he would have fitted about 8.8.

The application of larger diameter wheel rims also became a significant feature of the speedway bike. A larger wheel gave a greater 'arc of contact' - a longer strip of tyre tread in contact with the ground. This provided a more efficient drive on the loose surface of the speedway track which, in the early days could have been covered to a depth of four inches with cinders. The wheel sizes, 23 inch diameter for the front wheel and 22 inch at the rear, became standard for the first quarter of a century of speedway bikes. One of the leading tyre manufacturers began to provide specialty tyres, a narrow section front of 2.75 inches, with widely spaced and taller longitudinal tread blocks. This gave a quite 'spikey' effect that helped the wheel maintain the direction in which its rider steered it. A unique tread of 3.25 inches in width was developed for the rear tire. This had 'bands' of deep tread across the tyre and narrow longitudinal cuts. However, these bands of tread were not at right angles to the plane of the tire, they ran across at an oblique angle. This caused the tread strips in contact with the track to be square to the direction of the front wheel (direction of travel) improving the driving force on the bends when the machine

Two early photos of speedway action, probably late 1930s or early '40's

was cornering in a broadside. Many grass track riders also used these tires, but in the days when right-hand bends were also to be found on grass tracks, the angled tread strips were in the wrong direction for cornering to the right, and the most expert broadsiders were restricted to relatively low speeds on right-hand bends.

The size of the speedway bike's fuel tank became much smaller than other machines, as racing for just four laps only requires about half a gallon of fuel. An undersized tank holding less fuel of course makes the speedway bike relatively light. The speedway motorbike used methanol, or as the riders called it 'dope' which does not have the carbon content of petrol, and provides a 'cleaner' atmosphere for spectators. Methanol is mainly composed of alcohol and some other chemicals. It is faster burning and so cleaner, but it is only suitable for engines with a very high compression ratio, like the engine of a speedway motorcycle. The bikes used vegetable rather than mineral oils. All the oil that went into the engine of a speedway motorcycle was fed out of the crankcases on to the track in a 'total loss' system. On a road machine the oil is circulated round the engine and back to the oil tank for re-use. As a result the speedway motorcycle engine had clean oil running through it all the time.

The emphasis on reducing weight has always been a major consideration in the design history of the dirt-track machine. From the earliest days there was a quest to make the bike more compact and the frame tubing consequentially became smaller as new and stronger alloys became available.

4. Love's Labours

On her return to Burghfield Bridge Lodge, Fay found that her family home had been put up for sale. Within a month she and her father were living in a riverside hotel and her housekeeping role was over. Having become romantically involved with someone he met at the hotel, her father had made plans to travel abroad for a while. Fay therefore needed to find a new life, although she had more or less made up her mind about what she might do next. With the heady thrill of motorcycle sport still bouncing round her mind Fay rented a room in Coventry, the centre of trials country.

By the late summer of 1927 Taylour was making a living from prize money but felt she needed a steadier income and so travelled around the Midlands looking for work. Rudge Whitworth Ltd, one of the leading motorcycle manufacturers of the time gave her a secretarial position, but she did not always focus on her designated duties. She was to recall:

> ...I'm afraid I was often in overalls in the competition shop – Geoffrey Butcher *(the competitions manager at Rudge)* would periodically come and chase me back to the advertisement department where I belonged.

Clearly the secretarial work did not last long. Following the 1927 Olympia Show in London, Fay claimed she was elected, 'purely on merit alone' to ride as a member of the official Rudge trials team alongside Peter Blamire and Jack Amott, the latter was a former Rudge racer and a brilliant mathematician, but also an outspoken individual. Taylour may well a have been drafted into the Rudge squad on the basis of her talents, but the company would almost certainly have seen some promotional merit in using a female rider.

Sometime later, on a visit to the Rudge Whitworth factory in Coventry, Fay found a new, fast 500cc Rudge waiting for her. This was a more powerful machine than she had become accustomed to, and with this she went on to win the special Ladies' award in the London/Gloucester/London Trial in the winter. On Maidens Grove, the most difficult hill, the Rudge performed particularly well. However, the cup and gold medal did not compensate for her failure to gain top marks in the special acceleration test. Fay blamed the compression plate which had been introduced to lower the compression, for costing her the number one spot in that test. The plate made the bike easier to handle in muddy conditions but the male factory riders who tuned the bikes before the trials did not fit the plate to their machines. Their inaction with regard to Fay's bike was clearly a response to her gender and they must have thought that the plate would not effect her overall placing.

Taylour rode her motorcycle back to her lodgings as usual the night before the next trial. It had been tuned, prepared, and filled with petrol ready for an early start as she had to ride the 20 miles to Birmingham the next morning which meant a 7am rise. Before taking to her bed, she slowly and methodically dismantled the bike's engine and removed the compression plate. It was 3am before she finally slept and consequently arrived at the trial late thus incurring a fifty point penalty.

The hills were muddy and difficult. The 'colonial' section that riders had to traverse without allowing their feet to touch the ground was deep in mud, so balance had to be almost perfectly maintained throughout the ascent. Fay's fellow factory riders lost marks for 'footing', but she managed the climb smoothly and got through all the marked sections clean. Indeed, she would have won the event had she not had to carry the initial penalty for lateness. She had defeated her fellow competitors in terms of her riding ability and took the silver medal alongside her factory colleagues. After the trial Fay replaced the compression plate.

Winning and losing

As her career progressed, Taylour nagged her employers to enter her for speed events but they were adamantly against the idea. The Rudge company insisted that Fay's riding be confined to trials. For all this, she loved competition and often took surreptitious trips to events such as the grass-track meetings at Watford and small club races 'off her own bat' as she put it. On one of these excursions she met a 'handsome engineer' called Robert, who was completing his training in Coventry. According to Fay, she had always treated the efforts that the factory riders made to charm her with a sense of humour, adopting the role of 'one of the boys' even if she was the only woman on the weekly group expeditions. Before each trial she accompanied the men on practice runs round the circuits. Sometimes hundreds of miles from Rudge's Coventry base, she stayed in the same hotels as her team-mates, and although she claimed that on occasions she was obliged to push one of them out of her bedroom, she insisted that she never became intimate with the riders she toured with. However, Fay did see Robert a few times and went so far as to spend a weekend with him at his home in Scotland. Fay made the trip with her bike in the back of Robert's car, as she intended to race a few days later in Manchester, although not for the factory. Robert also had a motorcycle and they rode through the forests together. Taylour brings this romantic picture to a crescendo with Robert proposing marriage. However, she claimed that she evaded a direct answer and slipped out of the house at night, mounted her bike and headed toward Manchester for the next day's race, leaving a note that told Robert she would not return.

According to Fay, on reading the note the next morning Robert decided he would make the near 400 mile trip to see his beau ride. However, because he had little more than five hours in which to make the journey he scorned the use of his car, choosing to make an extended dash on his multi-cylinder motorcycle.

Completing this film-script like scenario, Fay, having satisfied her desire for competition by not only riding but winning the event, decided that she needed to go back to Robert. She did not wait to receive her prize before beginning the return trek to Scotland and reached the small village near to Robert's home close to exhaustion. Here, bizarrely, she decided to check into a guest house to wash and collect herself. However, on telephoning Robert's home at 11pm she was told (by who remains a mystery) that Robert left on his bike before breakfast, and that no one knew where he had gone, or when he would be back. Fay stayed in the village for two days trying to contact Robert without success. She then returned to Coventry to find a message marked 'urgent' awaiting her. It was a request for her to go to Warwick Hospital where Robert was being treated following an accident. He had arrived at the track where Fay had raced just after she left and had immediately made for Coventry. But having gone without food and sleep, seemingly sustained by his passion alone, he was in no condition for another long ride. Consequently he had crashed just short of his destination.

Friends, in what was to become a tradition, told Fay that she was a fool to have turned down Robert's proposal of marriage. He was a member of one of the wealthiest families in Britain and with his training completed, he was not likely to return to Coventry after he left hospital.

It appears that Fay had little time for regrets. She seemed determined to push-forward with her life, and she gave the impression that she was driven to pack in as much as she could in as little time as possible. She rarely seems to have given herself time to draw breath, nor did she make a habit of pausing to consider her actions. Fay rode her intentions like a run-away steed and dealt with what happened when it happened. It was an almost childlike way of managing her existence: she seemed to be always making up for something lost, or desperately looking for a means to make sense of her position.

The following illustrates Fay's attitudes to relationships. In her writing, Fay recalled her schooldays and picking flowers for someone she was in love with, although the person was never to be given the flowers as Fay was too shy to demonstrate her admiration in this way. There are indications that this was a same sex attraction, as she makes the point that there was no male presence during her school years and that it was usual for her peers to develop 'crushes' for older pupils and teachers, to the point of developing some relatively innocent, physical intimacy between themselves. This schoolgirl episode is not too dissimilar to her love for Fred, the garage mechanic, in that this too, for her, was not reciprocated. At the height of her relationship with Fred, Fay makes the observation: 'The urge to love refuses to be governed by the fact there's no one to love.' The desire for love and adoration, from individuals and the wider world, is tangible throughout Fay's recollections. She describes how while on the bus taking her to collect her father's car from the garage, passing through 'the little village where Mother was buried' she thinks of Fred who will be waiting at the end of her trip:

> Of his tawny hair, his good looking face, oh so good looking...suddenly something hits me in the back...It happens again as I'm driving home, re-living the hour just spent in the little garage. An hour of innocent conversation with Fred. But sixty minutes of heaven... "it must be lonely for you in that big house" he said. And I'd told him it was. But it isn't anymore!...those kicks in the back, the knocking on the spine, indicate that something new is entering my life...Sex for me, is still a word in the dictionary that follows the adjective male or female. I'm not curious. I'm not yet interested to probe the whys and wherefores of thoughts and feelings. I accept these spinal kicks for what they are, reaction to my thoughts of Fred. I would not want to know that this new sensation is anything but part of the pure and spiritual pattern that I want to kiss him, to be close, to touch him.

This story starts with a reminder of her deceased mother. Fay never felt she got the love she deserved from her mother, at least to the degree her sisters seemed to enjoy. Fay looked to her motorcycling platonic companionship with Fred to make up for this deficit and gradually that relationship becomes eroticised. However, again, the love is not returned, or the love she gets from Fred is not enough and eventually is lost. Motorcycling sublimates everything else; she becomes a devotee of racing and this passion quickly boils into something almost akin to a religion. But her account of events seems nearly always to portray her as steering very close to the boundaries of her own and others mortality. At the same time she sacrifices even the love she needs from others at the alter of her deity - the motorcycle - and she becomes a martyr to her infatuation for speed.

Unrequited love might be relatively hollow, but it has its rewards. Although the 'lover' may be intoxicated by the 'other', the indifference of the latter makes them a 'pillion passenger' in the situation. The lover is the one making the running and is therefore at least partially in control of the one who is unresponsive. The lover may be filled with a heady mix of emotions - hope, expectation and disappointment amongst others, but these imaginings, born of hope, are directed only by herself. Not unlike racing astride a roaring motorbike, an infatuated person struggles to guide the one-sided relationship; plotting a course, planning and anticipating the 'winning post'. Howver the relationship will never do exactly what is required or give the needed love (but they knew that from the start). From a particular perspective, the person doing the loving is involved in quite a selfish 'affair'. Relatively few chances have to be taken and comparatively little control is relinquished. When all hope is finally lost, there is the payoff of devastation that is heightened by such statements as '...and he married another', which seem to be made in a way that suggests disloyalty or even infidelity. For Fay at least, the energy this generates acts as a propellant to move on to the next relationship. In the years from 1927 to 1930 motorcycles carried Fay from point to point, on a personal circuit of infatuation, rejection and repeated infatuation.

Alongside this propensity to apparently seek out those relationships from which she must always lose out, Fay also appears to have engineered episodes throughout her life in which she reverses the roles. A constant for Taylour was a craving for explicit and perhaps unconditional acceptance (as with the ideal parent) and to be assured that this was 'real' she portrays herself as continuingly working to replicate expressions of devotion towards her, and seemed to expect this devotion to continue even after she had rejected those who offered her affection. Her stories of romance show her to have an appetite that caused her to kill-off love affairs just short of their crescendo in order that the process of adoration might be restarted with another suitor. So even if a relationship was to some degree a two way affair, she ultimately took total control by proving them to be one-way frequently claiming "he loved me, but it wasn't quite, although it almost was, the same for me". Her story about Robert is symptomatic of her attitude to relationships and love.

In the end it did not matter which part Taylour played. Both being the rejected and the rejecting had essentially the same outcome for her. Each enabled her to repeat the legend of Fred and end in a similar way - Fay speeding off on a motorbike, giving herself to racing.

Fay's amorous relationships may have been real or imagined, but to an extent she might be understood as having been addicted to the scenario of 'love's labours lost' as it is repeated over and over again. The almost assured outcome 'takes her right back to the track'. There was little doubt that she was hooked on speed and the danger that is its constant companion, but where she wanted this to take her was never quite clear to Fay. Certainly something seemed to compel her to literally 'get-away', and as fast as possible from a relationship of any depth, even though it might have involved a level of self-destruction as well as damaging someone close to her.

5. Cinder-Revver

High up in a stand at Stamford Bridge watching her first full-blooded speedway event, Fay viewed three heats of cinder racing, wherein the burning motorcycles were straddled by English riders, all of whom were relative novices. Watching the racers making courageous but unsteady progress, the new sport looked terrifying. However, she thought that as she had conquered the Camberley hills, she would be equal to the challenge the dirt-track presented. Enveloped by the aphrodisiac atmosphere of the vibrant, crowded arena, Fay believed she could do as well as the best of the men she watched. But her reveries were broken by the appearance of the dark, enigmatic figure of Lloyd 'Sprouts' Elder. Personifying a foreboding storm, the grimly daunting figure of the American Ace emerged from the pits on the far side of the track.

Born in the USA

The lanky Yank leant over his racing machine like a tall, thin gorilla, and started ominously circling the narrow quarter-mile oval, stalking its two long straights. Streamlined over his small tank, throwing the bike into the bend at high speed, he was noticeably faster and steadier than his British counterparts. Suddenly, on the far straight he opened up with a roar, like a panther straining for the kill. Fay found herself fearful for him and hoping that he would cut. She thought that he would be unable to take the curve at the speed he was making and go straight through the fence. A woman in the seat in front of Fay put her hands over her eyes.

Just before the bend, Elder appeared to have fallen off! The bike seemed to be moving across the ground, but rider and bike were still as one, leaning inwards at an absurd angle and skidding violently. Fay could not see how the American could avoid crashing. The skid, that somehow seemed to remain in Elder's control, continued all the way round the curve: a sort of fast, prolonged, purposeful slide. The recovery to near upright seemed incredible, but as if to demonstrate that there had been no mistakes, the American went into the turn at the other end of the track, throwing his mount over yet again until, once more, he was almost touching the ground. It looked to Fay like a weird and wonderful wheeled version of ice-skating; his front wheel was strangely upright. It faced the outside fence, but not in the direction he was circling. His back wheel was so slanted, that it looked as if it were trying to slide out from under him, as if he were riding on the rim. The machine leaned inwards, but it slid towards the outside, seeming to graze the fence. And, all the time, a fan-shaped plume of dirt was spewed back, viciously, energetically, causing man and vehicle to imitate a great, black peacock. As the turn progressed, the cinders making up the track surface sprayed the fence, giving the impression that the streamlined rider had sprouted wings. Elder's inside leg trailed from the saddle, his steel-toed boot extended beyond the sliding rear wheel with his toe lightly riding the track with almost balletic grace.

Sprouts Elder

The exhibition was totally slick, showing the excitement of new world speedway and bringing the culture of 'can do' razzmatazz into the grey world of a Britain yet to recover from the economic and social ravages of the First World War and already slipping into the mire of world depression. With the show over the crowd applauded loudly. Young women got up and made for the pits to call through the wire fence for Sprout's autograph. As the spectators melted away Fay sat alone in the great hollow stand in silence. Speedway looked petrifying, but she knew she needed to take it on.

World of leather

With the trial season concluded there was no rush to get back to the midlands so instead of taking the midnight express back to Coventry, Fay booked into a South Kensington Hotel and the next morning she visited the Stamford Bridge speedway office. The promoter, who Fay referred to as 'Mr Longford', had heard of Fay but told her that he did not believe that the dirt-track was for women. This was the start of a trek around the cinder-circuits of

London for Fay. At each venue she was given a variation on the same reception. It was out of the question that a woman might have the nerve and/or strength to match the speedways. Her final port of call was Crystal Palace. She reached the track in time to watch the racing from the stand. The British riders, who were not yet expert at broadsiding, made up most of the programme, which enabled the American and Australian racers to thrill the crowd even more. But there was one English competitor who seemed able to throw his mechanical stallion into the curves with as much abandon and aplomb as the overseas dare-devils. He also managed to beat some of the professionals, qualifying for the final - the Crystal Palace International. Fay watched the slim young son of Albion line-up at the off. From the start he took the lead. All the races were four lap events and he lead at the beginning of each of the first three circuits, but he was pushed into third on the first straight of the final lap, however he came through again on the final bend, looking invincible.

The following morning Fay made her way to a leather-wear sports shop in Carburton Street (Lewis's Leathers) where most of the speedway riders were fitted with leather racing suits and helmets. There were no other customers in the shop when Fay arrived. She looked at the walls which were studded with autographed images of motorcycle sport celebrities. She saw one of Elder, and recognised a few of the others and was pleasantly surprised to see an image of herself – a cutting of the story and pictures from *The Motor Cycle* magazine about her victories at Camberley.

She tried on different pairs of goggles and strapped a helmet on. The clumsy-looking crash-hat was quite comfortable. She had never worn bespoke head-protection as a trials rider. It was then that she noticed the Englishman who had won the big race at Crystal Palace come into the shop. Sammy, the shop owner, was with him. Looking at Fay, Sammy said, "This is the girl who won those cups at Camberley", pointing to the magazine clipping on the wall. The wiry racer looked at her with interest and asked her if she was thinking about learning to broadside. Fay quickly took the helmet off of her head and told him "Yes" and discovered the rider was Lionel Wills of the wealthy W.D. & H.O. Wills family, major players in the massive tobacco industry of the time. This was to be the start of a long and often intense relationship.

Lionel the lion

In 1996 Peter Wills, the son of Lionel wrote of his father being, 'one of those people of the inter-wars generation to whom the internal combustion engine was the apotheosis of civilisation.'

The photograph albums, which in effect record the life of Lionel Wills, are full of pictures of cars and motorcycles together with their drivers and riders. Many images of places where the cars and motorcycles had been, or could be, driven are also presented. On his collection of Bartholomew maps of the British Isles, numerous minor roads are inked over to designate the fact that he had driven on them. On another series of maps of the Alps he marked the small, twisting tracks ending on remote mountain tops which he had navigated.

Whether it was a motorcycle scramble somewhere in Britain, the Monte Carlo Rally from a start at Tallinn, or a remote meeting in the outback of New South Wales, all are recorded in photographs or maps, reflecting motor sport culture of the second and third decades of the Twentieth Century. The passion Wills had for this milieu is evident when one looks at a photograph of the Grand Canyon; the caption he placed under it warned 'Motorcyclist's Nightmare'.

Always maintaining the Corinthian ethic of the stoical amateur, the love Wills had for motorcycles dimmed slightly with age as the fuel of his ardour, riding, became less and less part of his life, but his years in the saddle were probably his happiest.

It has often been mooted that speedway's arrival in Britain was in no small measure due to Wills' involvement in the sport. The first dirt-track meeting staged at the Sydney Royale (the Sydney Showground in Australia) took place on the afternoon of 31 July, 1926. Ernie Buck won the first Main Event for solo motorcycles. It was during the 1926-27 season at the Royale that the young ex-Cambridge student Wills, during a visit 'down under' along with Mr. A. J. Stevens, the chief of the AJS motorcycle firm, saw an advertisement in a Sydney newspaper for a speedway meeting at the venue. Lionel's curiosity for anything to do with motorcycling drew him to attend. He was immediately enthralled by the whole broadsiding culture, having never experienced anything quite like it.

Wills sent articles describing the new sport back to Britain and these were published in some of the leading motorcycling journals. His vivid portrayals of what he had seen, spiced with his enthusiasm for the novel and thrilling form of racing, caught the attention of many of the readers and fellow aficionados of the two wheeled 'chargers of speed', indeed his depictions inspired the May 1927 Camberley event.

It was during the 1926-27 season at the Sydney Showground that Wills met Johnnie Hoskins. Later they were to work together in Britain after the Englishman had urged the Australian promoters to bring dirt-track racing to the UK. Almost diametrically opposite in terms of personality to Hoskins, Wills was a modest man, who was the first to understate his contribution to speedway - but he is widely acknowledged as the first British dirt-track rider. He once wrote, "The roar of racing engines is the music of heaven...and a fistful of twistgrip the very summit of desire..." He spoke and wrote of the sport as "...the supreme thrill".

Wills was to race at many of the same meetings as Taylour and he would often drive her to the tracks all over the United Kingdom in his family's convertible Rolls Royce.

During their first meeting Fay told Wills of her problems at the London tracks. Although she expected him to laugh, his sympathy for her plight lead her to confide that she intended to mingle in with the men at Crystal Palace on the official practice day, with her short hair tucked up under her helmet. Seemingly amused, Wills offered to help Fay with the plan, telling her, "The Crystal Palace is my home track…I'll drive you there".

Bends and gender bending

Some time in the early summer of 1928, having acquired a racing suit from Sammy, Taylour had a hook fitted to her factory bike for her right knee, in keeping with dirt-track fashion. Her employers would not have approved! She purchased a facemask too - in the days before visors riders wore masks to protect their faces from the flying dirt, but she also saw it as a means to avoid detection. On the practice day, Fay arrived with Wills at the pits. Amateur riders were making their way on and off the track all the time, there was no checking or security. The practice sessions did not produce fast speeds, with riders focussing on getting to grips with the powersliding technique and enduring many a tumble, but most of those concerned walked away unhurt.

The promoter, and track manager, the legendary Freddie Mockford, a great entrepreneurial pioneer of the cinder track, sat in his office set in the stadium terracing. Wills warned Fay that Fred was a very temperamental man, and that she would be wise to steer clear of him initially. While Wills distracted Frank, the Pit Marshall, Fay took her bike out onto the circuit. Coming into the first corner she leant the bike over on the turn and began to slide, but she swiftly fell off. Again and again she found herself having to pick herself up, but having slid a little further with each try. This continued until she was the last rider left on the track. By that time she had built the confidence to keep the throttle open while sliding and had discovered this was the secret of keeping the broadside going. She later wrote that learning to dive into the bends in a streamlined slide was a similar experience to learning to dive into a swimming pool.

With Fay still working out on the track, Mockford strode into the pits and yelled at Frank ordering, 'that lad', the last remaining rider, to be called in, fearing that any more wear and tear would result in the track not being ready for the racing next day. As Taylour was flagged-in the sultry sunlight that had illuminated the day was giving way to dusk. It was at this point that Wills told Mockford that Fay was a female. The promoter was both angry and shocked, and scorned the idea that a woman should compete against men.

On hearing of the promoter's position, Fay made her way to the stands to wash the cinder dust off her face for what she thought to be the first and last time. Shrouded in disappointment she felt defeated by the situation. However, back in the track manager's office Wills asked Mockford, "Why don't you book her to race?" (slipping in the small but definite fabrication that all the other promoters had signed her up). Recovering from his initial astonishment, Mockford probably saw the promotional potential and attraction of a woman rider, and found himself running after Taylour, calling, "Would you like to race here a week tomorrow?" He offered her seven days of practice before racing for him on the Saturday.

At the first opportunity Fay wired her senior manager, Mr Pugh, at Coventry and sought his permission to compete. Politely but firmly he refused, so she cabled her resignation to Geoffrey Butcher, the Rudge competitions manager, telling him that she did not intend to return to Coventry and ordered herself a real dirt-track racing bike.

This yarn of a breathless and immediate love for speedway and the resultant rejection of the trials competition was consistent with the way Taylour presented herself to the world, but not necessarily the entire truth. In later interviews with the press she often referred to being converted to speedway because it was relatively safer than trials riding and also paid better. The *Sydney Herald* (19 February, 1929) reported that 'an accident prevented her from further competitions' in trials riding. Later, in *The Motor Cycle* (25 September, 1930) she told 'Patric' a staff reporter of the time, that after the first Camberley dirt-track meeting she switched over to an OK Supreme machine the makers of which entered her for the 'Scottish' but a crash, and a displaced knee cartilage cut short her progress. Retreating injured and/or going for greater pecuniary rewards would not, of course, have fitted with the persona that Fay later built based almost totally on her love of speed and danger.

Pain and gain

Taylour witnessed an event that was to bring two facets of her future together in May, 1928 when Lionel Wills raced Australian Sig Schlam in the first 'international' at Crystal Palace. The pair were about as dissimilar as it is possible for two men to be in terms of physical stature. In temperament, background, psychological make-up and racing style they were also poles apart. But along with Fay they shared a passion for the power the track could ignite.

Despite giving up her employment with Rudge, Taylour managed to keep the company competition machine for a while, and her first rides were aboard that heavy trials machine even though it belonged to the factory. All that next week, in the early summer heat-wave of 1928, she slogged around the Crystal Palace track until at last, after tumble after tumble, she taught myself to powerslide. At her last practice session she had opened the throttle at the start of the turn, just after the usual cut at the end of the straight, and then held it open all the way round.

Wills and Fay soon established a friendship based on their mutual interest. However, although, according to Taylour, their relationship was generally understood to be founded on camaraderie, on a personal level Fay believed that they both felt a deeper, more intimate connection. They attended meetings together, but also shared the social life available to wealthy young men at the time, but Wills avoided introducing Fay to his parents. During that era this would have been the customary confirmation of his class that courtship was being undertaken and that he was 'walking out' with Fay. He kept their togetherness 'informal' and as such slightly illicit, by using the excuse that his family did not approve of his participation in the rough and dangerous sport of speedway (by implication suggesting that Taylour was rough and dangerous).

However, according to Fay this heightened his enthusiasm for their relationship and it probably did something of the same thing for her. Like his racing, the association with Taylour was spiced with an aura of illegitimacy, possibly even a form of symbolic rebellion against the conventions of the status group he was part of, which might well have felt suffocating to a young man whose generation straddled the boundary of tradition and modernity. Perhaps for Wills, Fay and the dirt-track were the last throes of adolescent defiance of parental expectations - although her respectable aristocratic connections and 'colonial' credentials made her something much more than a 'bit of rough', the likes of which the pale, pencil-thin, soft-skinned, public schooled, Cambridge weaned, boy-man Wills may have found harder to manage.

Taylour was unconcerned about the details, she was taken up with her new profession and that it included Lionel Wills was a bonus. She enjoyed being with him; she found that his six foot frame, patrician bearing, grey eyes and as she said 'fascinating mouth' kindled a desire in her that no other man would be able replicate. Although they were something of an odd combination, the retiring, slightly effete English son of privilege and the strapping, gung-ho daughter of a colonial copper, Wills provided Taylour with a companionship that she had never found with the factory men in Coventry. For Fay he represented the ultimate prize, and of course the potential of becoming the supreme loss. What Lionel got from his liaison with Fay is hard to tell. It may have protected him: he was the archetypal 'soft toff' and it would not have been surprising for him to have received a certain amount of 'sledging' at the hands of the tough Australian and American riders he rubbed shoulders with, directed at bringing his 'manhood' into question.

After broadsiding bends all week Fay was rewarded with her first dirt-track contest. But she had been working on a smooth track, unsullied by a programme of racing, and the roughed surface of competition was to hold a few surprises for her.

Taylour's initial taste of proper dirt-track competition came on 9 June 1928, in front of a packed Crystal Palace. Fay's entry into the 'naked in tooth and claw' world of cut-throat speedway contests had been heralded in The Daily Mirror of the previous day. Under the 'la-de-da' strap-line, 'Eve on the Sport Field', it announced, 'Miss Fay Taylour, the only girl to try speedway racing, will make her debut at the Crystal Palace track to-morrow.'

A top Australian rider took the track alongside Taylour that evening, the great international Ron Johnson, astride his mighty Harley-Davidson. Although born in Scotland, Johnson moved to Perth, Western Australia, as a boy, taking on the work of a lumberman when he left school. When he came to England in 1928 he had a short spell at Salford under Johnnie Hoskins, before signing for Crystal Palace (the side that in 1934 became New Cross). Johnson was blessed with a very light frame, but was exceptionally strong and had been a good amateur boxer in his earlier years. Unfortunately, he did not always have the best of luck - his speedway career cost him some toes and fingers. Johnson was recognized as a scientific racer, using logic and tactical acumen to enhance his riding. (Later he was to reach something of a peak in his career when he was to make the highest score in the Test series riding for his adopted country against England in 1934).

As Fay surveyed the track before her first serious ride, it looked deceptively smooth as the big rake circled it before the contestants lined up. Her race was to be run over four laps and Fay received a 280 yard start on Johnson (the Palace track was 449 yards to the lap).

Taylour had persuaded her uncle, Lord Riddell (owner of the News of the World), to watch her first competitive outing. He was given the starting flag and asked to signal the 'off' of her initial race. "What do I do?" he asked. "Just drop the flag", he was told. His Lordship, showing all the qualities of his class to do exactly what they are told, literally dropped the ensign and it floated to the ground! He was amazed at the crowd's reaction (raucous laughter). Taken with the atmosphere that energised his own enthusiasm he proclaimed in his most definite and plumy tones, "I must send my reporters here" and soon after he bestowed the News of The World Trophy, the first of a number of prizes that would be donated to the sport by newspapers.

For all the muddle, the race finally got under way and Fay went off like a rocket, but she immediately discovered the ruts that had developed over the earlier races, and noted that her heavy bike would not be able to ride the surface as effectively as the special light machine on which the Australian was pursuing her. But before the first lap was over it was clear that Fay's ability had been underestimated. As she took the last bend she still had 120-yards in front.

For three laps Taylour held on to her lead and at the beginning of the final turn she was still in pole position. However the ruts and her inexperience took their toll. Her front wheel went into a terrible wobble, which she fought for several yards but the bike eventually somersaulted. Johnson zoomed past as she lay motionless on the track - the crowd went silent. But, she came round, and although still dizzy, picked herself up and waved to the cheering fans. She was their darling from that moment - a 'plucky' girl, duelling with the men, astride a bucking, growling, pounding mechanical beast. In those days that would have had more than a whiff of eroticism for many of the adherents to speedway.

The second heat was much the same story. Once more Taylour understood that with a lighter machine, like Johnson's, the outcome might have been different. As it was, mounted on the Rudge trials machine, she was unable to match her better equipped opponents. But Fay was now the sweetheart of the speedway. The caption in the morning papers took the immortal virgin/ temptress stereotype as its headline, 'Eve invades the dirt-track'. *Motorcycle* of the 14 June, 1928, told how she did well 'going into some real slides' but related how on the last lap, with Johnson still about 100 yards behind her, Fay had fallen off, remounted, and got going again just as Johnson crossed the finishing line. However, she had given a good account of herself, particularly considering it had been just three weeks since she first saw a speedway track.

Taylour had hoped that after her efforts Riddell might have bought her a specialist bike, "But" lamenting her uncle's inability to discern her obvious prompt, she groaned, "all he produced was lunch at the Savoy. He hadn't taken the hint when I joined him in the stands after crashing and explained the unsuitability of the bike." "Are you hurt", he had asked, and seemed surprised when his niece said "No". However, she admitted, "I was, a little, but the crowd loved an unhurt exit."

Track woman

Motor Cycling of 13 June, 1928 celebrated Fay's baptism of the cinders:

> The prospect of watching a lady rider, Miss Fay Taylour, matched in a handicap race against a star such as Ron Johnson was chiefly responsible for the excellent crowd at Crystal Palace Speedway last Saturday.

In subsequent press articles Fay began to build herself an image, telling of her interests in music, dancing, tennis and how she had represented Berkshire as a hockey player. Her capability was put down to her experience in sporting trials over 'freak roads'.

At that time there was nothing to prevent a woman from riding on the track. The speedways, seizing on anything for publicity, took full advantage and engaged a number of women riders, but the situation was tenuous at best. The following week saw Taylour continuing to take tumbles as she continued to push herself beyond her skill level. An increasingly annoyed Mockford, before once more booking Taylour, told her, "If you fall off again women will be barred from the dirt-track forever". He let her know that, "the ACU comes back from the Isle of Man on Saturday" and as such their attention would be squarely on speedway events[15]. The Track Tsar told his female investment that at the next meeting, "I've got a very strict ACU Steward." Mr. A C Pickering was doing the rounds at that time and was known to be both strict and impartial - but mostly strict - and would be watching Taylour with a particularly jaundiced gaze. So Fay was back on the practice track for yet more punishment. On her next competitive outing she put on a much better show. She had managed to borrow a light Rudge Dirt Track Special from Wills and managed to stay in intimate contact with it for the whole meeting.

Taylour's popularity grew as the novelty of her performance became general knowledge and promoters were quick to contact her as the new audience for speedway packed the tracks. The sport was sexy in every meaning of the word. The bronzed, muscled and gleaming Australians met the Americans, so reminiscent of the rough-rider heroes of the Western movies, hugely popular at the time, head to head on the speedway. The thrill of these encounters was made more real by the spice of danger that was an ever present fact of speedway, and a constantly implied attraction in the advertisements for the meetings. The drama of the nascent crash was always a consistent element of any event. Tens of thousands of spectators were keen to see the connoisseur riders from every corner of the exciting pioneer countries undertake demonstration rides and match races (there was no team racing in the early days of the sport). Amongst all this Taylour proved to be an added draw and she showed herself to have become a highly adept rider when she appeared at Hove, near Brighton. The following appeared in a local newspaper *(see over)*. According to Fay 'It paid to advertise'.

At the Hove meeting 6,000 turned up to witness Fay (described in the local press as 'a young girl') 'easily' defeat local champion and top English rider, Les Barker in the mile. She was the only rider of the afternoon that did not seem likely to fall at some point, and her time of 1 minute 50 seconds was faster by far than any of the other handicap performers.

On the last Saturday in July 1928, Taylour, now being introduced in the national press as 'the famous woman driver' was at West Ham's huge stadium in the Docklands of East London. With a 5 second start she won her event, reaching 42.45 mph, a top quality performance on the Custom House track.

Fay's fame was becoming a double edged sword as it had become the subject of widespread debate. However, Jack Marshall, in *The Illustrated Sport and Kennel* (2 August, 1928) was supportive in his piece 'Women and Dirt Track Racing'.

Within one hour of this journal being on sale last week, I received a call at my office from a Mr. Ernest 'A' , who was perhaps one of the earliest Dirt Track riders in this country. Mr. A , who has not ridden for a long while, confessed himself in agreement with my remarks, except that he considered I was a little wrong in advocating women riding cycles on speedways.

There is a lot to be said for Mr. A's criticism, and indeed much to be said for his plain statement affecting rivalry on the track, but surely a rider such as Mr. A must realise, with his experience, that women riders - such as Miss Fay Taylour - also know how to race motor cycles on dirt tracks.

The lady in question, with a four minutes[16] start last weekend, beat the field with more to spare than her original time limit. She beat the field easily when odds were five to one against.

MISS FAY TAYLOUR ENGLAND'S LADY CHAMPION SPEEDSTER

RACES

LES BARKER

Hove   **Dirt-Track Race Meeting**   Hove
              Sports Stadium
              To-Day At 3pm

SEVENTEEN THRILLING SPEEDWAY EVENTS

J. Willimott
England
Versus
Sig Schlam
Australian Champion

Charlie Datson
World's Record Holder
Ron Johnson
West Australian Champion

Thirty-six Speed Kings
In Duel after Duel

EVERYBODY'S GOING TO SEE MISS FAY TAYLOUR TO-DAY

Special Bus Services every 5 minutes from Castle Square via Brighton Stadium

Get a bus, get a Char-a-banc, get anything so long as you get to the big Speed Meeting at Hove To-day

---

Advertisement in local Hove newspaper

In early August Fay took her first major scalp defeating A.R. Frogley in a mile match at Crystal Palace. Taylour was given a 5 second start, but she scarcely needed this advantage as she covered the first circuit in only $^2/_5$ of a second outside the track record, and won comfortably at an average of 36.22 mph. This was a fine effort but it needs to be compared to the speed produced by Paddy Dean[17], one of the foremost Australian riders at the same meeting. From a flying start he covered a quarter-mile lap in 21 seconds, a speed of 42.85 mph, and thus equaled the record held jointly by Art Pechar[18] and Charlie Datson. Dean's time for the mile was 1minute 26 seconds (41.86 mph), and he thus beat Pechar's earlier record by $^3/_5$ of a second

At this time, it seemed that many pundits had little idea of how to react to Taylour's activity beyond long-winded patronisation and crass stereotyping. A fine example of this was an article, ' *weekly discourse on Dirt Track Racing and interesting talks with Leading Riders - Cinder Celebrities No.1 Miss Fay Taylour*', printed in the *Auto Motor Journal*, 16 August, 1928 penned by 'Steve' and entitled *Cinders:*

I start this series by being the perfect gentleman in putting the ladies first.

I met Miss Taylour at the Stamford Bridge track on a practice afternoon, and my first impression of her was, 'what a business-like little person!' Dressed in riding boots, complete with steel 'toe-cap,' black leather breeches and jacket, crash helmet, goggles and gauntlets, it was indeed a transformation when the headgear necessary for cinder riding was discarded and disclosed the smiling countenance of a lady. Of course, the vanity box was put in evidence immediately, and after her performance with this magic apparatus I was introduced.

"Interview? Why, yes, certainly. What do you want to know", were her first words, said with vivacity, and like the little sport that she is, she entered into the spirit of the thing and told me a few facts about herself.

Miss Taylour is a charming Irish girl with auburn hair, clear bright eyes and pretty clean-cut features usually associated with athletes. Her father, who was an officer in the Royal Irish Constabulary saw considerable war service, has just recently married again, and seeing that before this event Fay was her father's housekeeper, she is now released to satisfy her desire to make a name in the motoring world.

Her experience on the 'cinders' has been short. Even so, she can hold her own with a good number of the men. As is natural, the controversial matter of whether it is dangerous for girls to ride on dirt tracks came up during the conversation, and there is a lot of truth in the way Miss Taylour puts it: "It is no more dangerous than horse riding, flying and other similar sports."

"Seeing that you are Irish," I said, "supposing for a moment your temper got the better of you during a race, and—well— and you lost your head? What then?"

"But," said Fay, "I am unique, one of the favoured few without an Irish temper."

Well, she looks it!

She is a keen motorist and drives a Morris Oxford Coupe. Recently there was an argument with a lorry, which she upset. She now contends that cinder riding on a motor-cycle is more safe than motor touring on the roads. Her hobby is motoring in all its branches, and she has won many trophies in reliability and speed trials.

Fay is a most popular rider with the crowd, and a win by her is the signal for thunderous applause. Incidentally, Art Pechar has been coaching her in the art of broadsiding, and sure, m'lads, she can do it!

"Marriage? Ah, yes, but my ideal has not yet arrived."

Please don't rush and ask me what constitutes her ideal. I don't know!

It was during the latter part of the summer of 1928 that heavy rain overnight in North-West London had an advantageous effect on the Greenford dirt-track, facilitating higher speeds than were usual for the circuit. A report in the *News of the World* named Taylour 'the prominent lady rider' as it told of her participation in a mile race. With a 5 second advantage, riding a borrowed machine, Fay finished with close to her original handicap, averaging 42.45mph. She followed this with a fine three-lap (1.5 mile) race with the popular if incongruously named, J. Sloman

Woman in a man's world

As Taylour was beginning to make a name for herself in speedway, she was the subject of an article, *Girls on the Dirt Track* (25 August, 1928) here she had an opportunity to voice her right to compete in the light of the growing doubts about women's 'suitability' for dirt-track competition. It is reproduced at length below as it is a fine example of the duel manner in which Taylour was presented to the public. On one hand she was regarded as a top class rider, able to match men in performance and personality, and on the other as a 'fine exemplar' of the 'fair sex' – a very contrived depiction struggling to find an acceptable place even given the rather contorted ways women were portrayed at the time. Fay was described as being both different and the same, feminine but masculine. As such, the following is full of stereotypes used as escape routes during the then chancy activity of eulogising women's achievements in male environments. Fay dramatises her entry into the sport as being an instant conversion.

"Why shouldn't women race?" asks Miss Fay Taylour, in this exclusive interview. Her own exploits on the dirt track would provide a conclusive answer, if all other girl motor-cyclists were like her.

I found Miss Fay Taylour, the only woman dirt-track racer, in the centre of the field at Stamford Bridge.

It was a strange scene. Thundering, roaring, racing motor cycles flashed past, practicing for the evening's events. Crash helmeted, leather encased figures hurried to and fro. Mechanics in their white overalls, grease splashed, brawny-armed, and horny-handed, wheeled slim, silver machines to and from the paddock.

Miss Taylour straightened her back from examining her mount and pushed a sun-browned hand across her white forehead, smoothing into some semblance of order her delightfully wavy, brown shingled hair.

"You want me to tell you something about myself? Well, first of all, let me say that I feel most horribly dirty!"

I smiled and thought she looked perfectly topping, despite a little spot of grease on her nose, in the neat riding kit that accentuated her slim, boyish figure.

A voice came from behind, and a well-set-up young fellow caught Miss Taylour's sleeve.

"Feeling all right, Fay?" he said softly, and did I detect a note of anxiety in his voice?

She laughed merrily, "Fine, thanks, Jim!" she said.

I watched his retreating form. Was it sweetheart or brother?

"How did I come to take up this sport?" she rattled on. "Well, you see that corner of the stand up there? I just ran up those steps six weeks ago and caught my first glimpse of dirt-track racing. I knew right away that was the stuff for me. I went straight back to my firm, Rudge Whitworth's and said to the competition manager – that is the man who arranges what events the firm shall enter machines and who shall ride them -

'I'm going to ride a Rudge on the dirt track as soon as possible'

'You're not!'

I said, 'I am!' And that's how it happened

"I expect you noticed in a certain newspaper lately that one Pressman considered women were physically incapable of competing in dirt-track racing. Isn't it ridiculous?

"But this critic hadn't seen little me! He only saw a number of women motor-cycle riders giving exhibitions to show what they could do, and this newspaper man thought they were real women dirt-track racers.

"After all, why shouldn't women enter, if they have the physical strength and nerve, their people approve, and they are allowed to compete by the authorities? I'm sure my father would much rather have me dirt-track racing than smashing round Brooklands at a hundred-and-fifty miles per hour or flashing through the air in a plane.

"Do you find the steering hard to pull over the curves?"

"Not a bit! Yes, I've had one or two spills, but as far as being windy – well, you're down before you know anything about it!

"But it's horse riding that I love. I come of a horse-loving family, and if I were given the choice between a good horse and the best motor-cycle in the world, I know which I'd take".

Demons of Speed

"Oh, please excuse me, but I do feel so dirty. I simply must go and have a wash." She flashed me a smile from her Irish blue eyes and was gone.

Later, I watch two motor-cycles tearing round the track at nearly forty miles per hour, broadsiding almost to the ground at the curves, sending the cinders splashing in all directions, sliding, skidding, roaring, two tense leather-covered, helmeted, goggled figures riding to win.

The crowd began to cheer wildly on the last lap. A man behind me laughed.

"He's playing with her," he said.

Came the answer sharply: "Rot! Miss Taylour's riding a darn fine race!"

I started. Surely one of these juggernauts was not the jolly, laughing little girl I had chatted to a bare half hour before?

The judge's flag signalled the end of the race. The machines slowed down. Goggles went up, helmet came off, to disclose a laughing face, ruffled shingled brown hair, and dancing Irish blue eyes. Yes it was she!

Can girls compete in dirt-track racing? I know the answer now.

Taylour continued to show her prowess and although she lost a match race with Harry Lewis, one of the best of the English riders of the late 1920s, she gave him something of a race. Lewis had not been threatened by Fay from start to finish but she was only a second behind him, riding 'exceptionally steady'. At the same meeting she put up a much more convincing performance against G. Everness, sliding boldly into the corners. Despite the fact that when Everness fell he was only a few yards behind, gaining slightly, Taylour displayed fine control of her machine, and made such good time, that it is likely that Everness could not have beaten her in any case.

On 22 August Johnnie Hoskins told the world: 'It may be hard to name the King of dirt track champions but the Queen is certainly Miss Fay Taylour'

Identified as 'an English girl' Taylour was at this point said to be capable of holding her own against male riders, having competed against all comers on the previous Saturday at Lea Bridge, London. There she won both her heat and the semi-final, but fell when she was in a good position to win the final. She also raced and beat Tom Croombs, one of the best English riders on the track at that time and a considerable achievement for Fay. Tommy, as he was known, was a small, light and reserved man who left his job as a plasterer in New Malden to become a pioneer among British speedway riders with Brighton. He was one of the few early English riders to race a Peashooter Harley successfully. After moving from Brighton he broke the record for the Lea Bridge track in 1928 beginning his rapid rise to fame. He quickly became a scratch starter in many handicap races. His method of almost standing on his right footrest when going round the bends was reminiscent of Frank Arthur. Like Arthur he kept very close to the white line, becoming known as the 'White Line Wizard' because of his ability to hold the inside of the track at top speed. The quiet Croombs thrilled the Lea Bridge crowd for two years before joining West Ham in 1930. He would represent his country on numerous occasions and maintain his status as one of Britain's top riders well into the 1930s.

At this point Taylour was claiming that the most vociferous criticism of her racing activity was coming from her own sex, and she invited all women to see her demonstrate that dirt-track racing was not just a man's sport. Almost as if to accommodate Fay's summons, the Salford track declared that women would be admitted without charge for the Monday night opening, at which Taylour was scheduled to be matched against a good local champion. Lionel Wills was also on the list of riders competing in that meeting. According to Taylour:

> Lionel drove me to many of the tracks, sometimes racing himself though we never matched against each other, which may have been by design for the promoters linked us romantically.

Wills would often surprise spectators by driving up to the pits in a Rolls-Royce with his motor-cycle on the cushions of the back seat. At that time Wills had the burning ambition to overcome his friend, the crack Australian, Charlie Datson.

Sig Schlam, another fine rider from 'down under', who was also due to ride at Salford commented, 'Those Manchester boys are shifting...and I'm going to turn everything on and leave it on.'

6. Dirt-Track Queen

Before racing at Salford Fay Taylour was being lauded as 'Queen of the Dirt Track' and the 'Broadside Queen'. Johnnie Hoskins was announcing her to be 'as capable a rider that she can hold her own against most men and has beaten, among others, Tom Croombs, a rider of note.' So the confrontation with Ron Johnson, the young, highly talented Australian, in the challenge match was eagerly anticipated.

A woman at Salford

Despite inclement weather conditions in Salford, about 20,000 people witnessed the opening of the new dirt-track at the Albion Greyhound arena, near Manchester, on Monday 27 August, 1928 which was controlled by the Albion Speedway Company.

The track was expected to be one of the fastest in Britain. The main attraction of the evening was Taylour, and in her heat in the City Hall Cup persuaded the watching reporters to proclaim her as 'a brilliant exponent of broadsiding'. She delighted the crowd by easily defeating the male competition. Unfortunately for Fay, in the third semi-final the 'lady champion' as she was to be nicknamed by the local media, led the field for three laps at a lightening pace, but was let down by her machine on the last bend.

Eric Langton, still at that time associated more with T.T. riding than his exploits on cinders, took the City Hall Cup, setting the track record with 1minute 35 seconds for the four laps.

The match races between Ron Johnson (Australia) and Taylour (who was designated as a Londoner) and Lionel Wills (also presented as a London racer) and another rider whose name would feature in the history of dirt-track racing, Oliver, the brother of Eric Langton, were abandoned after two attempts respectively.

Wills, for whom the speedway was an all embracing distraction from his upper-class background and responsibilities, had arrived at the track at the last minute with his machine, once more, on the back of his Roll-Royce. He put up a determined show making several good recoveries before crashing badly in the in the last race. He was thought of as a capable rider but Fay, his constant companion, was beginning to be seen as being a more controlled racer, with an instinct and sensitivity for the track that Wills to some extent lacked. But as she was perhaps moving ahead of Wills in terms of ability, her attachment to her almost constant chauffeur was growing.

The day following the start of Taylour's northern campaign, on Tuesday, 28 August *The Star*, following the proclamation, 'Women on the Speedways' endeavoured to continue the debate that had been rumbling on since Fay's first appearance on the speedways:

The decision of the majority of track managers to ban lady riders despite the proved proficiency of at least one has focussed public attention on the position of women in motor-cycle sport. In compiling a list of the best speedway racers in the country I would include the name of Miss Fay Taylour.

Male applicants for racing permits are inevitably serious in their intentions. Women applicants for speedway honours are greater than many suppose, but what a sorry lot they are! The majority are merely moneyed, bored and brainless young women looking for excitement and have never ridden a motor-cycle.

It seems speedway could deal with no more than one woman on the track and if others came along they were expected to somehow be 'the completed article'. From the modern perspective it is difficult to see quite what was so frightening about the possibility of women coming into speedway racing. The subject was written about in terms that ranged from twee endearments to outrage and disgust. These feelings might be put down to macho attitudes and the male fear of losing face by the possibility of defeat by a woman, but that seems a little simplistic and even trite. The arguments about safety might be more convincing if it was not a fact that speedway was a sport where injury and, at times, death, were occupational hazards that were accepted by all from the moment one laid tyre to track. No, the attitude of the media and promoters, which was not widely shared (or at least voiced) by the riders, had deeper social explanations and more complex psychological roots.

After Salford Taylour was seen as a dashing and clever rider, who seemed to refute the assertion that considerable physical strength was a prerequisite if a machine, travelling at speed round the corners, was to be safely controlled. She also challenged, by her very presence, the notion that the dirt-track was essentially a place for men only. Fay was given the credit of being the superior in skill in each of the Salford races in which she took part. Her cornering was daring and performed at speed, and she appeared to have the ability to cope at critical moments, such as when finding her path blocked on a bend.

It is the skill involved in dirt-track racing that has always been its main attraction; the testing of human ability in contest. On the face of it speedway is not as sophisticated as other forms of motorcycle racing. It is, basically, going down to the first bend and turning left. This vision of running round in circles has often been used by enthusiasts of other forms of motorized racing as an analogy with which to dismiss speedway, but it really does not do the sport justice. Dirt surfaced tracks were, and are harder to 'read' than paved surfaces. The speedway riders tended to produce two or even three racing 'grooves', other motorcyclists riding on paved circuits usually create only a single racing line. Dirt tracks often changed dramatically during the course of a race or meeting, and a decent racing line early on might have been much less effective later in the proceedings. Learning to read a track and set machinery up to suit the prevailing conditions took considerable experience and expertise.

In the first years of speedway competitors often found themselves moving in a bunch at high-speed. Negotiating the 'mobile chicanes' created by these conditions required a high degree of skill and compensates for the deficit of right hand turns on a track.

Speedway machines were and still are relatively unsophisticated when placed alongside other racing motorcycles, but this simplicity brings with it demands on riders unique to this type of competition. There has generally been less concern with technical development relative to other forms of motorcycle contest. The main objective in speedway is that riders should compete against each other on equal terms, because the emphasis in the sport is very much on racing, not the machine. This should be compared with road competition where technical developments, inboard telemetry, fuel and tyre considerations and pit stops have ensured that the sport is less and less about driving and racing, and more and more about computer technology and design and seems to have taken the edge off of racing in recent years. Speedway on the other hand, despite its many shortcomings, has always been about real head to head, wheel to wheel, person to person competition. Its initial fascination for the public was that it put men (mostly) on machines and they fought for a result, calling on their will, strength, physical power, racing instincts and ability and not so much the technical superiority of their machine. It was a true contest of the spirit, bringing out the higher human qualities of judgment and courage, whilst applying the reactions and intelligence of the rider. Speedway allowed the riders to go to the edge and the audience to witness their collective adventure and individual daring. It is these characteristics of speedway, its intimate, primal qualities, together with its almost tribal nature, that might explain the panic about being 'invaded' by women. The dynamic of a man staring aggressively into the eyes of another male is not the same as a similar face-off confrontation between 'gender representatives'. This, at the time would have been a symbolic challenge to a great swath of social, personal and psychological conventions, stretching from political institutions to bedroom interactions. Who comes out on top questions our notions of virility and expands the traditions of eroticism - a frightening prospect for a society in the last throes of an Empire premised on Victorian repression.

In the late 1920s the opinion was being formed that there seemed to be no reason why other women should not enter the dirt-track lists, as Fay did not appear to be physically exceptional. According to *The Evening Chronicle*, 30 August, 1928 she was not an 'Amazon'! However, Taylour herself voiced scepticism on this point saying that the sport was 'too unladylike' although she had her own means of dealing with this. 'Patric' in *The Motor Cycle* (25 September, 1930) told his readers, 'She admitted that one of her chief pleasures while racing was to be able to clean-up and get into 'nice clothes' after riding at a meeting.' She told the journalist:

> Even if I look tough in my kit…I like to look like a respectable example of womanhood when I'm off it; I don't mind confessing that I take care of my complexion by applying a thick coating of cream before I ride, and wiping it away, dirt and all, afterwards. It's often been a source of wonderment to people why the dirt seems to have a greater preference for my face than anybody else's – that's the explanation.

Although, by making such statements it seems as if Fay was colluding with the sexist environment in which she lived (even though there is little else she could have done), in fact there was no shortage of volunteers making the point that 'unladylike' activity might not mean undermining the prevailing gender stereotypes. For example, the *Manchester Football News* (1 September, 1928) claimed that, 'Fay Taylour Keeps touch with the Feminine World', and went on to make the case for Fay's presence in speedway:

> Noise of roaring engines, of excited spectators, of riders dashing about the pits. Above, a cold, grey sky; below, a muddy swamp, and, chilling us, drenching us, a pitiless rain. And it was in these circumstances that I first met Miss Fay Taylour, the wonderful dirt track rider.

> She was standing in a corner of the pits trying to wipe off the dirt which had flown into her face during her previous race. Her hair was streaming over her face; there were spots of the track all over her; her leathers were covered with the mud which her wheels had flung up. And as we were introduced she brought from some mysterious pocket in her riding kit a small mirror and a powder.

> My face must have registered disapproval. "What is the matter," she asked. "Don't you approve of women riding on dirt tracks?"

> I hesitated - and was lost. Here in front of me was a charming woman, a woman who obviously, despite the strenuous sport in which she was engaged, still retained all her feminine characteristics. .

Rare Riders
I compromised. "It is not," I said, "that I disagree with women riding on dirt tracks. My only argument is that so few women are able to hold up a machine on a track that the woman rider must inevitably remain a novelty. How many women, given the time and the opportunity to ride, could hope to ride against the men?"

"You think," said Miss Taylour, "that a woman riding in these filthy things (she looked down, at her leathers) must lose something, that she must grow coarse. Will you see me after I have finished racing and then judge, for yourself?"

I promised, and as I promised the microphone announced a challenge race between Miss Taylour and an Australian. I went into the centre of the track to see it. There was only one rider to watch. It was the Irish girl. The Australian fell but even so he would have had no chance against the woman, for she was riding with a skill and judgment that many a man would have envied.

We resumed our talk after the race. The rain was still falling and the track became more impossible every minute.

"You may not believe me" she said, "but I love this game. I used to ride a lot in reliability trials but I have given it up for the speedway. It is more thrilling, not so exacting, and it pays better."

Miss Taylour was called away for another race. Half an hour afterwards I called at the office for her. Was this, I asked myself, the same girl whom I had seen in the dirty riding leathers? She was in a brown costume. Her hair was neat and shining in the electric light. Her eyes were sparkling and her skin was without a blemish. She carried a hand bag. "Well?" she said. I raised my hat in complete surrender.

Over the Top.

We wormed our way through the crowd. The rain was still falling. It did not seem to trouble Miss Taylour. We got to the safety fence surrounding the track. She thrust her handbag into my hand and started to climb over the wire. I followed. The faithful journalist must never lose his quarry.

We saw a race from the centre of the track and then we made our way to the pits where Miss Taylour had stored some struts for her machine. It was another nightmare that awaited us. Autograph hunters by the score. Little pieces of dirty paper, autograph books, programmes, cards - all were thrust in turn into the girl's hand as she willingly signed her name, in the pouring rain.

We escaped. Scurrying through the rain Miss Taylour gave me a piece of chocolate. "A little boy gave me three bars because he liked me," she said. On the way back to the office more autographs. My pencil was looking alarmingly worn.

There was no peace for us. Another crowd of admirers gathered round. I gave a despairing look round and prepared to say goodnight. "Have I convinced you," asked Miss Taylour, "that women, can ride on dirt?"

"You have" I replied briefly. "Do you mind telling me your age?" "Guess" she said. And I leave you to do the same.

The above is typical of the struggle the media had with Taylour, or more specifically managing the actuality of a woman in a 'man's world'. Her achievement was difficult to understate and it was 'good for business'. This led to two options, portray her as a kind of 'track babe', a 'gritty gal' straight from the pages of 'Bunty' - or a 'Daughter of Lesbos', something that the media of the time had no means of presenting or dealing with. In the end the usual sexual stereotype was customised and used (probably unconsciously) to create suspicions about Fay's sexuality (and were not uncommon in the realm of gossip). This was not just about the fact of homosexuality being unpalatable to the public at that time. British society in the 1920s was unable to contemplate (or even perhaps to begin to tolerate) models of female autonomy implicit in Lesbian life-styles. That would have felt (and maybe would have been) intimidating to power structures premised on male hegemony. However, reading some of the popular press reports of the exploits of women in contemporary motorcycle sport, one is left with the feeling that we have not really come that far since Taylour's day.

For all this, by the time she rode out at Middlesbrough, Fay's public image had been established and she was being hailed as the 'Daring Girl Rider'. A good crowd demonstrated that speedway might have a longer life on Teesside than many people had imagined, it being an area long noted for its adherence to soccer. In the north generally speedway was flourishing - at the White City, Manchester, the dirt-track sport was threatening to supplant the greyhound racing that had spawned it, and speedways elsewhere were often run on three nights a week.

Taylour's first appearance at Cleveland Park Speedway, Middlesbrough, on the evening of 4 September, 1928, saw her beat several of the 'crack' British and Australian riders. She carried off the biggest prize of the evening and was the star of the meeting. In terms of machine control and daring, few of the male competitors could equal Taylour. She approached the corners at breakneck speed and after broadsiding brilliantly, demonstrated remarkable acceleration out of the bends.

However, perhaps the most interesting encounter at Middlesbrough that evening was not between male and female. What intrigued the crowd was the encounter in which Taylour came face-to-face with another woman rider with a growing reputation.

Eva

Eva Askquith was the hardy daughter of a butcher from Bedale, North Yorkshire. She was as skilful with horses as with motorcycles in her younger days, winning cups for riding in local shows and at point-to-point events.

Eva had learnt to ride a motorbike whilst serving in the army but never got a chance to ride what was supposed to be her first motorcycle, a small two-stroke which she and a girl friend bought for £3 out of their savings. The friend was riding it round a field when it caught fire and was destroyed. Eva bought the first of her own machines in 1926, a 250cc New Imperial. This was followed by the purchase of a faster model, an HRD and after that she got herself a special TT AJS (a machine that was not really suitable for her) which she rode in the grueling Scott Trial in Swaledale, acknowledged as the biggest and most demanding one-day trial in Britain. Just to complete the course was a physical feat in itself, with its huge gullies, torrential streams, rocks, mud, water holes, bogs, bracken, heather and atrocious gradients. The Scott never failed to take its toll of even the best and most courageous competitors. Every rider ached from head to foot by the time they got to the finish; most were almost dazed with fatigue and it was enough for most competitors to be able to say that they had finished the course. Eva Askquith, at the age of 21, did just that in 1927, despite falling from her 'Ajay' many times on her way to winning a second class award. Oliver and Eric Langton were in the same event, riding 596cc Scott machines, as was Alec Jackson[19] on a 490cc Norton. Oliver won the Bailey Trophy and the Denham Award and Alec gained the special award. Oliver and Eric, with Tommy Hatch, carried off the Scott Trophy for the best amateur team.

Eva entered the Scottish six-day trial and won a competitor's medal, awarded for finishing and she came second in a trial from York to Edinburgh and back which had to be done in 24 hours. She purchased a Velocette, and this helped her rise to fame in grass track racing, reliability trials and hill climbing at Post Hill and at Dalton Bank. At Dalton Bank she crossed the finishing line at the top of the huge hill on one wheel in an almost vertical position. A photographer captured this spectacular feat, the picture appeared in the next day's newspapers with a caption, 'Girl rider's spectacular feat' (there is nothing modern about 'wheelies').

Recording the fastest time at a Post Hill event in the ladies' class against Marjorie Cottle (Raleigh), Edyth Foley (Triumph) and Taylour (Ariel), Eva was awarded the Ladies Trophy.

Eva also took part in sand meetings but she never really liked these sprint-type events. It was the 'flat-out' hill climbs that she really enjoyed, although grass track racing on the Harrogate cricket ground provided her with an immense amount of fun and success.

In 1928, just as the majority of dirt-tracks were closing down after a fantastic season, two circuits, Leeds and Southampton, were surprisingly opened in October. Leeds speedway held its first-ever meeting on 14 October. Eva had been there as a spectator and the following week she was a rider, winning her heat in the Junior Handicap from the two second mark, but finding her grass track Velo not really a suitable machine for the dirt.

Dirt-tracks built in stadiums intended for greyhound racing, like the 402 yard Leeds oval, were always at a disadvantage as compared with cinder circuits which had been specially constructed for speedway, because it was impossible to give the track anything other than long straights and short radius bends. For all that, Leeds drew weekly crowds of 10 to12, 000 people.

Leeds speedway opened again on 30 March 1929, and Eva was able to put in further appearances. Instead of using the old Velo, her mount was now a specialist dirt-track Douglas. Eva was not too tall, and had short legs and the new bike with its low frame was well suited to her.

At the time Leeds was operating, Saturday meetings were taking place all over Britain at Barnsley, Birmingham, Bolton, Cardiff, Exeter, Glasgow, Leicester, Liverpool, Manchester's Belle Vue and White City, Nottingham, Rochdale, Sheffield, Southampton, Crystal Palace, Greenford, Harringay, King's Oak, Lea Bridge, West Ham, Stamford Bridge, Warrington and Coventry. The previous year several managements had staged two meetings per week, on Wednesdays and Saturdays. The enthusiasm for dirt-track racing was massive.

Eva's initial races on her new Duggie, purchased entirely out of her prize money, were heat victories, but she was soon making finals and often winning events although she also had her mishaps. At High Beach, in the first heat of a scratch race, she was sandwiched between two riders in a triple collision on one of the bends but, although badly shaken, she insisted on taking her place in the re-run.

Askquith thought nothing of sticking her bike in the guard's van of a train at Bedale, changing at Northallerton if necessary and going into Scotland, the West Country or Wales - anywhere where there was a speedway meeting she could enter. Nothing seemed to daunt her.

Eva Askquith on her Douglas
(photo courtesy of John Sommerville)

After appearing at Wolverhampton she made the headlines when Mark Sawbridge of the *Wolverhampton Express and Star*, reported on 4 September, 1929:

A true Yorkshire lass, born at Bedale, is Miss Eva Askquith, who made dirt-track history at Wolverhampton last night by being the first woman to ride on the cinder path at Monmore Green.

With her grey-blue eyes and soft brown hair, Miss Askquith, in common with many other women who have made a place for themselves in mechanical racing, is in her every-day dress the essence of femininity and even in her workman-like racing kit she somehow manages to retain her essential womanliness of appearance.

Her fortune on the track at Monmore Green last night seemed to bear out what she herself believes - that few women have the strength of wrist and hand to compete with the strongest men riders on the dirt track.

She simply was not in it with 'Westy' Westwood who has so great a knack of horizontal riding at the turns. 'Westy', however, regards Miss Askquith as a worthy opponent, and gives as his opinion that the reason she did not do better was to a great extent due to the cause which is apt to upset many first-rate racers - dislike of the track.

"I have only been riding on the dirt-tracks since March", said Miss Askquith at the stadium just before her race. "In all, I've had about three years with my motor bicycle. Before that I'd never been on one and I used to borrow other people's when they weren't looking and ride round a field to learn."

Miss Askquith is one of our few women riders in England, or the world for that matter, who have appeared in both hill climbing contests and dirt-track racing. Unfortunately, however, she has not been as successful in the latest sport as she was at hill climbing, which is probably due to the fact that she has reached such 'heights' - in more senses than one - at hill climbing.

Post Hill at Leeds, one of the most dangerous and steepest test hills in the country, is Miss Askquith's favourite spot. Here she is at home, both on the hill and with the people. Yorkshire Sunday afternoon crowds shout themselves hoarse as heat after heat and final after final has been won by Miss Askquith, against some of the cleverest and most daring male riders England can produce.

Eva once said that she thought that the people in her home town of Bedale felt she was 'crackers' for being involved in such a dangerous sport, but she did put Bedale on the sporting map of Britain during the 1930s. She was certainly a celebrity of her day. The Eva Askquith archive in the town's museum contains a signed photograph of the nationally popular comedian Tommy Trinder, dated Edinburgh 1930, dedicated to Eva with a message hoping that her career would 'skid' along successfully.

Performing in front of a 17,000 crowd at Brough Park speedway, Eva won the first round of a match race against Gordon Byers[20], the 17 year old Newcastle Champion (who was later to become a top Wembley Lion). Gordon won round two, but before the decider of the Golden Helmet contest could be staged, Eva was involved in a triple crash and sustained a cut head which put her out of action for the remainder of the programme. However, she was one of the very few to defeat Byers, the record breaking Golden Helmet winner and undaunted she was racing again the next evening at Gosforth speedway. The great 'Smiling' Jim Kempster[21] was there too as well as Charlie Barrett of Wembley, who before taking up the sport, practiced by racing round the cinder path surrounding a gasometer. His father was a Gas Works manager in Devizes.

Eva rode in the victorious Leeds team against Sheffield at Owlerton on 31 July, 1929. In one of her two rides as reserve she finished second in the fastest race of the evening. Leeds won 35-28 on points.

After winning a match race at the Crystal Palace at 42.41 mph, Eva made her bow at Lea Bridge speedway in East London and broke the ladies' record by over five seconds. Her next engagements were three consecutive rides at Wembley, West Ham and Southampton. Eva easily defeated woman rider Sunny Somerset at the Empire Stadium. At West Ham she took on the Hammers captain, the formidable 'Tiger' Stevenson.

Harold 'Tiger' Stevenson earned his nickname from his determination to succeed despite countless mishaps early in his career. He was introduced to the finer techniques of speedway by Sprouts Elder, whose sweeping, spectacular style he emulated and later refined. Even when more efficient and austere styles prevailed in the sport, he persisted with the old extravagant broadside. 'Tiger' was to lead the West Ham side on many occasions. Alongside Bluey Wilkinson and Tommy Croombs, Stevenson was to become one of the West Ham elite riders, a group of the very highest quality and would be nominated to race Ron Johnson for the British Match Race Championship of 1933. Stevenson won both legs and became one of the few Londoners to reach Star Class. Recognition of Stevenson's achievements of that season came when he was made captain of England for four of that year's Test matches, leading his country to a 3-2 series victory and scoring double figures in all the matches in which he rode.

Although before 1930 Stevenson had not matured to the formidable rider he would one day become, he was amongst the best of the English riders in the late 1920s. However, at Lea Bridge Eva won the first heat of the match race at 38.38mph, but 'Tiger' won round two although at a slower speed. The crowd eagerly awaited the decider. Eva got the result by one length; a truly fantastic victory.

With her characteristic determination and courage Eva made her debut at Southampton. Her match race opponent was the famous 'Sprouts' Elder, in front of a huge crowd. 'Sprouts' at that time could be ranked in the top five racers in the world, riding his factory tuned Douglas machines which were among the fastest track bikes on the face of the planet. He dominated the initial race, but Eva was never far behind. Race two saw the Yorkshire lass tearing round the track in the lead after a good start. The two screaming Douglas' echoed through the Banister Court Stadium. Sprouts favoured a counter punch tactic, a kind of cat and mouse game. He rode like the genius he was, his Duggie seemed to be cornering on its flywheel. Elder had laid his machine over at an amazing angle in trying to catch his female opponent and over-slid. However, he left things a little too late, misjudging Eva's speed and she went on to win in 82 seconds. With things level the American was now on his guard, and very much being forced to take things more seriously by the girl from Bedale: he won the decider by two lengths.

Eva wooed the crowds that loved to see her beat the men in match races. She, alongside her closest rival Fay Taylour, became a big attraction on all the northern circuits. But some of her best rides took place at Wembley. In 1929, the first year of speedway at the Empire Stadium, Eva beat Fay 2-0 on 4 June. Taylour was soon to get her revenge defeating Eva 2-1 on 27 June. Art Warren beat Eva 1-0 on 8 August, Askquith beat Sunny Somerset 1-0 on 29 August, and Geoff Taylor beat Eva 1-0 on 7 November. This was a fine competition record but overall, at what was considered the centre of speedway on the Wembley track, Eva had bettered Taylour 3-2. Johnnie Hoskins, quoted in *Speedway Star* (3 February, 2001) told how:

> Eva was the opposite to Fay in terms of personality,…but also a brilliant rider. They gave added interest to the sport at a time it badly needed publicity. They rode against the men at tracks up and down the country, but it was when they met in opposition to each other that the sparks began to fly. Even the star riders leaned over the pit gates to see Fay and Eva hefting their big Douglas machines and racing with utter abandon to the finishing flag. Fay would hold up the start of a race while she adjusted her hair, applied a little lipstick or exchanged a few words with officials on the line. Eva never worried about such, what were for her, trivialities. She sat watching and waiting for the starter's gun. I never could make up my mind which was the better rider of the two.

Askquith's adventurous spirit knew no bounds for, as the 1929 British season drew to an end she set off for a spot of dirt-track racing in Spain (with Charlie Barrett and Cliff Parkinson[22]) where the spectators would throw rotten tomatoes at the riders they failed to take a liking to. The Spaniards gave her a rousing reception at Barcelona speedway where she appeared several times (on posters in Spain she was known simply as 'Miss Eva'). Following a short visit home, she sailed to South Africa to compete at Ellis Park speedway,

Johannesburg where, on her first appearance a 15,000 crowd saw her in a match race against Joe Sarkis, the South African Champion. Over £1,000 was taken in gate money a substantial sum for the time. The South Africans called Eva 'The Yorkshire Rose'. She was the first female dirt-track rider in South Africa, and when told by a local reporter that most women there confined themselves to pillion riding she replied simply: "You cannot get much fun out of that!" She also rode in Australia and Denmark. In Copenhagen, accompanied by riders George Reynard and Alex Jackson (who would one day manage the England team) her riding caused a sensation. The Danes flocked to see this young lady of 23, who had the stamina and strength to hold a fast and heavy racing machine on a speedway and, what's more, to ride it at speeds that did her great credit. The ride on that Copenhagen circuit was spectacular and Eva simply had to go almost flat-out, cling on to her Duggie and hope for the best. She met the 'Great Dane', Morian Hansen, the Danish Champion. He was a tough man who never wore goggles. There are many hair-raising stories of his determination, and his seeming indifference to hard knocks and pain. The calm yet determined Dane was one of the best riders of the few to come out of continental Europe in the early years of speedway. He made several visits to England before he joined West Ham in 1931 and moved to Hackney Wick when that club was formed in 1935. He also had a spell with Wembley. During the Australian speedway season of 1935-36 he broke his jaw in his first race, but did not let this interfere with his riding. He wintered in England in 1936 and qualified for a commercial pilots licence. When the Second World War came Hansen joined the RAF and was decorated with the DFC and the George Medal. Always a brave rider, he proved to be an equally courageous warrior.

Eva Askquith's name pulled a record crowd of over 10,000 on her initial appearance in Denmark. In her first race she defeated the two male riders, after which came a few losses. However at the next meeting she had become more accustomed to the circuit and secured several more victories.

A giant of a man in a trilby-hat always appeared at the Copenhagen meetings. He was the attendant Doctor named Ove Bevdixen, a very likeable and happy person, who tested all the riders' hearts before they started to race. According to Eva, 'He was one of the greatest sports I have ever known.'

Back again in Yorkshire, in April 1930, Eva prepared for the English dirt-track season. Returning to England after a very successful Danish tour, she was in demand and she raced on tracks as far apart as Glasgow, Exeter, Coventry and Wembley. At Leeds, her home track, the local fans gave her a warm greeting; the programme was headed 'WELCOME BACK, OUR EVA'. Apart from John Lloyd and Eric Langton on Rudges, every other rider was Douglas mounted.

To those who knew her well, Eva Askquith was a remarkable person. It was difficult to accommodate her reserved, sensitive and peaceful nature given her persona on the tracks, tearing round the confined space of British speedways at an awe-inspiring 42mph.

Moving on

In the Middlesbrough match with Askquith, Taylour proved herself the better woman on the night, and won in the excellent time of 1 minute 10 $^4/_5$ seconds, conceding six seconds to her rival. However, Eva was riding a much heavier bike than Fay and at that point had not perfected the powerslide technique to the level Taylour had achieved. Instead of throwing the bike wide into the turn, Askquith rode round the inside with bent knee. Ironically, with the arrival of shorter wheelbase bikes some years later, most speedway riders broadsided in much the same way.

Eva and Fay shake hands at the start

Although hampered by her unfamiliarity with the track, and the fact that it was smaller than some she had become accustomed to, Taylour not only performed her broadsides as well as most and better than many of her male colleagues, she won the handicap and bagged second place in the scratch event. She also managed to extricate herself from a nearly impossible situation when she 'snaked' out of a couple of bad skids with a coolness and assurance reminiscent of Fred Fearnley[23] and demonstrating her complete control of the bike.

At the same time Sig Schalm showed himself to be a growing presence in speedway when he succeeded in beating his own record for the Middlesbrough track, taking second place in a heat in 1 minute 20 seconds. Fay and Sig would meet again down under.

Taylour's exploits continued to become the object of national interest. In *Dirt Track Notes and News* in *The Daily Express* (5 September, 1928) Fay was described as 'a pretty girl of twenty-four, with auburn hair', but the column also recorded the fact that she had hit over forty miles an hour at the Crystal

Palace, beating men from a level mark, and was 'doing missionary work among those of her own sex in Lancashire'.

The *Evening Chronicle* (10 September, 1928) reflected on Taylour's growing status:

For the Films?
What is to be the future of Miss Fay Taylour, the dirt-track rider, who has won such golden opinions in Lancashire and the North through her clever and plucky exhibitions?

Quite frankly Miss Taylour admits that she does not know herself. At the moment she is considering with some perplexity whether to accept an offer to go on the films; sign a contract to ride on the Continent; pay a visit to Australia; or try her luck in America.

Whatever may be her decision (writes our dirt-track representative) she is determined not to sever her connection with British dirt-track racing entirely, and has no desire to suspend her riding until the close of the official dirt-tack racing season - the end of October.

British Film Chance
"I am bound by contract until the end of September, and after that I hope to have a month of independence," she told me.

"During that month I want to be able to travel about to almost any track I please, and there are a number in different parts of the country which I have yet to visit. Therefore I have no desire to settle anything for October. The question is, what am I to do with myself during the winter?"

Miss Taylour told me that the film offer had been made by a British company, and the proposed film would probably be 'shot' in England. I understand from Miss Taylour that her riding, would also play a part in the film, which may, I believe, be one of the talking variety.

In *The Evening Chronicle* (3 September), 'Kick Start' seemed to buy into the 'cult of personality' that was developing around Taylour, arguing in the piece, *Idols of the Track* that:

What the 'Fans' wanted was, Personalities and Not Pot-winners.

The sudden cancelling in Manchester recently of a dirt track meeting caused something of a stir. It also drew attention to the fact that the dirt track 'fan' is becoming critical, and insists on 'star' performers.

Miss Fay Taylour is another idol with the 'fans'. She has personality, pluck, and skill, and, win or lose, there's always a cheer for Fay. In her case, the element of novelty - a woman shining in an essentially masculine sport, also enters with telling effect.

The more personalities and novelties in dirt track programmes, the better. And heat events should be reduced to a minimum, even if this meant running some of them off privately.

All star programmes every week are an impossibility. But an attractive alternative would be a programme consisting of semi-finals and finals only for the various cups, and challenge races freely interspersed with novelty and exhibition turns, not forgetting the comic side.

The population of Britain were indeed very keen to support the highest quality of speedway, but it was considered as least as much an entertainment as a sport by those who were paying their money to watch it. Characters like Taylour, who could supply competition, intrigue, novelty value and perhaps a whiff of scandal were therefore very much needed.

Douglas muscle

Taylour rode out at the Crystal Palace meeting in September, 1928 on a gleaming, brand new, dirt track Douglas. The Duggie's power and Fay's skill astounded everyone. Douglas motorbikes were manufactured in Bristol by the firm of William and Edward Douglas from 1907 (sadly, the firm went out of business in 1957). On this extraordinary machine specially designed by Freddie Dixon, the record-breaking Brooklands and TT rider, Fay would become one of the few women riders to adopt the spectacular 'leg-trailing' style of broadsiding, on the outer rim of the track. This was Fay's third meeting at Crystal Palace in mid-September and included a match race with Joe Francis, one of the best riders of his generation. From the rolling start she promptly left him, and he fell from his Ariel in trying to catch her. Another start was made, and the same thing happened. After a third start, Joe's exhaust, pipe came adrift from the port, and he slowed down to wrench it off and throw it away. After a fourth start Fay's petrol pipe broke and the small tank lost all its juice in about half a lap. The organisers would not hear of the race being run again. Given the fact that the contest was restarted three times because of Joe's troubles, Taylour probably should have been given at least one restart, but she pleaded in vain, and Joe was announced as the winner. The crowd, according to the *Motor Cycle* (22 September) 'kicked up a shindy at this', and in response the race was declared void.

At Liverpool Speedway, on a September Saturday evening, rain detracted from the quality of the racing, but the riders did their best and provided a good programme. Taylour received a great ovation for her fearless riding with Keith McKay in a Silver Armlet final. She was beaten by inches in a match with the pioneer Australian as she ran home second to McKay.

The *Leicester Mercury* (28 September) reported 'Eve Competes on The Dirt Track'. The evening before Taylour, who the Mercury called 'the first woman to compete in the sport and world's woman dirt-track champion', had been beaten in each of the three events in which she took part, but it seems her performance at the Leicester Stadium was a 'a wonderful exhibition of feminine daring and skill'. Fay, who was described as a 'small, petite figure', was given a 'hearty reception' when she made her initial entry on the track to ride in a challenge race against Arthur Sherlock, the well-known and talented Leicester rider.

Fay and her Douglas
Photo courtesy of John Sommerville

Unacquainted with the track, Taylour was allowed to ride round twice before the race with Sherlock. When the pair eventually set off for the race, as Fay went into the first bend her machine skidded and she was thrown. Sherlock, who was riding some distance behind what the *Mercury* called 'his fair rival', and having given his opponent a few seconds start, pulled up, and the race was re-started. Again Taylour had trouble with her machine, and the competition had to be postponed. However, the race was finally run and for the first two laps it was a real fight. Taylour resolutely held the lead, refusing to be intimidated by the constant threat of Sherlock roaring in on her. But he timed his challenge perfectly on the bend in to the third lap, coming out in front. Taylour bravely held on to Sherlock's heels and raced full-out to the very end. But the Leicester man had taken the momentum and won comfortably. The record of the night's racing told the story:

Challenge Races
A. Sherlock (Leicester) beat Miss Fay Taylour Time, 1 min. 32²/₅ secs

Fay also rode in the Golden Helmet Competition and the Senior Race, but was beaten in the heats.

Across the sea to Ireland

As winter closed in Fay crossed the Irish Sea for the first time as a racer. The *Belfast News-Letter* (8 October) heralded her return to the Emerald Isle under the strap-line,

Belfast Speedway...Star's Dashing Performance at Windsor Park Track...Lady Champion a Favourite. Miss Fay Taylour's Display in Speedway notes - Powder puff on the dirt track.

Attired like a 'crack' - leather breeches, coat, crash helmet, and mask - Miss Fay Taylour gave a demonstration of broadsiding at Windsor Park...Her display, daring as it was skilled, at once established her a prime favourite with the spectators – most of them women – who greeted her every subsequent appearance with applause. She had several spills, but an attendant would help her to re-start her machine and she was off again in a moment to the accompaniment of a thunder of applause. She rode in five races altogether and won two heats, she was unplaced in the finals.

Taylour gave an exhibition of riding to provide a prelude to the meeting, which opened with the Ulster Speedway scratch race over five heats of four laps each. Taylour covered the four laps in 1 minute 55.5 seconds. Norrie 'Cyclone' Isbister, winner of the first heat, found Taylor a dangerous opponent. He made a bad getaway, and when he fell his chances of finishing second seemed remote. Although Fay had taken the lead, Isbister quickly remounted and passed her before the line was reached.

Scotsman Norrie 'Cyclone' Isbister was present at the first ever dirt-track meeting staged in Scotland. He was to recall that initial Caledonian event at Celtic Park at a time when Speedway was unknown north of the border, but a respectable crowd turned up. The first race included Sprouts Elder, Stewie St. George from New Zealand and Ivor Creek. Norrie recalled standing at the fence and watching the racers coming out of the bend and saying to himself, "these 'so and so' guys are mad, no way, I don't want to know this thing". He told Keith McKay, "I'm not here!"

However, in later years he was to promote the Ashfield Giants, drawing crowds sometimes of up to 26,000, creating the tremendous atmosphere for which that track was known especially during big international meetings, like

Scotland v England. Norrie passed away in November 1999, aged 93. He was a regular supporter of the sport up to his death and a true legend of Speedway.

In the Belfast winter of 1928 Taylor and Isbister met in the second heat. Fay fell in the first lap but Norrie, ever the sportsman, pulled up. Taylour's second toss left him to finish by himself. In the final it was Isbister who took a tumble and it was with apparent reluctance that he was prevailed upon to wheel his machine past the post. The results demonstrate how the evening went for both Isbister and Taylour:

Ulster Speedway scratch race

Heat winners
Cyclone Isbister (Scotland)

J. Cummings (Scotland)	Rudge	Time 1min 52 secs
Larry Coffey (Sandbrook)	Douglas	1min 49 ½ secs
Miss Fay Taylor (Birr)	Rudge,	1min 55 ½ secs
Evan (Liverpool)		2min, 6secs.

Final
1, Coffey; 2, Isbister; 3, Miss Taylour   Time 1min. 51secs.

International Challenge Race.
The first heat was won by Larry Coffey, and in the second Isbister beat Miss Taylour. Coffey had the final to himself after Isbister came to grief.

From Ireland to Salford

The *Daily Dispatch* (9 October) carried the news:

Fay Taylour Misses Boat and Too Late for Dirt Track Races.
Miss Fay Taylour, who is leaving shortly to ride on dirt tracks in Australia, missed the boat by which she was to travel yesterday in order to race on the Salford track last night. She crossed from Ireland in a cargo steamer in an effort to reach the track in time for racing, and sent the following telegram to Mr. Hughes, manager of the track:-

'Missed steamer. Crossing by L.M.S. cargo boat leaving Dublin 1 pm to-day. Arrange for my mechanic for fast motorcar or aeroplane to meet me Holyhead.'

Must appear Salford to-night.
An aeroplane could not be obtained and a fast motor-car was sent to Holyhead, but Miss Taylour was just too late to ride in any of the races. She reached the track just as the last heat of the Salford Handicap had been started, but she immediately changed into her riding kit and gave a demonstration.

Taylour recalled that episode as being instrumental in opening her eyes to the likes of Hoskins:

I'd been visiting Ireland and intended to catch the mailboat from Kingstown to Holyhead on the morning of racing, and then on to Salford by train. My bike would be at the track. But I missed the ship because I forgot that Kingstown had changed its name to Dun Laoghaire though everyone still called it by the old name, and when the little train from Dublin chugged out of the station I was still on it, and then suddenly saw the pier and the ship and realised I was leaving it behind. When I got back the ship had sailed, and I was told there was no other sailing till the evening. Efforts to find a plane proved futile and I could have sat down and cried if crying were a more active pursuit. I just *had* to reach Salford.

It was unthinkable to let that track down. Fans were my friends and these were very special. Their cheers when I raced there before and won a heat, and then their sympathetic groans when my bike conked out on the last lap as I was leading in a final made me promise to return. I would have to find a way of bridging that seventy miles of water...and I did.

At 1pm I sailed in a small open castleboat with a cargo of pigs, dozens of them all standing together in the centre, and the poor creatures were sick when we started lurching about after leaving the harbour. Luckily I'm a good sailor because there was nowhere for me to be sick except with them. It was raining, but when the weather cleared up the pigs cheered up. It was quite fun, and the skipper made his old boat go as fast as it could. I'd wired to the track manager to have a fast car or aeroplane to meet me at Holyhead from where I'd have to cover the best part of 200 miles. Racing started at 8pm.

One of the track helpers was there with his sedan, and he was a good driver but I'll never forget that trip. It was lurchier than the cattle boat, and I watched the time all the way for it was a race against the clock. If I could get there before the racing finished I'd be lucky. I changed into my racing togs in the back of the car and got more bruised in that process than I might on the track. And then we arrived – just in time for me to give a demonstration which was better than nothing, though I begged for the programmed match race to be put on. I then received ten pounds appearance money only, and asked the promoter to pay for the car trip out of the saved match race money which would have amounted at the least to between five and ten pounds. He called me a bushranger, and I knew there and then that I was no match for the promoters even if I could tackle the toughest riders.

Questions were still being asked about the involvement of women in speedway racing and *Motor Cycling* (10 October, 1928) at least seemed to be on Taylour's side:

There has been a lot of discussion as to whether dirt-track racing is a suitable sport for women, and many have poured large bucketfuls of cold water on the aspirations of many of our prominent girl riders. The chief stumbling block seems to be the amount of strength needed to hold a machine in a skid. Sprouts Elder is one of those who thinks that no girl is strong enough to do it, but on this point I disagree. There are many of our girl riders who can more than hold their own with the opposite sex when it comes to hard work on rough stuff. As for speed I recall that Col. Stewart[24] shared a Brooklands record with his wife, while for sheer hard riding there are many men who wish they could equal Fay Taylour's prowess at Camberley. Fay, of course, seems to be the only girl who has taken up the game seriously. Good luck to her! I fail to see why girls should not ride on cinders if they want to, and Fay's popularity with the public is evidence of the fact that their appearance would not prove a blight on a programme. In this connection, I hope to give, very shortly, Fay's views on the subject. They are extremely interesting!

However, Fay had no time for analysis at that point. After appearing at Edinburgh, Taylour gained the ladies record at Brandon (Coventry) in mid-October in front of 4,000 Saturday night spectators. Her best lap was timed at 20 seconds and her total time for four circuits was 84 seconds. Later Taylour won the Brandon handicap race from 2 seconds in splendid form (C.L. Davies was second).

Laurence H. Cade, in *Allsports Weekly* (20 October, 1928), four months into Fay's speedway career, told of how her early efforts in the sport were 'such as to discourage her', but that she had become 'better than many of the male exponents'. Cade saw Fay as a courageous rider who took risks, was more at home on a 'senior' than a 'junior' machine, and having no fear of speed was able to accelerate into the curves. But at the same time he asserted that she was 'a true feminist, extremely graceful on a dance floor, and a charming young lady'.

For Cade, who identified Fay as 'An all-round sportswoman' who 'played hockey for her county - Berkshire - and is good at lawn tennis and golf', it was evident that she had modelled her style on the method adopted by Billy Lamont. 'To her' he eulogised 'the wide bends are 'skid centres' and the straights for accelerating to the speed required for a proper broadside'.

There were certainly elements of Fay's riding that seemed to mirror the style of Billy Lamont, but while she did take calculated risks, she never had the reckless fire of Lamont.

As the winter of 1928 closed in, Cade argued that Taylour had earned a place among the heroes of the Speedways. For him, dirt-track racing was no pursuit for a woman, but Fay seemed the exception to the rule. He explained that she had overcome a tendency to wobble on the turns and had 'learnt to shift the cinders on the bends and was able to skid her back wheel' as well as any of the English riders. Fay had achieved this standard because she took chances and made herself proficient in the track arts, despite falling many times in the process.

Taylour had competed in handicaps, and the time allowances she received had to be continually adjusted because of the great progress she made. Cade saw that her courage might have suggested a degree of masculinity, but argued that she was seen by fans and the media in a positive light.

Looking back on her first experiences of the speedways Fay wrote:

I could have hung up my crash helmet now if I'd been racing to prove that a woman, after all could conquer the art of dirt track racing, or 'dracing' as it was fondly nick-named in those days. But the challenge remained because I was never satisfied that I had yet shown my best which only time and experience could develop. The sport was still new, and charged with romance. The ambulance men on the infield were frequently in action and one could never be sure of not taking a drive with them. Film stars ran off with handsome daring riders, and fans who were packing into the stadiums in crowds of from twenty-five to eighty thousand were roaring themselves hoarse. There was magic in the air, and the enormous fun of racing at new places was worth any nervous strain.

The boys were all signed up with a 'home' track, but I roamed all over England, also to Scotland, Wales and Germany, as the spirit or invitation moved me. New tracks had sprung up everywhere, and it was no longer difficult to be accepted now that I'd proved my worth as a rider and draw-card. It was difficult, however, to get the promoters to pay the appearance money I needed. They were shrewd enough to know that the sport was far too precious to me to use as a negotiating hammer, and when I engaged someone to act as manager they refused to talk to him! The manager, incidentally, turned out to be less useful still, for when I arrived at a far-away track and looked for the newly-ordered engine that he was supposed to dispatch it was nowhere to be found. Later I learned that it was sitting in his pocket in the form of a converted cheque!

But I raced on regardless, putting every penny and pound aside that I could. Sometimes I didn't even have a penny to save such as one of my visits to Salford near Manchester.

Fay was certainly hooked on something. It may have been a simple love of the sport, but in the last analysis there was probably nothing 'simple' about Taylour. She certainly was deeply concerned to grab the limelight and seemed motivated by notoriety. Fame is an intoxicating liquor and the harder one looks at Fay's life the more one becomes convinced this was her addiction. She was desperate to be known, but also appreciated as extraordinary, even wonderful. Whilst she broke many a mould, it is uncertain how close she got to this ephemeral goal, although for Taylour this begs the question - could she ever be famous enough to meet her own standards? And of course the problem with fame is that it is fleeting. Like so many things in Fay's experience, glory was a fickle lover – but perhaps that was (or is) it's most alluring quality.

7. To Australia

Towards the end of 1928 it became public knowledge that Taylour would take to the dirt-track racers of Australia during the winter and so face the vast crowds thronging the speedways 'down under'. This meant meeting the best riders on the planet. According to Cade (*Allsports Weekly*, 20 October, 1928), speed seemed to have no terror for Fay, as she had the valour to tread on the gas when she was approaching a curve. During the 1928 season in Britain, Taylour had proved herself in venues as diverse as Ireland, Brighton, Manchester, Liverpool and Scotland so it was logical for her to continue her progress in the sport. That meant going to Australia.

After the spring of 1928 speedway mushroomed all over Britain, and was now beginning to develop into an organised business. But as in all business, expansion is necessary and given the seasonal nature of the sport, those who made a living through the tracks had three options: find alternative employment from the end of one season to the beginning of the next, live off of any prize money they had accrued, or cross the world. Some riders would maintain constant employment migrating from the realm of the Southern Cross just as the warm winds of spring blew across the British Isles and then returned as the shrouds of winter descended over the Northern Hemisphere.

When that first season of speedway ended in England in the late autumn of 1928, the Australian riders returned home for their summer season. According to Taylour, she was speaking to Johnnie Hoskins, and she told him, "I'd like to see Australia". The entrepreneurial Australian, never one to miss a trick although he was to spend much of his career condemning the idea of women being involved in the sport, offered Taylour an appearance in Perth.

But in another version of events the Australian rider Charlie Datson, who Patric in *The Motor Cycle* (25 September, 1930) described as Taylour's '...patient guide and mentor during her fledgling days at the Crystal Palace track', had suggested that she see the Australian promoters in London with a view to gaining some contracts to ride-out the winter at the dirt-track hotbeds of the likes of Adelaide and Sydney. But Australian patriarchs of the ovals were not keen on accepting Taylour in this most masculine of sports in a country where the dictates of male chauvinism still held sway. However, as was his wont, Hoskins broke away from the convention and offered Fay some encouragement by arranging for her to journey to Perth, Western Australia. She told Patric that she took a Douglas and a Rudge. The Douglas was a state of the art machine and very much her secret weapon because it had proved itself superior on the dirt to the widely used Peashooter.

There is some indication that a trip to the home of speedway had been on the cards for Taylour for some time even before the early winter of 1928. *The Evening Chronicle* (3 September, 1928) had predicted Taylour's crusade more than a month earlier than Cade. Under the headline, 'Adventurous Girl – Australian Trip for Dirt Track Racing – Miss Fay Taylour makes Speedway History' the article reported that 'the pretty Irish girl' was, 'leaving England next month to race on the Australian tracks' and that:

> She will be the first British rider, man or woman, to leave Europe for the express purpose of competing against the Australians at their own game.

> When I saw her to-day she confessed that the idea of racing in Australia had a particularly strong appeal for her.

> She told me that details of her trip had yet to be arranged. She may travel to Australia under a contract with either Mr. Frank Hunting of International Speedways or Mr.Hoskins, who opened the Salford Speedway, both of whom were responsible for the growth of the sport in Australia.

> "But whatever happens," she said, "I am going to try my Rudge out in Australia. I particularly want to make the trip."

Peer's Cousin

Miss Taylour has that carefree disposition typical of her race. Cousin of a famous millionaire newspaper peer, she has in her a strong sporting spirit. "True", she will tell you, "I make money on the track" - since she started dirt track racing a few months ago, her riding expenses have been £350 – "but if I didn't love the riding itself I am certain money would not prompt me to appear on any track."

Miss Taylour, charmingly dressed, looks very unlike a dirt-track rider. Yet her record on the Speedway is one which many a hundred riders covet with envious eyes. She has beaten first-class men, including Australian cracks, at various centres, and at the opening meeting of the Salford track gave an exhibition of daring riding that was cheered to the echo.

She has ridden at the White City, Manchester, and the Rochdale Speedway, and will be seen at the Salford Speedway again on Monday night next. She likes the Manchester crowds, their enthusiasm, and their sportsmanship, and hopes to ride again in Manchester before she leaves for Australia.

The Evening News (8 November) made it official:

> Miss Fay Taylour, the woman dirt-track rider, is leaving England for Australia to compete in races there. She means to come home through America and to race in New York.

> Miss Taylour, who will take two motorcycles with her, is Irish, dark, blue-eyed, and distinctly pretty. Her nerves must be made of steel for when racing she often laps at 45 miles an hour, making fierce looking broadside skids in cornering. She has ridden on equal terms against men and beaten them.

On the 20 October Taylour turned up for her heat of the Special Scratch Race at Crystal Palace with her 1929 dirt-track Douglas, received only that morning and she had yet to even ride it, let alone race. The Palace Potentate, fiery Fred Mockford had refused to let her do any practice laps, so Fay went more or less carefully in a handicap heat and bagged second place. Then in a scratch heat Fay came up against W. Harris, Bill Bragg, Leslie Barker, and Joe Francis. Francis gained the lead on the first lap, but hit a bump, wobbled badly, and thus allowed Fay to pass him. However, Francis made an astonishing recovery, but did exactly the same thing on the next lap this time crashing to the ground.

Fay tore away from the field and won easily in 1 minute 32 seconds, clocking an average speed of 39.13 mph. In the final Taylour was matched against Roger Frogley, Arthur Willimott and Dick Bellamy. Willimott's machine refused to start, and Frogley won comfortably and in style in 1 minute 30 $4/_5$ seconds (39.66 mph). Dick Bellamy came in second and Taylour third.

An interesting snippet from that meeting was that Mr C.L. Smith, the announcer, in bidding good-bye to the spectators, said that the track would re-open on Saturday, 30 March, 1929 and in the meantime flood lighting would be installed.

Six days and more in Europe

After Taylour's northern glories and before leaving for Australia, Lionel Wills put a proposition to Fay. She recalled the proposal as follows:

"How about doing the International Six Days with me", he suggested as we drove back from a weekend's racing in Manchester.

It sounded delicious, although it was a reliability trial and not a race. The start would be in Munich, Bavaria, where we would first spend a week. Then we would drive over the most beautiful passes in the Austrian, Italian and Swiss Alps, with a hotel stop every night at such romantic places as Oberammergau and Chamonix, touching also Savoie in France and finishing up in Geneva.

"Why not", I said though I'd have to find a different type of motorcycle.

The P&M agents offered me a Panther bike, and Lionel produced entry forms; and when competitors' numbers were issued he grinned and said: "look! They've given us consecutive numbers"! It meant we would ride together and finish the day's run at the same time. His student brother was also competing but would be riding with his friends in a different section as he had a much earlier number. His hotel vouchers were also different, mine and Lionel's were the same.

At Munich our bikes were checked and sealed and locked away by officials, and we spent much time sitting around in beer gardens listening to orchestras. Lionel, with a huge tankard of beer in front of him always – he loved beer – while I drank coffee out of those brown handle-less pitchers that seemed to give it more aroma. In the evening we went to theatres or night clubs, and to the official ball two nights before the trial started, or to a bit of it. Lionel didn't dance, he sat watching, but after I was partnered by an attractive official who flirted a little he said, "let's go". The evening was barely under way, and I loved dancing, but I let him take me back to the hotel. We were staying at the Bayerischer Hof.

Marriage never entered my head now. I'd forgotten that I once thought I was on the shelf. Lionel was there all the time and I made no effort to secure him. I loved him but I wasn't in love, that ecstatic state that is very wonderful but never lasts. And yet, even with that awareness, I was to demand such a state of myself before I would say 'yes' to anyone. When you are happy you find people attractive just as happiness draws them to you. I was happy racing and quickly found men attractive, but just as quickly the attraction faded if they took too much for granted. With Lionel it was different. He was one apart, and those two weeks in Europe could not but enhance my feelings for him. Side by side in glorious weather we rode through the trial, and if my cycle engine wasn't singing the right tune or a nut worked loose he was off in a flash to fix it. Past dream castles we went, and then climbed high in the Austrian Alps, pausing at the top of one pass to look down through the tops of pine trees to a lake far below.

"We'll come back one day", he said seriously, "when we do not have to ride on!".

In the evenings we ate our well earned meal together at some quaint foreign inn or hotel, having first handed our motorcycles in to the official checking area from where he always insisted on carrying my kit bag. Then, less seriously, he would joke each time he produced our vouchers for accommodation. The porter or room clerk always wanted to give us a double room, and Lionel would say, "tomorrow I'll say 'yes!" The second last night, in a row boat on Lake Maggiore, I took great trouble to tell him I was not in love with him though I felt closer to him than ever before. Why? Why did I go to such contrary lengths? Was I afraid of a proposal, or was I now making an effort to secure him on the lines of my older friend's advice? 'Never let a man you're fond of know that you care' she'd warned me before leaving for India with her army husband.

Next night we were in Geneva with the riding finished, and after a leisurely wash and change Lionel ordered dinner to be served in his room. We had just finished the last course when the peaceful tete-a-tete atmosphere was rent apart. Without any warning the door burst open and in stormed the young brother whom we had not seen since the trial started. He was tired and agitated, and still in riding kit, and he threw himself full length on the spare bed, dusty boots and all. He'd taken a wrong turn during the afternoon run and got hopelessly lost, then after arriving very late at the final check he found his hotel accommodation given away and all the hotels full. It was lucky his brother had a double room! Lucky too that Lionel's threat had not left me roomless!

Next morning Lionel arranged for our bikes to be railed back to England. Whether we'd won medals or not did not seem important. "I'm tired of riding, let's take a train to Paris!" he'd said, "and fly home from there".

The train broke down near Dijon and we reached Paris in the middle of the night. Hotel accommodation was no problem but the porter at the reception desk shook his head sadly, as all the others had, at our request for two singles. In the elevator, however, he cheered up, and before showing us into our separate rooms he smiled slyly and wished us a *very* good night. Within a split second Lionel appeared from nowhere like an apparition. "No wonder he wished us such a good night", he laughed, "he's given us adjoining rooms!"

Though such causes for mirth were rapidly vanishing they still existed for us, and Lionel had further fun up his sleeve. We'd had to spend another night at the hotel before getting a flight, and now at the airport he engaged the roving photographer to take a picture of us stepping on the plane complete with weekend suitcases and happy smiles. He arranged for it to be mailed to London, and a week later told me the sequel with great glee.

It arrived at breakfast time with the first post. "Ah! Week-ending in Paris", he exclaimed, and handed it around the breakfast table. There was stony silence, all that could be heard was the munching of toast, and the deeper the disapproval the greater was Lionel's amusement. The young brother had already reported that we rode together throughout the trial. It was bad enough for the future head of their austere firm to be a dirt track rider, but to be friendly with a woman who raced motorcycles was the last straw, and my name was muddier than ever. "Mother even called you a scarlet wench", said Lionel laughing hysterically.

In this respect I couldn't share his amusement though I loved his rebellious trait of not caring a hoot what anyone thought. I wished his mother could have formed her opinion other than by mischievous hearsay, but it didn't really worry me, only made our friendship more private and precious.

We had parties with Dormouse *(an old school friend of Fay's)* and her friend Walter to whom I'd introduced her some time previously. Walter Braidwood had been at Cambridge with Lionel, and also raced motorcycles, and now had a repair shop in North London. He and Dormouse fell in love at once which perhaps accounted for her long visits to her older sister who was now practicing medicine in London with her doctor husband.

Walter also raced cars but gave up the sport to become a doctor and marry Dormouse.

My other school chum, Norah, who completed a course at a horticultural college in England after leaving school, was now back in Ireland at her home in Ballyshannon. I had no home any more but that suited me. The stepmother's attitude had changed somewhat. She was becoming less sisterly, and Derryquin, the new house in Lymington, though home for Dordy (*Fay's pet name for her Father*) could never act as such for me nor indeed for Enid who was working hard at University College London to obtain her medical degree. But we were welcome for visits, and I found the attractively furnished two-story house typical of Dordy who had an eye for good pieces at auctions. His old desk was there with its pleasant woody smell, and the grandfather clock that was said to have been dug out of a bog in Ireland; also the family silver, with the familiar marmalade pot decorating the sunny breakfast table while the bacon and eggs kept warm on the old copper stand with the lighted methylated wicks underneath.

And, as of old, Dordy had built a garden and tennis court and was busy putting them into shape. He had joined the Lymington Royal Yacht Club having taken up sailing again, and was competing in club races. Before I was born he had done much yachting in the seas off County Cork and Kerry, and Derryquin Castle featured intimately in his memories of those days when Mother was his sweetheart and later his wife. Perhaps that is why he called the new home Derryquin.

"Goodbye dear! Take care of yourself" he had driven me to the station after a three day visit. I was due to race in Hamburg, Germany the following week, and then the next stop would be Australia.

Hamburg seemed grey and dull though there was all the usual excitement in the racing, and when I left for London there was an incident at the railway station that marred the farewell and left me hurtfully perplexed. A woman dashed down the platform and joined the small gathering that was seeing me off. She was hysterical and someone pushed me on the train telling me not to say goodbye to one of the racing officials.

"Why"?

It was explained that the excited woman was the wife of that official, and she was jealous of me.

Of me! I was no film star or raving beauty, I was a sportsgirl riding a motorcycle, and of all the men at the racing track he was the one I'd noticed least!

I didn't try to sort it out although an identical incident had occurred in England a year earlier, and it would happen again many times. I would not have been able to sort it out then anyway. I was far too engrossed conquering motorcycles to think about conquering men, and I had no delusions about my looks – or perhaps I had. I grew up with the idea that I was quite plain, and as a young child hated my face in the mirror. But it didn't worry me, no one told me I was ugly, and with a pretty blonde sister each side of me how could I expect all three of us to be pretty? I was the middle one, and brunette. They were blonde. And I still had the belief, though without any complex, that I had nothing to boast of in looks. I did not rein in my smiles or my friendliness, and now I'm wondering if such innocent friendliness and enthusiasm for the racing was not just as maddening to a jealous woman as a calculated and flirtatious sophistication.

Would my manner have been entirely different then had I known the contents of a letter written by my mother when I was nine years old? Only recently I read this letter, one of many kept by my father through the years and handed to me at his bequest when he died. It was written to him from England where Mother had taken us to show us off to her relatives and close friends. She wrote: "People seem much struck with Fay's looks, and everyone here considers her the best looking of the lot". If a child grows up with the idea that she is good looking her manner and behaviour must surely be affected with this knowledge. And what of the child with the opposite idea? Shall she lack social confidence but get praised for being unspoilt?

How many parents remember their thoughts as a child, how they were formed, and what effect they could have on their future? I remember now because I have had to think back as I write. And I realise now too that it was not until I landed in sex-conscious America, decades later that I fully understood why many men liked me.

Euripides and the Trojan woman.

On 24 November, 1928 Taylour left Euston at 11am The labels on her trunks and baggage bore the legend, 'Fay Taylour, Australia'. She had been sharing a flat with two other women for some time and had spent most of the previous evening packing. Arthur Simcock[25] the TT rider, had called to give Fay some information and advice she required. Then another friend had turned up to receive instructions about selling her car followed by a visit from her father. Worrying about his own father's wanderings, her father told his racing daughter that should anyone in Australia called Taylour claim relationship she was to 'take no notice'. The telephone rang constantly when Fay was not making calls herself. All through this the gramophone sang out incessantly. The whole episode reflected her excitement and almost childlike last minute response.

Taylour's only companions on the trip to Australia were her new Douglas and the Rudge as a standby, with a reserve engine and a box of spare parts.

She travelled alone and on 'spec', with very little money. She had a few introductory letters and recommendations, but no racing engagements apart from the one that Hoskins had arranged. This was the sum of Taylour's support for her adventure. She had told the *Daily Mirror* (24 November, 1928) that she was sailing from Liverpool on the *Euripides*. She booked a return passage so that whatever happened she would be able to return to Britain. At that time such an undertaking would have been challenging for a man, but for a woman it was almost without precedent. Taylour had the distinction of being the first, and at the time the only British dirt-track rider to take on the Australians at their own game, in their own land.

As Fay boarded the ship the struggle to define her to the world continued. When it was suggested that long before the end of the voyage she would become engaged to some millionaire, she instantly replied: "That would be impossible – all the really nice people are already married." This, along with the number of 'evening frocks' she took with her to Australia, was seen as evidence that Fay was 'essentially feminine' even if she did ride the dirt-track.

Fay seemed to think that there was only room for one woman on the speedways, it was after all her unique selling point. As she sailed for the other side of the world, Britain was given the message loud and clear; she had to be an exception to the rule - In a letter to *Motor Cycling* (5 December, 1928) Taylour wrote;

> To the question 'Can a woman ride on the dirt,' I answer emphatically 'Yes', and the more I ride the more I hope to prove it; but the question of it being a woman's sport is quite another matter. Judging by the number of girls who have taken it up, my answer to that is 'No.' I am sure - in fact, I know - there are plenty of girls who say they would love to race on the cinders. But how many of them would be strong enough to hold a slide?
>
> I am not superhumanly big or strong for a woman, but 1 am decidedly above the average, and am blessed with perfect health, which probably accounts for the fact that I feel no strain when riding. Also I had done a certain amount of rough riding before I took it up, and speed events always appealed to me.
>
> Therefore, if a woman wants to take up dirt-track racing seriously, she will have to be very healthy and strong, and if there were ever enough women to have a ladies' meeting they would have to be capable of broadsiding to make it worth watching.
>
> There is one more drawback where lady riders are concerned. Supposing a girl has all the necessary qualities and the desire to become a dirt-track rider, then her parents will probably interfere, or her best boy will object, or, again, if she is married I guess her husband would not hear of it. None of these difficulties lie in the way of the men. I myself, am lucky, since my father, my physical fitness and the track authorities permit me to ride. And I thoroughly enjoy it!

For all this, as far as the media were concerned Taylour never took 'advantage of woman's privilege' and was being put 'in the same class as those of Spencer[26], Datson, and Sprouts'.

A few days before his return to Australia Johnnie Hoskins, 'bigging up' his new and novel investment, commented that Fay's 'dash and skill' and her 'International standing' would 'take the fans by storm inside a fortnight', and that Britain would need to think itself lucky if the Australians let the country have her back again.

By now Taylour was calling herself Irish, perhaps because a fellow colonial might gain more sympathy than a 'winging Pom' in Australia. She was about to enter into another phase of her own effort to build an identity in a context far removed from her roots and original station in life. But she was taking a well trodden path familiar to the ex-pats of empire wandering over the great British domains looking to find a place and/or a role in that world. Once more her actions contradicted her personal claims - her individual labels of identification were in opposition to her direction and action in the world.

HELLO, ADELAIDE!

MISS FAY TAYLOUR (Douglas).

Fay in the 'SA Speedster' of 1929

8. Super Sig

As Fay Taylour was finding her way into the world of motorcycle competition, 10,000 miles away another rider was making his name, one who Taylour would meet in competition at the very pinnacle of both their careers. In November, 1927 a press reporter wrote a warning:

> If Sig Schlam does not cease showering the spectators with cinders, the management will be forced to shake them as they leave the gate in order to return their track.

On 26th of the same month, Sig Schlam was nominated to ride a Harley in the sidecar events at the Claremont track, Western Australia, as well as riding solo. But, due to an over zealous handicapper who insisted that he start the sidecar race (his first) from his solo mark of three seconds behind scratch, Sig did not compete, nor did he ever nominate for a sidecar event again. That same night however he won the State Championship from Charlie Datson and Ted Kinnear as well as lowering the five lap record to 2 minutes $21^2/_5$ seconds in the handicap final.

A press report of December 1927, 'The Rising of a State Champion', commented on the ascent of Sig;.

> It is not until we recall our memories that we realise that scarcely twelve months ago, Sig Schlam the present State Champion and idol of all speedway fans was practically unknown to most of us and was classed by the handicappers at least, as a mere novice.
>
> Sig made his debut in the Association Novices Handicap and was second limit man, having a start of practically three quarters of a lap on the back markers. He won his heat in easy style and was well ahead in the final when he did that sensational skid which earned him so much comment. It might be stated for the benefit of those who did not have the pleasure of witnessing this event, that while riding a big twin Harley, he encountered a skid that threw his machine flat on its side. He held on to it in this position for a distance of about twenty yards, and then by a combination of skill and good luck, managed to bring himself into normal position. From this he continued on and rode into the second place.
>
> He also showed his extreme daring on the same day by winning the long jump, an event which required much daring and skill.
>
> Even then the majority of followers, as well as many other riders would not recognise Schlam as a good rider and he was obliged to carry on without financial or verbal encouragement. This seemed to spur him on to even further success as may be judged by his following achievements since the opening of Speedway.

Champions Scratch Race	Eight firsts out of twelve starts, including the Silver Gauntlet, the Silver Sash and State Championship.
Match Races	Two firsts out of three starts.
Track Records	Holder of every track record for solo machines.

These achievements seem outstanding when we consider that they are only backed by about twelve months of experience, but when we study Schlam's great daring, combined with his wonderful skill and personality, we can expect even more from him in the future.

Schlam the Man

Sig Schlam was born in Kalgoorlie, Western Australia on 5 February, 1905 to Mr. and Mrs. Leopold B. Schlam of Boulder and later of Yarloop, a small milling town. Yarloop, one of Western Australia's most important timber centres, is about 80 miles south of Perth on the fertile coastal plain near the foothills of the Darling Range. Yarloop is also at the heart of some of Australia's best agricultural country and is especially favoured by dairy farmers and citrus growers. Sigsmund Leopold, who would always be known as Sig to his family and friends, was raised and educated in Yarloop. His father was a manager of Millars Timber and Trading Company which had built the town of Yarloop and ran the milling operation there. The young Schlam therefore came from a respectable family, and although they were around the same age, Sig and Fay were as different as Aboriginal chalk art and Dublin cheese.

Sig was one of five children. His brother Ron and a sister Joy were born after him: Winston and Cyril were his seniors. Winston, or Win 'a real gentleman' won the King's Prize[27] for rifle shooting in 1930. Failing eyesight eventually forced his retirement in 1980. Cyril became a speedway star in his own right and during his brief career he was known as a daring and skilful rider, who gave no quarter and would, unlike his brother Sig, sometimes push himself beyond his capabilities often crashing to the ground as a result. Once, at the Sydney Royale, he was informed that the track was more challenging than it appeared at first sight. He was advised to follow the track custom and ride slowly around the circuit at the start of the meeting, allowing himself to get a feel for the surface and let the fans take a look at him. However, Cyril roared out on the track in his usual style, hammering around at full bore and unofficially broke the track record in the process!

Cyril began his speedway career in the 1928-29 season and quickly went through the ranks to 'A' grade. He rode a 500 AJS with a TT works motor, sold to him by Sig. On 9 November 1929, he beat his illustrious brother in two match races taking the first encounter by one length and the second by two lengths. These performances were not often replicated. Cyril fought hard to better his flying sibling but was never to achieve the standard of riding perfected by Sig. Cyril's uncontrolled racing temperament probably got in the way of him becoming a champion and he retired from Speedway in 1930 after an accident at the West Australian Cricket Association (WACA) ground where he suffered a spleen injury.

After the completion of his primary and secondary schooling, Sig had been sent to a University in South Africa by an uncle. It was there that he met and married Constance, who later presented him with two daughters. But he pined for his homeland and he returned to Western Australia and Yarloop before completing his studies.

On his return, Sig, like most men in Yarloop at that time worked for Millars, then went to Perth where he was employed as a Motorcycle Salesman with Gordon's Cycle and Motor Company - early in 1926 he was selling Norton and Excelsior (Big X) machines.

During that year he took his father from Yarloop to Perth in his 1925 Harley-Davidson and sidecar, to watch the State Grass track Motorcycle Championships at the Royal Showgrounds at Claremont, in the Western Australia Motor Cycle Association (WAMCA) Carnival. While watching the events he told his father that he could do better than the contestants, so he detached the sidecar from the big Harley-Davidson and transformed himself from spectator into competitor and thence into victor, winning the races in which he entered as well as the long jump. Sig was anything but a large man and when one compares his physique to the enormous bulk of a giant American 1,200cc V Twin Motorcycle, it is surprising that he could hold the machine up, let alone guide it round a track at high speed and consistently win races aboard it, not to mention take it for short flights in long jump events!

After the competition he promptly re-attached the sidecar and drove his Dad back home to Yarloop!

In the WAMCA Carnival at the Claremont Showgrounds on 9 April, 1927 Sig Schlam on a Harley-Davidson scored the following successes:

1st in the 600cc and over Handicap
1st in the State Long Jump over a distance of 27 feet 7 inches
2nd in the Novices Handicap (unlimited).

He was at this time referred to as a 'newcomer' to the sport although he was a member of the Harley-Davidson Motor Cycle Club.

Claremont

Speedway racing started in earnest in Western Australia during the spring of 1927 under the direction of promoter John S. Hoskins (although there had been motorcycle racing on the circuit the previous year). Having successfully promoted Speedway at tracks in New South Wales during 1926, he was in the process of expanding his interests. Hoskins travelled to Perth early in 1927 and attended the WAMCA Carnival at the Claremont Showgrounds on 9 April, probably in search of talented riders to fulfil his plans for Speedway in Western Australia. There were about 7,000 spectators present on the day and the Carnival was described as a 'Splendid Success'. It had a relatively lengthy programme of nineteen events, one comprising no fewer than five heats, each with eight competitors. Apparently the event was staged and completed without a single delay or snag.

The day's events included obstacle races, (towed) Surfboard riding, Motorcycle Long Jump, Musical Chairs, Point-to-Point, Sidecars and Solo Grass Track races over and under 600cc. Although there were many falls, no one was more than 'winded' in the course of the day.

This was an environment in which Hoskins felt very much at home and he was to recall that he had not experienced, 'a better programme staged or seen better or keener competition amongst the riders. The speeds for the track were splendid and the finishes brilliant'.

Hoskins calculated that motorcycle sports on a bespoke speedway in Perth would have the potential to attract crowds of 20,000, on a par with horse racing if a track could be found capable of holding machines moving at 100 miles per hour, instead of the 50 miles per hour on the grass circuit that Claremont[28] offered

Johnnie Hoskins.

prior to September 1927. For Hoskins, dirt-track competition was no more dangerous than horse racing, and it would be free from the influences associated with organised gambling (although a good many informal wagers were always part of speedway), providing a family atmosphere and thus its own particular audience.

Following months of negotiations and arrangements, Hoskins managed to get a cinders track laid around the outer boundary of the grass arena of the Claremont circuit. There was wire netting atop the fence and electric lighting around the outside of the perimeter fence.

At 8 pm on Saturday, 10 September, 1927, the starter's single barrel, sawn-off, 12 gauge shotgun blasted and the first ever official speedway meeting under lights was in progress in front of more than 15,000 cheering spectators.

Peashooter power

It was late in 1927 when Johnnie Hoskins imported another New South Welshman, Frank 'Dubbo' Brown, mounted on a Peashooter Harley. To fit in with this class of machine, Schlam began to enter either his BSA Sloper or a Peashooter Harley.

Brown attempted to lower Sig's latest 3 lap record of 1 minute 20$^1/_5$ seconds on 24 December, but could make no less than 1 minute 24 seconds.

Sig rode the 'Shooter for the first time on 14 January, 1928 in 'The Flying 350', a match race in which he was pitted against Brown. The race was to prove a close run encounter, ridden with all the commitment and speed that the two rivals could command with Brown winning by two lengths. The Peashooter had arrived and Sig took the hint.

The Harley-Davidson Peashooter had been developed specifically for board track racing. In 1925, Harley-Davidson factory rider Joe Petrali, who would become one of the most successful dirt-track racers for Harley-Davidson, and one of the best racers of all time in America, began a five-year reign as the winning rider in the AMA Grand National Championship. Petrali raced the Peashooter in the USA. It was a 350cc machine, and at 290 pounds it was a light bike, which gave it superior handling. It was readily adapted to circuit racing in Australia and became a mass draw in the Newcastle area of New South Wales. Aussie pioneers Charlie Spinks and Frank Pearce, were the first big stars at the Brisbane Exhibition Ground to make good use of the bike during its first season of 1926-27.

The 'Shooter was a phenomenal machine and practically the pioneering motorbike of Australian dirt-track racing. It excelled during the early years of organised speedway and was, for a long time, the only early motorcycle specifically designed for the sport. The 'Shooter is widely regarded as the first ever, true thoroughbred racing speedway machine, rather than a modified road bike. Later machine designs, right up to the contemporary period, have clearly been influenced by the Peashooter and the machine remains one of the all-time famous, favourite dirt-track motorcycles.

Most of the top Australian riders of the 1930s, including Vic Huxley and Englishman Frank Charles[29], began their careers on the Peashooter, which in the 350 cc capacity range was clearly superior to anything else for many years. On the 556 yard Sydney Showground, Tommy Benstead[30] won many prestige events on his Peashooter, even though he raced rivals on heavier 500cc machines. Its original colour was army green, and in its speedway trim it had 'U' shaped handlebars nearly facing the ground, as if to hunch its rider forward while power sliding on dirt-tracks.

Although riders like Huxley, Spinks and Charles often took corners with the throttle wide open on the Peashooter, it had a cut-out button mounted on the left handlebar. The throttle was not easy to control in any other position but wide open, in consequence speed and control often relied on the use of the cut-out button rather than the throttle. One bold exponent of cut-off button use was, Charlie 'Daredevil' Spinks[31] who was known for his habit of actually stepping off in impossible situations using the cut-off button.

The Peashooter was also present when the sport was introduced to England in 1928. Riders to use the Harley included Frank Arthur and Buzz Hibberd[32]. However after the initial season in the UK, the British twin cylinder Douglas (known affectionately as the 'Duggie') the type that Fay Taylour took to Australia with her on her first tour, outclassed the American bike. But the men who rode the Peashooter will forever be associated with the machine. One of the most famous was Colin Watson. Watson, who had been a fine amateur footballer was born in Ilford, Essex, of Scottish parents and was to become one of the most experienced riders in the pre-Second World War period. Although he had been wounded in the First World War he made impressive strides after taking part in the historic first speedway event at Kings Oak in 1928 and held several records for that track. Competing under the banner of International Speedways Ltd. from 1929, Watson first rode for White City and Harringay and joined the successful Wembley League side, skippering the team from 1930. He was also popular at Wimbledon, where he competed successfully in handicap events. Watson was not a spectacular stylist, but he was one of the safest and fastest of the home-grown riders of the pre-1930 era. In 1929 he began to ride the $2^{3}/_{4}$ Peashooter Harley having bought his machine from Frank Arthur. Watson swept the board at the start of the 1931 season, but concussion in the last Test match of the 1933 season prevented him from reaching his true potential in the years to come although he did skipper England for a while.

On 13 July, 1946 Watson was seriously injured at Bradford in a second-half scratch race. He crashed, hitting a lighting standard by the safety fence in the process. His machine had dragged him, head down, for about sixty feet. Watson was rushed to hospital with a punctured lung and fractured skull; he was unconscious and on the critical list for weeks. A calendar month later, during the qualifying round for the British Riders' Championship at Custom House, an announcement was made to the 60,000 crowd that Watson had taken a cup of tea and eaten a slice of bread and butter. But Watson would never ride again. A benefit was arranged and over £2,000 was raised. The 60,000 gate was about 15 percent higher than the average attendance at West Ham Speedway at that time.

All the way to Wayville

On Tuesday 17 January 1928, Charlie Datson, Sig Schlam and Arthur Pidgeon boarded the Trans Continental Railway and went to Adelaide to contest the Australian Speedway Championships at the Wayville Track. They took Datson's dirt-track Duggie, and Sig's the Sloper and 'Shooter' with them. Pidgeon was given the task of taking care of the machines.

Sig won the second heat of the Australian one-mile Championship from the Queensland champion, Brisbane's genius Victor Nelson Huxley. Although seemingly a daring rider Huxley never had problems with staying on board his bike. He was a master of the general theory of racing, which was to drive fast for the corner, then to shut back for a brief second. Timing being everything, the lull would be followed by a powerful dive for the line, jockeying a way through the crowd of riders with the same thing in mind.

Starting his dirt-track racing career in 1926, Vic Huxley was one of the pioneers of speedway. He learnt to broadside in Brisbane, where he was born on 23 September 1906, and became one of the greatest exponents of the art. He really began to impress riding the Harley Peashooter, becoming an overnight sensation at the Ekka speedway, and also at the Toowoomba Showground and Davies Park in Brisbane. Huxley came to Britain to ride for International Speedways in 1928 and turned out for Wimbledon, White City and Hall Green (Birmingham) gaining the lap record for both Wimbledon and White City. He then joined Harringay in 1930. He became almost unbeatable in the first few years of speedway, breaking records all over the world including the one-mile standing start for Davis Park and the World's flying start record for the third-of-a-mile track. Huxley won eight £100 Championships and the Golden Helmet on a number of occasions. He successfully defended his Championship title against Colin Watson but lost it to Jack Parker. In his career 'Hux' captained the Australian teams against Great Britain and won more than 5,000 races from 1926 to 1936.

In a mile international contest on that mid-January Tuesday in Wayville, the tall thin American Sprouts Elder, who was rated as the fifth best rider in the world, defeated Sig Schlam by 15 yards. Schlam rode his BSA Sloper 33 against Elder, who was riding $3^1/_2$ HP Indian 4 valve racing machines at the time. Schlam was also beaten by Alby Taylor in the two mile championship at a track record speed, by 10 yards. However, in the final of the Australian one mile Championship, Schlam, this time on his Peashooter, led Taylor throughout the race and won the event in a fast time of 1 minute $9^2/_5$ seconds. A prize of £200 came with the victory, a substantial amount at the time.

Alby Taylor was a local Adelaide truck driver who rose from virtual obscurity to become a crowd favourite within months. He had the advantage of racing a bike supplied and maintained by an Adelaide motorcycle agency.

Prior to the staging of the 21 January, 1928 meeting at the Wayville Track (Speedway Royal), Alby Taylor held the one-mile track record at 1 minute $9^1/_5$ seconds and was also the holder of the prestigious Silver Gauntlet. In the same year he defeated the great Vic Huxley to take the Australian Two Mile Championship and prize money of £200.

Taylor added a victory in the Gold Sash final to his achievements on the same night when he defeated Harry Mangham to collect a further £20. He had also achieved a second place in the One Mile Championship and achieved a new two-mile track record.

A letter from Adelaide

A letter, purporting to be from Sig Schlam about his experiences in Adelaide, was printed in the *Hoskins Weekly* (a journal created, published and edited by the indefatigable Johnnie). The letter was written to John S. Hoskins.

Dear J.S.,

In my last letter to you I forgot to tell you much of the track, it is hard on the straight with sand on the corners, and it holds much better than cinders, although slightly heavier. The riding looks spectacular, although I think our own track much harder to ride - but you sure hurl down the straights into the corners at frightful speed (So it seems!!). I'm fairly game, but I went out in practice this week to turn the Shooter flat, and the motor (*in this context means motor cycle*) seemed to hurl into the corners so fast that I dropped my bundle and buttoned (*to throttle off or hit the kill button to temporarily cut, or stop, the motor*). It took me four tries to get the 'guts' and even then I cursed myself for a silly fool and it took me all my will-power to leave it on, and when I got in - Oh Boy! - the world went mad. The motor lay flat on the ground. I couldn't see anything but a dim white smudge that must have been the fence and it hurled round that corner at close to 200 miles per hour (so I thought). Charlie said "Don't button" -1 couldn't. He said "Take her in flat and just steer her where you want to go. You can slide and you can ride a Shooter. They're easy". I had mentally agreed with all that, but he forgot to mention that the motor would bounce two feet in the air and was going to get so low to the ground.

I realise now that your yarn of Billy Lamont cutting his hands on four inch pegs was not all 'OXO'[34].

I got out of the corner O.K. and have done it since and still get a thrill, but that first time, when I was as white as a sheet with fear in a cold sweat, my eyes popping out and a sick feeling in the tummy - and then getting out in one piece and on top was a thrill I wouldn't have liked to have missed. I thought I knew what sliding was - I didn't. Sprouts is in wonderful form and has two very fast motors. I consider him as fast as (*Paddy)* Dean, but he's a bit weak and hasn't stayed put yet. He's as good as Dean to watch. Charlie (*Datson*) is feeling better and looking better. He's borrowed a couple of Jones' motors, so ought to go well. We're sick of the place - nowhere to go and no Speedway Office at all. The town is Speedway mad.

Monday - Charlie riding a 2³/₄ Douglas, jumped a chain in the first lap of the Championship.

In the 3¹/₂ class, riding one of J. Jones' fastest jobs, his ribs went again and he took it easy.

I found the BSA not fast enough in the 3¹/₂ Championship.

In the 2³/₄ Championship Huxley fell going into the first corner so I won my heat without trouble.

In the Silver Sash my BSA was just too fast for the Douglas Dean was riding - 100 yards from home on the last corner, I went into a big slide and Dean took my back wheel away from under me and won easily.

-*Sig*

Another letter from the Wayville Track, Adelaide read:

Dear John E.S.S,

Boy, if you could only get the crowds at Claremont they get here. Twenty thousand rolled out to see Sprouts, Charlie and I do our stuff - the most enthusiastic, cheery mob I ever saw - not a groan or a hoot from anyone. Sprouts went on with his 4 valve, 3¹/₂ and opened my eyes in the Preliminary. Sprouts rides his 3¹/₂ flat on the ground round the whole two corners and is rather spectacular. Charlie's ribs were not quite right so he took things easy.

I went out in the Scratch race with Len Stewart[35] and someone else. Len drew the inside position and I middle. I drove the BSA flat all the way, but owing to the fact that Benzol is absolutely unavailable I couldn't use my fuel and the motor died badly on the corners. However, Len turned within two seconds of the record, with me a length behind, so I was fairly happy with my ride. I was unable to get a preliminary as Arthur (*Pidgeon*) was changing sprockets.

In the handicap I was standing Len up 3 seconds and a few others 16 to 30 seconds. I passed Len on the beginning of the fifth lap and kept it all on, but down the last straight Len shifted on that Norton: it fairly flew, and he won by half a wheel. In the Semi Final I fell owing to the safety fence. This misnamed monstrosity consists of a netting hung on steel spikes, three feet away from the pickets and when the back wheel smacks the fence it bulges in and therefore when the wheel runs along the wire it strikes the steel strut and throws the back wheel right out into the middle of the track - and then - whack - head on.

The picket fence is painted white, and there is not even calico over the inside mesh fence, so of course it is quite invisible.

Sprouts attempted a record on his 2³/₄ and failed quite horribly, somersaulting his motor and knocking it about badly. The BSA got initiated into some hair raising sliding.

Charlie and I are quite ready to trot back to the old joint and spread ourselves around.

The BSA firm is treating us royally. All the others are exceptionally friendly and will do anything as long as we pay for it.

Well, I've given you a very disconnected kind of letter to read (if you can). Regards to all from Charlie, Arthur and Self.

-Sig

Sig Schlam at speed!

Schlam's glory in Adelaide was contrasted by Charlie Datson's relative lack of success, which probably had much to do with his sickness, injury and the problems he had with his machines. But his lack of luck did not end in Adelaide. During the 1927-28 season at Claremont Speedway, Datson was plagued by ailments and accidents - on two occasions he fell due to front fork breakages on the Peashooter.

Schlam and Datson returned from Adelaide in early January, 1928, and were hailed as conquering heroes. The Claremont Speedway meeting on 18 February, 1928 was attended by over 20,000 people looking to welcome their lads home -probably a record for any evening sporting event staged in Western Australia.

At this time, Schlam and Datson were challenged by the visiting Frank Brown from Sydney, New South Wales, another Peashooter rider. Before they went to Adelaide, Brown had not recorded any great successes on the Claremont track, but on that evening in February he turned the tables on the local racers. Brown defeated Schlam decisively in two match races and on both occasions he created new track records.

The riding styles of Brown and Schlam were quite different. Sig rode the track better and hugged the inside line, while Brown would swing out wide on the bends but at the same time he would broadside back again, often managing to maintain, or even take the lead. This aspect of Brown's riding was seen to better advantage in the match and handicap events, when he displayed an uncanny ability to steal leads from what appeared impossible positions on the inside or outside.

On 10 March, 1928, Brown broke a rear axle on his Peashooter. In order to compete against Syd Parsons in the semi final scratch race, Schlam was obliged to scrounge a rear wheel. Two weeks later Sig won the 'A' grade handicap from 2 seconds behind scratch using the same back wheel. He gave the front position riders 13 seconds start and came home in front. Following his return from Adelaide Schlam had only won two handicaps prior to that victory. He had broken the track record several times but could do no better than second place, although he was fighting hard in every race. This caused some of the fans to question the veracity of the handicapper. However, the following week Sig won the handicap again, conceding more than half a lap to the front markers.

A few lines taken from the programme tells the tale of a remarkable victory:

> All the limit men were travelling at such speed it appeared that Schlam never had a hope. In the first lap he seemed not to have gained a yard, the second lap saw the field a little nearer. In the third lap it looked most hopeless but in the fourth he got within striking distance and with a hundred yards to go and three men to pass, he just managed to win by the merest fraction.

At a special Easter Monday afternoon meeting in April 1928, Schlam raced the BSA Sloper for the last time. His results show why - he was defeated by Charlie Datson by a length in a match race and beaten by Dunne in the scratch race semi final. Although Schlam was known as the most consistent rider of the 1927-28 season on the Claremont track, it was apparent that the BSA Sloper was ageing technology and not really up to the pounding it was taking. The Sloper was certainly a five-lap machine, as it took four laps to wind up to its peak speeds.

To Britain

Schlam, Datson and Ron Johnson headed for Britain on 10 April 1928 led by Hoskins who was looking to expand the market for dirt-track racing. The extrovert promoter had established speedway in Australia, but it was no more than an embryonic sport in the United Kingdom, however the first meetings were proving to be extremely popular with fans and riders alike. The dirt-tracks in Britain were (and are) much smaller than the vast Claremont Circuit. These tracks received a great deal of criticism during the first British season because they were considered much more dangerous than road racing circuits. The actual width of the High Beech Track, for example was only 15 feet and this made overtaking perilous relative to Australian tracks. Some motorcycle firms refused to supply racing machines to dirt-track riders as accidents on the cinders would create adverse publicity. By 1930 however, almost all British motorcycle manufacturers offered 500cc dirt-track models, although they were nearly all basic stock machines with modifications.

In July 1928, Len Dean, Secretary of the Harley-Davidson Motor Cycle Club of Western Australia, received a letter from Sig Schlam. Much of this missive was given over to Sig's homesickness but part of the content provides an insight into the Australian's initial experience of the Speedways of Britain, and in particular the competition the Aussies encountered:

Dear Len,

As you have already seen in *Motor Cycle* we all had a very disappointing day at our initial public appearance. Ron (*Johnson*) stopped after three laps (couldn't forget Claremont I suppose). I managed to get into the final after breaking a chain when I'd gone half a lap.

Charlie got a most wonderful ovation - his Douglas (a brand new one and some iron let me say), didn't like the rain and took three out of the four laps to really get going - and then Oh Boy! If the Claremont crowd had seen him on that fourth lap they'd have cheered him to the echo too. I, who have seen Paddy Dean and Huxley go, have never seen riding like that last lap. Frogley (his opponent and England's best), was over a quarter lap ahead when the bell went for the last lap. As if in answer to all our prayers (we were all praying, I think), the Doug suddenly ceased its spluttering and spitting and began to burble and whine like an angry bee. Into the first corner he went, the ashes showering over the crowd, screening them momentarily from sight - what a wonderful corner that was. Then up the next straight the motor, now thoroughly wound up, screaming out its challenge and warning to Frogley who was not so far ahead now as he should have been. On came Charlie - surely he was not going to go into the last corner that fast, surely he would not button. He was mad. Didn't he realise that he was doing over 60 miles per hour on a $1/4$ mile track? Did he ever imagine he could steer a motor round a sharp corner like that at that speed? Yes, he was either going to get round or break his neck in the attempt. On the last corner the women had screamed and the men had shouted warnings at him - on the bend however not a sound was heard, even the women were silent - they'd just fainted. My hair stood on end, but I couldn't turn my head away. I couldn't move. In went Charlie, his motor lay straight down and heaved the track over the fence in one tremendous wave. He got around - don't ask me how, I don't know.

As soon as he straightened up, the tension lifted and crowd went mad. Frogley won by five yards.

Although the names of Australian riders such as Vic Huxley (who had seven machines and two mechanics with him), Paddy Dean and Stewart St. George were frequently mentioned in press reports, the West Australian trio of Schlam, Datson and Johnson had not made any impact by the end of June 1928.

Parts of a letter written home from Sig in early October 1928 tell of the trio's development, but also of the growing pressure of the tour:

Charlie's iron is fast alright, but it's got nothing on my new one (Douglas). Ron has also got a new one, too, and gee they all go. I wish they could do them justice. I've got something at last too fast for me - on these small tracks.

Ron has gotten himself a wonderful reputation in the last fortnight as being a wild man. A week ago he caused a strike in the pits because he wiped out a chap, Eric Langton[36] a TT rider, with the back wheel of my Doug, while getting through and then on the next bend, he wiped a guy's front wheel away while getting around him. The mob decided not to ride if Ron rode again, so he didn't compete in the final. That was at the Salford Track.

Later, Ron and I went to Middlesbrough and found his new Doug waiting for him, with loud prayers of thanksgiving from me, and he proceeded to go mad.

He left everything on and ran up the local champ's back, got chucked off and the bike stood up and tore down the straight flat, leaped the safety fence and dived into the crowd.

I was more fortunate and put up the fastest time for the night and won the scratch race.

The last night at Manchester, Ron came out and the local heroes who drew him in their heat quaked at the knees. When they heard a faint moan coming they shut off and hugged the grass while he howled by - he just about cleaned up the programme.

The English lads don't like the Shooters but have to admit that there are no 350cc jobs and only two 500cc jobs better for the dirt.

I'll be glad to get back to Aussie for some sun and air.

We have all been raced so much that we are not interested in tracks, bikes, promoters, money or anything. Sleep is the only thing of which we can't get enough. When we first arrived, these toy tracks seemed funny, but after five months of turning your motor round in circles, they give you the bellyache, as well as being dangerous. The motors are lying down so low on these circuses that you have no hope of going inside a fellow who falls off. You can only hope to get around the outside or hit him, his motor or the fence.

Eric Langton was mounted on a Rudge 500cc when the incident with Johnson occurred. The Rudge frame was fitted with brackets, gussets and straps which prevented it from flexing in road conditions. Langdon drilled these fittings to lighten the overall weight of the machine, and provide more flexibility, thus making it more suitable for dirt-track racing.

Sig Schlam and Charlie Datson returned to Western Australia in November 1928, fresh from their triumphs in England, but disenchanted with a raw deal they had received from one or two promoters. Datson's motorcycle was accidentally forwarded from Britain to Adelaide, South Australia and on his first ride at Claremont on 15 December he was forced to use a borrowed and strange machine as his mount.

Schlam made his return to Claremont Speedway on 1 December, 1928, to a tumultuous welcome from his many fans who had turned up to see their favourite in action. At that event he demonstrated that he was still the Schlam that had left Australia months before, but he had gained a professional polish on the well tuned, more powerful dirt-track Douglas. He won £66 in prize money in his first three December meetings. A writer at the time commented on the 'new' Schlam:

> Schlam is a great rider and it is hard to understand why he is not more popular with the crowd. He takes care of himself and his machine and very seldom has to retire from a race with engine trouble. He is certainly awake to all the points of the game, but we have never seen him do anything unsportsmanlike on the track. He is out to win every time, no matter whom he is pitted against. Evidently a lot of the public seem to think that when he is racing against a rider whom it is pretty certain he will beat, Schlam should not show him up, which is an utter fallacy. The prizes are there to be won and a rider would be foolish not to ride his very best.

> In the early days of the sport, Schlam, when in a chivalrous mood, did 'swank' once or twice and was beaten; he knows better now.

By the start of 1929 Sig Schlam was one of the best, perhaps the best, all-round rider Australia had to offer. On his home track particularly, he was a mighty force to be reckoned with. The people of Western Australia knew that whenever the growing legion of British riders sent representatives to prove themselves in the 'colonies', Sig Schlam would be in the front line of Aussie power. Not many people early in 1929 expected that the 'old country's' advance guard would consist of a lone rider, and no one thought that rider would be a woman. But whatever, it was Schlam who waited to defend the honour of the southern hemisphere.

9. Fay v Sig

Fay landed in Western Australia in January, 1929 to a grand reception, but it was the tall gum trees and wide open spaces that grabbed her imagination. She immediately took to the mixture of the pioneering spirit combined with the magnificent vastness of the natural environment. But she might have seemed a tad odd to many of the locals, with her accent, seen by at least one commentator as being 'the cultured one of London or Southern Ireland', and when she chose to use 'a French phrase, it is with the inflection of France'. Fair dinkum perhaps, but by Australian standards Taylour would have seemed a very strange 'Sheila'.

Her first race in Perth at the famous half mile track of the Claremont Showgrounds took place on Saturday, 5 January. She beat the local star Frank Brown in a match race, clocking an average of 52.7mph - a more than notable lick in those days. In fairness to Brown it should be pointed out that he was mounted on a $2^3/_4$ machine, whereas Taylour, with a $3^1/_2$ motor, had the advantage. For all this, she had assumed the lead early on in the race and was never headed, winning with relative ease. She finished her first race as the winning rider.

Her time for the three lap encounter was 1 minute $20^2/_5$ seconds, the track record being then 1 minute 17 seconds. It was a slick pace given that it was almost as hard to hold a machine in check at 50 mph on the loose surface as it would be to accomplish a similar task on a hard track with the engine revving at near the 100 mph mark. In the 'A' grade event Fay was well in the lead, again looking a comfortable winner, but she made the mistake of confusing the flags and came to a standstill, thinking the race had finished. However, with the exception of Sig Schlam's 54.3mph average, Taylour registered the best time on an evening when some of the best of Australia's riders were in good form. She delighted the huge speedway crowd with her ability to slide, and 'turn on the taps'.

In *The Motor Cycle* (25 September 1930) Taylour told of her feelings before her first race on the Perth track where the average speed over the nearly half-mile circuit was close to 60mph. Ever the doyen of the seductive double-entendre she remarked:

> I don't mind admitting I was nervous about it at first…but as soon as you've got the feel of a big track it's infinitely preferable to a small one. For one thing, provided the lap is the right shape, you can enjoy a slide, because you can stay in it

After the meeting it was reported that Taylour intended to attempt the 1 minute 17 second track record for three laps, which at that time was held jointly by Ron Johnson and Sig Schlam. *The Daily News*, (Wednesday 9

January, 1929) concluded that, 'It will be interesting to see how the male element will stir should the record be lowered by a woman'.

However, at that point one of the principal events at the following Saturday's meeting at the Claremont was seen to be the match between Taylour and Alf Chick, in the scratch race. It was expected that Chick would need to make the pace to overcome the woman racer. The riders would be mounted on machines of equal horse-power and of similar make. The *Daily News* looked forward to the race as 'a thriller and a keenly contested one' that 'should have the crowd on its feet from gun to gun'.

Claremont dawn

From the first days of the Claremont track there were complaints about the quality of the lighting which was too widely spaced and caused very dark shaded patches on the track. This was of considerable danger to the competitors and an annoyance to spectators.

This lighting problem was soon rectified, as was a difficulty caused by the Brass Band which began playing at the same time as the track announcer gave the results on a megaphone.

During the 1927 season, the admission rates were two shillings (2/-) for adults and 6 pence (6d) for children - admission to the Grandstand an extra 1/-.

In the contemporary period the motorcycle events at Claremont Speedway were usually given a more low-key promotion (except for Test Series) than Saloon Cars, Speedcars, Super Modifieds, etc. On the opening night at Claremont Speedway, six cars participated, all under 1100 cc, but these received no mention in the press reports following the meeting.

The motorcycle riders at that first event were all members of motorcycle clubs in the Perth area. Their mounts in these very early dirt-track events were no more than stripped down, stock, road bikes, some actually ridden from the racers homes to the track. The types of bikes used bore some classic names such as Douglas, Indian, Harley-Davidson, Super X Excelsior, AJS, Velocette, Norton, FN, Calthorpe, Omega, Chater Lea, Ariel, BSA., Royal Enfield, Sunbeam, Triumph, New Hudson and James. All were chain drive to the rear wheel and most were fitted with hand gear change on the side of the petrol tank.

Prizes were generally excellent both with cash and trophies. Handicap race prizes were £25 for a win, £12 for runner up and £5 for third place. The winner also won a trophy, usually silver or silver plated. If a record for the event was established, the rider also received a Sterling Silver record badge bearing the event time, date and name.

For the first three meetings, there were no power restrictions placed on solo motor cycles and, unbelievably, several machines with capacities from 1,000cc to 1,300cc participated against others as small as 200 cc. Following the third meeting on 1 October 1927 (which had been cancelled the previous night due to a power failure), a limit of $3^1/_2$ Horse Power or 500 cc was placed on solo motorcycles in handicap events. This limit was to apply for most races held at Claremont after this date.

On the opening night at Claremont Speedway in 1927, the three lap, rolling start track record was set at 1 minute $27^1/_5$ seconds. This was something of a feat given the conditions of track, lighting and standard of the machines being used. But when the record was set by a diminutive country boy, mounted on a 1,000 cc Harley-Davidson, the time was phenomenal.

This 'Country Boy' was a 22 year old, slightly built and agile young man. Five feet tall and weighing eight stone; he was classed as a novice motorcyclist by speedway organisers, officials and reporters alike. Sig Schlam had made his first mark on the speedways of the world.

Tactician Taylour

Assessing the Claremont track Fay had calculated (correctly) that she would need to broadside at a higher speed on the huge Aussie track. She had envisaged most of her time would be taken up with demonstration rides in Australia, which she thought would give her time to acclimatise and achieve the kind of speeds she would need to compete. But almost from the start she was involved in match racing and as such felt very much a beginner, and not too safe in spite of the many good performances.

A match race was organised between Taylour and the renowned Sig Schlam, the West Australian champion, again at Claremont. This was Schlam's home turf and he was the master of his domain. It seems Perth was looking forward to the contest. Taylour noted an advertisement (full-length and block letters) almost daring her to fail:

> **THOUSANDS MARVELLED AT THE HAIR RAISING FEATS EXPLOITED BY MISS FAY TAYLOUR AT LAST WEEK'S MEETING.**
>
> **NEXT SATURDAY NIGHT THIS FEMININE WIZARD OF THE CINDERS WILL ATTEMPT TO LOWER THE TRACK RECORD AND DEFEAT SIG SCHLAM (THE WEST AUSTRALIAN CHAMPION).**
>
> **CAN SHE SUCCEED WHERE OTHERS HAVE FAILED?**

Schlam was indeed a mighty competitor, seemingly way beyond Taylour in class and experience. Five meetings into the first Claremont Speedway season he was hailed by the press as 'The Unchallenged King of the Cinders'. His first three-lap record was 1 minute 28 seconds on his big Harley-Davidson on the opening night. In a later race that same evening he achieved 1 minute $27^1/_5$ seconds, this equated to a speed of 49 miles per hour. These times were made on the cinder track aboard a 1,000cc Harley-Davidson.

By 14 December, 1929, riding a Douglas Speedway machine, Schlam lowered the record to 1 minute 14 seconds during a scratch race. This represented an average speed of approximately $57^1/_2$ miles per hour and $^4/_5$ of a second faster than the 1936 track record for the same distance, achieved on an improved machine running on an improved track.

These facts do not show the likes of later record holders to be inferior riders; rather it illustrates the quality of Schlam, and supports those who argue that he was the greatest Western Australian dirt-tracker of speedway's pioneering days.

Fay gave an interview in Perth on 3 January 1929 (a couple of days before her first appearance at Claremont). During the interview Fay said, "Like all other racing motorcyclists, I decided to try the thrills of the new sport and made my debut at the Crystal Palace, London, aptly enough in view of my present visit, in a match race with Ron Johnson, a West Australian." She also informed her interviewer that she was a cousin of Lady Riddell, the wife of the wealthy owner of the *News of the World.* Here Fay was laying out her credentials, firstly as a 'trackwise' competitor but also as a person with aristocratic connections. This gave her a wide range of appeal and made her something of a social curiosity.

However, while Taylour's riding capabilities were generally conceded, there was doubt as to whether the woman rider could defeat a male racer with the quality and experience of Schlam, 'champion of the Western State'. He was not by any means the most popular man with local fans,

Claremont advertisement from this period

often taking the role of the villain in the Hoskins inspired, underlying pantomime. Certainly a section of the crowd delighted in seeing him defeated, but they were rarely gratified.

The proposed match with Schlam was an opportunity to provide a high profile England versus Australia race on Australian soil, Fay being the first rider to make the trip from Britain (British riders did not compete in numbers in the Australian season until 1930). The speedway press reported that everyone was waiting to see who could defeat the canny, and almost unbeatable Schlam. He held the lap record for his track, which had stood for over a year. The Claremont circuit was twice as large as the tight English ovals Fay had been riding throughout her dirt-track career and it is therefore unsurprising that Taylour felt her paring with Schlam was a ridiculous mismatch. Although she had brought the latest fast speedway bike from Britain with her, Schlam also had an advanced machine.

False start

To the consternation of those looking forward to the scheduled Claremont confrontation between Taylour and Schlam, a few days before the event an announcement was made that Fay would not be taking part in the racing on Saturday, 19 January. Fay claimed that the omission of her name from the programme was due to a whim on the part of a Mr. E.L. Baker (a director of Speedways, Ltd.). She expressed her disappointment at being left out following a disagreement between herself and Baker concerning the match race which he had suggested should take place between her and Schlam. She had asked that the prize money should be increased to £50, but Baker refused. Fay protested:

> This is not an unreasonable amount…as there would have been only one match on that occasion. The statement issued by W.A. Speedways is inaccurate. It is said that I did not fulfil my engagements for the first night. That is not true, because as a matter of fact I had no engagements. Before I reached Perth, Mr. Baker without obtaining my consent, advertised me to appear in three races in addition to the necessary preliminaries. That was expecting too much of me after a 40 days' sea journey, and in view of the fact that I would be riding on a strange track under strange conditions. I told Mr. Baker that on the day I arrived. Unfortunately, I am not under any contract with Speedways. I have come here and brought my two machines from England entirely at my own expense. It was most unfortunate that the armature shaft of my magneto should have broken last Saturday, and I was quite as disappointed as the public. I am still anxious to appear next Saturday, and Mr. Baker knows I am quite prepared to ride in any event under the same conditions as last week, except as far as an international contest is concerned.

Baker responded by saying that although he did not intend to follow Taylour's example of 'engaging in personalities', he thought it necessary to correct some of her remarks. He insisted that her complaint that she was entered in three races on her first appearance on 5 January without her authority was ridiculous. He went on to say that Fay seemed to regard the company's action in so entering her as impertinence but, through a Perth friend of hers, the management was asked to enter her for such events as they thought fit. As such, Baker said that Taylour was accordingly entered for the match race, scratch race and 'A' Grade Handicap, these being the three principal events and those which every visiting rider competed in, thus giving them the opportunity of winning the maximum amount of prize money. According to Baker, although he met Taylour on her arrival a few days before her first appearance, and saw her frequently after, she did not ask for the nominations to be withdrawn. He claimed that it was only after she had won her match race against Frank Brown that she told him she had been advised not to start in the other two events. He continued:

> Regarding Miss Taylour's statement that she had not been allowed to ride because she had asked for a £50 prize for her match race with Schlam, this is only partly correct. Miss Taylour demanded a substantial sum as appearance money, to be paid provided she appeared, and on top of this the very substantial prize of £50 for the match race. The management was unable to accede to these extravagant demands, feeling it would be unfair to put her in a position so very different from the other professional riders. She has caused the public great disappointment as she was expected to appear in five events, three on January 5, and two on January 12, but only finished in one. Last week her performance was particularly disappointing. She was advertised to attempt to break a track record and also to ride in a match race with Chick. Her machine broke down, and, although she had two machines in the State, and should know how highly sensitive special dirt track machines are, she had only taken one to the ground. All experienced riders, who can afford to have two machines always have both in readiness. When engaged in attempting to break a track record, which is considered a special attraction, a competitor should take every precaution to see that the engagement may be fulfilled.

The proposed race was as potentially good for Sig Schlam's career as it was for Taylour and the promoters and motorcycle manufacturers. Sig worked for Mortlock Bros Ltd, Perth where he became a Harley and BSA salesman. He rode his first speedway races hoping to win enough prize money to bring his family to Perth from South Africa. His plan was to race until he, his wife and children were finally settled in Australia, then retire from competition to focus on his sales career. But it appears that such was his success on the dirt-track thoughts of retirement were abandoned.

Ripper riposte, recriminating reply

On 21 January Fay published a 'rejoinder' (in the *Daily News*) to Baker's statement about her involvement with W.A.Speedways Ltd.

> In reply to Mr. Baker, I would point out that although he flatters me by putting me on the same plane as men professional riders, he had definitely agreed, the day I arrived in Perth, to withdraw my nomination from at least one of the races for which he had entered me before my arrival here. I pointed out to him then that I would not ride under customary match conditions. It was up to him, therefore, knowing the keenness of speedway patrons, to advertise the fact at once.

> In regard to his statement concerning my 'extravagant demands' I might point out that I have already laid out £500 by coming to Australia, towards which Mr. Baker's company has contributed nothing. I fail to see that the so called substantial fee of £30 for my first appearance, and five percent (£33/2/5) of the gate receipts for the second, can be termed 'extravagant', nor can the suggested prize of £50 for an international race be classed as such.

> Mr. Baker said that the public was keenly disappointed as a result of my inability to compete as advertised, but I assure the public that my disappointment is as keen, or keener. However, I have prolonged my stay in Western Australia with the express purpose of keeping faith with the public by riding next Saturday night under the auspices of the W.A. Motor Cycling Association, many of whose members are riders themselves and do not consider my demands 'extravagant'. I am racing against Sig Schlam in a special match race. It has been advertised that I brought two machines from England, but only one was brought for racing purposes. I assure the public that I have made ample arrangements to enable me to ride next Saturday, even should anything happen to my racing machine.

It seems that public opinion and that of the media (probably manipulated by Hoskins) supported Taylour's position. Firstly they all seemed to feel that too much had been asked of her on her first night appearance - taking part in the three events would have potentially meant 19 laps, assuming she won all her heats of the 'A' Grade Handicap and Scratch Race. It was agued that for any rider (male or female) after journeying from the UK to Australia with only four days in which to recover, such a debut would be considered exceptional.

Secondly, Taylour's request of £50 for an International Match Race with Sig Schlam was not considered excessive, even though this amount was to be paid on top of appearance money. At the same time, the attendance at the speedway on the Saturday night, 5 January, was greater than the average attendance for previous Saturdays probably as a direct result of the advertised involvement of a 'Lady Rider'. On Saturday, 12 January the attendance had been even greater. It was argued this was because patrons, 'having witnessed this lady rider's prowess as a motor cyclist, realised that she was equal to our best, and wished to see more of her'.

It was suggested that if Taylour had been paid £30 as appearance money and £50 for a special International Race, in effect £35 more than the ordinary match race, this would have been easily recovered from the additional attendancees leaving Speedways Ltd very much in profit. In any case, £50 for an International Race was not seen as excessive.

On arrival in Australia Taylour had requested to be withdrawn from at least one event included in the 5 January meeting. This was done, but, without any prior notification to the public. The only attempt to accommodate the paying customers was an announcement that another rider would take Fay's place. In the two events in which Taylour did appear, she clearly demonstrated her ability as a dirt-track exponent and was immediately accepted by Speedway fans as a likely rival to Schlam. Unfortunately, on her second appearance (12 January) when greater numbers of spectators turned up to see her, machine trouble eliminated her entirely from the programme.

In the past there had been numerous occasions when 'star' performers had been advertised to appear, and at the last moment failed to turn up, or suffered some disability that had prevented them fulfilling their obligation; in fact one of these occurrences had happened quite recently prior to Taylour's appearances in Australia. It is unlikely that Taylour's absence was seen as anything more than disappointing, but also an occupational hazard

According to the *Daily News* (21 January, 1929):

Motor cycle racing in this State has taken on well, and no doubt those responsible for its continued popularity (the riders) should be given greater consideration. Instances have occurred in the other states of disputes between riders and promoters which at times have very nearly ruined the sport. Let us remain free of such instances in this State.

Taylour had intended to leave for the Eastern States, but had been keen to take part in a race against Schlam. She realised that many Speedway patrons might have felt frustrated at some of her previous showings and was anxious to put up a particularly good exhibition at Claremont, since this would be her final appearance in Western Australia. She had of course learnt her trade on the smaller tracks of Britain where the average speed hovered round the 36 mph mark. But against Frank Brown in her first match race she registered a fine win. Of course Taylour could have used her Rudge after the failure of the Douglas, but this would have meant the loss of the one advantage she had - advanced technology. So for all her rhetoric about her duty to the public, Fay may well have put glory before honour.

Public opinion, together with the prospect of a lucrative payday caused the WAMCA to come to the rescue and arrangements were finally agreed for what looked like being one of the big events of 1929 at Claremont. Apart from her race with Schlam (where both riders would be mounted on machines of similar make and horsepower) Taylour also intended to attempt to lower the existing Claremont track record for three laps.

Advertising for the event at Claremont began to focus on Taylour's involvement. In *The Call* (25 January, 1929) it was boldly proclaimed that Fay would 'go to the ball' albeit a week late.

WA MOTOR CYCLING ASSOCN'S MONSTER ANNIVERSARY CARNIVAL

INTERNATIONAL MATCH RACE

MISS FAY TAYLOUR VERSES SIG SCHLAM

POSITIVELY LAST APPEARANCE OF

MISS FAY TAYLOUR

MISS FAY TAYLOUR

MISS FAY TAYLOUR

BE THERE!

CLAREMONT SPEEDWAY SATURDAY

BEST OF ENEMIES

From the inception of speedway in Western Australia, Hoskins imported ace riders from New South Wales. Charlie Datson rode a Douglas dirt-track motorcycle and although they were carefully publicised in programmes and by the media as arch-enemies, Sig and Charlie became the greatest of friends, on and off the track. Charlie had a reputation as a skilful trackman when he arrived at Claremont and he was used time and again in match races billed 'WA versus NSW'.

Within a few weeks of Charlie arriving in WA, Schlam and Datson were to appear in their first match race meeting with a £15 prize. Datson made the pace from the off, but Sig was in the lead as the half lap mark was passed. At that point Schlam's bike started skidding allowing Datson to come back to him, but Sig would not surrender the lead. To the delight of the locals, Schlam beat the man from Sydney over the three laps, crossing the line about 15 yards in front of Datson in a time of 1 minute $25^1/_5$ seconds. In doing so he had proved, in the vernacular of the district that 'groper lads (young men who fished for that particular 'denizen of the deep' off the coast of Perth) can't be outdone'.

A record crowd was anticipated for Fay's meeting with Schlam, which was to mark the peak of Taylour's speedway career. The organizers, the Western Australian Motor Cycle Association, claimed that the amount of prize money offered for the meeting was the largest speedway purse ever offered in the State. The local boy's encounter with 'the international champion' and the confrontation between Sig and Alf Chick, considered to be Schlam's most dangerous opponent, certainly would have whetted the appetite of local support.

On the run up to his date with Fay, Schlam was showing some good form. Up to and including the meeting on 12 January, 1929, Sig had recorded 16 wins, 5 runner-up spots and a third place in heats, finals, scratch, match and handicap events. His best time for three laps was 1 minute $16^4/_5$ seconds (a track record) and he had recorded 2 minutes $21^2/_5$ seconds for 5 laps

At the 12 January meeting, Schlam had excited the big crowd when between the pits and the finish line. He dropped his machine right over so that it appeared for a fraction of a second that he was riding with his left shoulder touching the cinders. Then, with a super-human effort, he righted himself. However, his skill (or fortune) at the following meeting let him down, because when he put the Douglas down it did not come up and he suffered a rare fall though fortunately escaping injury. In the press reports, Schlam was made out to be something of 'the villain of the track' an angle the press frequently used.

> Sig Schlam is not too popular with a section of speedway fans. Why? I don't know! Evidently they cannot appreciate clever riding, or are unduly biased in favour of other riders. In one of the events, Schlam fell and this one-eyed body of partisans started to hoot. When Schlam threw off his colours and walked over to the fence and climbed through, there wasn't a sound, and it is said that a couple of conscience-stricken humans made off; but Schlam, his racing finished for the night, had only hopped over to sit beside Mrs Schlam, who was generally to be found in the same seat, taking an interest in the racing.

Westralian showdown

> Taylour recalled her pre-match feelings

> Perth Western Australia – I am being driven to Claremont Speedway by an official. My tummy is on fire and the banner across the street terrifies me. It reads: 'Fay Taylour will race Sig Schlam in International Match Race - England versus Australia'. Schlam, the West Australian champion is said to be unbeatable. I am afraid because I know I must ride that big half-mile track on full throttle, harder than my limited experience knows how. The official tells me that the fans will take their stop watches to the track to make sure that the race will not be 'fixed'. I had ridden against a top rider the week before and shown I could power-slide the loose-surfaced turns and win, but that win was easy. My engine was bigger and faster and I did not have to use full throttle. It is Schlam's home track and he holds the lap record.

The *Hoskins Weekly* (2 February), the promoters own journal, reported the programme:

Drawn by the fact that Miss Fay Taylour would be making her final appearance on the Claremont track and competing in an International Match Race with Sig Schlam, and that a Special Challenge Match Race was to be contested between Alf Chick and Sig Schlam, the attendance at Claremont on Saturday last was one of the largest for the season. In conjunction with the above two Special Match Races, a strong supporting programme was arranged by the W.A.M.C.A on whose account the meeting was run. In view of the slight disturbances which had taken place between Speedways Ltd. and Miss Taylour, her re-appearance was eagerly awaited by the crowd, and when she did come on to the track was accorded a very strong welcome from all sides of the ring.

It was a warm evening and a very large crowd had gathered. As was customary, the programme opened with the 'B' Grade' Handicap, on this occasion being termed the 'Colts' Handicap. Cyril Schlam made his debut in the third heat, he was something of a 'local hope' at the time. His spectacular style, together with being the brother of the rider who was, around Perth anyway, 'universally recognised as Westralia's greatest dirt track find', created a deal of interest in his performance.

Cyril won his heat, but was only capable of third position in the final. Hartree, who ran second in the fastest heat, won the final, with Patterson second.

The Challenge Match Race between Alf Chick and Sig Schlam followed the Colts' Handicap. For many this was the 'star turn' of the evening. Over the previous several weeks much comment had been heard as to who would be the likely rider to lower Sig's colours. With the news of Taylour's arrival, some thought she would have that honour but most (with Fay being a woman) pinned their faith on Chick. Schlam was the clear favourite to win over the three laps, although at the previous meeting Chick had beaten Schlam and lowered the record in the process.

If it were not for Alf Chick, Schlam's record for that season would have been much more impressive than it was. On the occasions when Schlam had been beaten in solid fashion, Chick was the one to administer the drubbing. The last time they had been pitted against one another in a special match race, Chick's machine ran like a gun. Alf had secured the lead early on and he had romped home by a good 8 lengths, setting up a fine new record for the distance. However, to many, on that occasion, it had seemed that Schlam's machine had lacked something of its usual kick. Certainly, at points, Sig had appeared to have been unable to make up the yards separating him from the flying Chick, although several times he had come close to drawing level and taking the lead. Chick's success had followed a change of strategy over the weeks prior to the January showdown. He had previously made a practice of keeping well on the outside and riding high on the fence. But early in 1929 he had realised the wisdom of getting the inside running and keeping it. That said, Schlam had made it known that he meant to capture Chick's record.

From a good even start, with Chick on the outside, the two set off, but by the time half a lap had been run, Chick was in the lead and riding superbly. Schlam appeared to wait for a wide swing on Chick's part at 'Fowl House' corner, but although Chick went a little wide it was not wide enough for Schlam to get through. Passing the post for the first lap Chick was about two lengths ahead. He held his lead at a lightning pace for the next two laps, with Schlam drawing very close to his rival on several occasions. During the last half lap the cheers of the crowd welled up into a crescendo, and as the post was passed, with Chick in front, a cacophony of yelling, applause, motor horns and sirens filled the atmosphere, that along with the roar of the racing machines became almost corporeal, such was the approval of Chick's victory. Chick had won by about three lengths, in a time of 1 minute 17^1/$_5$ seconds.

The International Match Race was next. Taylour, on the 3^1/$_2$ Douglas, rode a preliminary lap, receiving a warm welcome from the ringside. After circling the track both riders came to the post, astride identical machines, both had been bought at the same time from the Douglas factory in England.

While it was hard to tell when they were both mounted, Fay was taller and physically sturdier than her opponent that evening. An article in November 1927 headed 'A Word for Sig' reported:

> As Sig Schlam will tell you, the penalties of being small are far from few. When people see the celebrated 'Sig' lapping the cinders at 50 miles per hour, few of them realise that he is a little over five feet in height, but in everyday life he is being continually reminded of the fact. Recently, when charged at the Police Court with committing some minor breach of the traffic regulations, Sig tried to explain to the Bench how ridiculous their laws were, and at the same time looked as if he would succeed.

However the next morning the newspaper account of the case read: 'Much amusement was caused in the Traffic Court yesterday by the gross impertinence of a diminutive youth named Sig Schlam.' It seems the reporter was unaware that Sig was a married man with a family.

On another occasion, Sig was chatting with strangers in Mortlocks. During this conversation (Sig's penchant for discussion caused him to be nicknamed 'OXO'[34]) the question of speedway cropped up. One of the strangers was full of praise for Schlam, who had won the Silver Gauntlet at the previous meeting. As soon as he got a chance to get a word in, Sig admitted to being the object of this person's acclaim. After having congratulated Sig and wishing him future success, the stranger turned to one of his fellow travellers and said:

> If he had told me that that fellow over there was Schlam (pointing to a man whose height was something in excess of six feet) I could have believed him, but to think that a little weed like him could glide that big Harley around the track is beyond me.

Track war

They got off to an even start, with Taylour on the inside, but both riders immediately clapped on speed. At the first bend, Taylour took a slight lead, but at the half lap Schlam appeared to be gaining a little. As the post was passed for the first circuit Fay, riding brilliantly, was in front by about three lengths. During the next two laps Taylour slightly increased the gap between her and the little Aussie, and passed the post at a particularly good speed, registering 1minute 17 seconds (54.9mph) and receiving a massive ovation.

Later, Taylour made an attempt to lower the track record, but was unable to equal her Match Race time, registering 1minute 17⁴/₅. But overall she had ridden exceptionally well.

Following the Match Races came three heats and the final of the Open Scratch Race. Walker, Chick and Schlam were the heat winners. In the final, Chick lost a lot of ground in the first quarter lap, but managed to recover and pass Walker for second place at the end of the first lap. In the next two laps he was unable to catch Schlam, who passed the post about four lengths ahead. Schlam's time was 1minute 18 seconds (an average time of 54.7 mph). Schlam simply outrode Chick in that race, and was again the holder of Claremont's Golden Helmet.

The heats of the 'A' Grade Handicap went to Schlam, Mason, Walker and Datson, with Parsons and Dunne qualifying for the final as fastest runners up. Mason was unfortunate in his heat for, after passing the post at the finish he came down in the path of Parsons and was temporarily removed to the casualty ward. However, he appeared in the final, but once again hit the cinders. The final was ultimately secured by Parsons, with Datson and Schlam filling second and third places respectively.

Fay covered herself in glory by leading Schlam for the whole three laps and, in spite of a heavy track, achieved the fastest time of the evening. She had equalled the lap record, lowered by Schlam in the previous week after it had stood for 12 months. At the end of the meeting she informed the crowd over the stadium intercom system that she was leaving that night for Melbourne. The fans expressed their disappointment - it seemed they had hoped to see more of her. Although she could not stay her performance endured. Fay's time was one of the best ever recorded on the track. She concluded that perhaps being scared was an advantage and remembered:

> The fans leap the fence to congratulate me. I am the first, and only rider that season from the British tracks, to race in Australia. It is 1929. Dirt Track Racing had been an Australian sport for years, but it was only a few months since Australian promoters had invaded England.

Good Cop, Bad Cop

In the *Hoskins News* (2 February, 1929) a letter from 'Inglewood' was published (dated 28 January 1929) entitled 'Should Schlam be Excused?' The letter was apparently responding to views like that was published in *Hoskins News* in a section entitled *Criticisms*:

> Miss Fay Taylour certainly vindicated all the criticism. We notice that, in fairness to Schlam, his motor was not going well (very often) but Miss Taylour's Doug showed a decided miss in the engine too.

> Wonder how many of the fair sex of W.A. will try their luck on the cinders after seeing Miss Taylour's exhibition?

Reading between the lines of the diatribe from Inglewood, see below, it seems to propagate the 'good cop, bad cop' relationship (as promoted by Hoskins) between Schlam (bad cop) and most other riders he faced in competition - all part of the show in Hoskins' terms. For all this, the following does confirm the quality of Taylour's performance against Schlam. As Fay noted on a press cutting detailing the race, at this time she 'had been racing on the speedways for a mere few weeks! Schlam was a professional veteran, and he was racing on his home track'.

> Dear Sir. - I would like to ask your opinion concerning the fairness displayed by some of our local contemporaries when commenting on the various races at the Speedway, and particularly when referring to Match Races, in which Sig Schlam is the 'leading light'.

> During the past three or four meetings several scratch races and match races have been run, some of which have been won by Schlam and some by Alf Chick. Going back to the first Match Race - Schlam v. Chick; Schlam won this comfortably. Then later on Chick beat Schlam in a heat of the scratch races. Although Chick won this race in convincing style Schlam was excused on the grounds that his motor was not going too well. Although from memory I think that Schlam's time in the Match Race run first equalled Johnson's old record. Then came the Match Race, Chick v. Schlam, when Chick was mounted on his Douglas. He beat Schlam and incidentally lowered the record: Schlam, not too far behind. Again comment published claimed some slight failing on the part of Schlam's machine. Although later in the same night he beat Chick. Then above all came the Miss Taylour-Schlam Match Race. Miss Taylour beat Schlam in 1.17, the fastest time for the night, Schlam again being excused on account of his motor not being quite right. Yet, in his Match Race with Chick he wasn't too far behind and the race time was 1.17 1/5. In the final of the Scratch Race Schlam registered 1.18. Does it look as though there was much wrong with his mount? I don't think so but do think that instead of excusing Schlam's machine those responsible for writing the matter in some of our locals should give credit to the performance of the better man. Many thousands of Speedway goers have been waiting to see who would beat Schlam, and no doubt some of those who follow the racing are so disgusted as I am to read of such excuses when they should be giving Chick all the credit due to him. Yours, etc.

Hoskins replied:

To 'Inglewood.' - Yours to hand as published above. Yes, we agree with you that comment published from time to time in some of our locals is very one-sided and particularly in relation to our 'local star', Schlam. Schlam, since the opening of the Speedway at Claremont, has, without doubt, been the outstanding performer, but this does not place him in a class of unbeatables, and therefore, we, like yourself, think that Alf Chick has beaten Schlam on conditions of equality, and if any leniency is to be shown it should be handed Chick's way and not used as a means to excuse Schlam for not being able to hold his own against new blood. In relation to the Taylour-Schlam Match Race, we could not see any reason to believe that Schlam's motor was not running too well. The track certainly appeared a bit heavy, but this would operate against both riders, and as far as times go, Schlam's time must have been 1.18 or faster, for he was not too far behind Miss Taylour at the finish, and she registered 1.17.

We thank you for your communication. — Editor

Star quality

The outcome of Fay's battle with Sig Schalm was little short of revolutionary in any context, but in the colonial milieu it was close to a cateclysmic event in the realms of dirt-track racing. There can be little doubt that she did herself a lot of good, her victory over Schlam certainly generated a keen female following during her stay in Australia. But more than this, she had created the foundation of a legend within the new and growing phenomenon that was speedway, an activity that carried the trappings of both sport and theatre. It was, first and foremost an entertainment but Taylour's ability to tap into all its facets meant that she was certainly a celebrity off the track and a star on it.

Fay Taylour demonstrates her broadsiding technique

10. Aussie Odyssey

Immediately after her successful Saturday night in Perth, Fay Taylour boarded a train to start on her 1,300 mile Australian odyssey. On a Tuesday evening at the end of January, 1929, Fay stepped off the West-East locomotive in Adelaide. She was met by a bevy of sponsors including Messrs. Judd and Wilde (Vacuum Oil Co.), Claxton and Cooke (S.A. Motor Sporting Club), and the 'representative' of the *South Australia Speedster* and immediately made it known that she intended to ride in Melbourne on the first Saturday of the following month. She was booked to appear at Hede and Cowley's Exhibition Dirt Track. She also announced that she had sold the Rudge special dirt-track motorcycle that she had brought with her to Australia to Cyril Schlam, so was reliant on her Douglas and the one spare engine. Cyril had used that machine to race at Claremont on the last Saturday in January.

Brimful of enthusiasm

After making sure the Douglas was safely transferred to the *Melbourne Express*, 'Brimful of enthusiasm and wearing an evidently permanent smile of happiness', Fay recalled how she was keen to start at Speedway Royale (that would become the Royal) in Adelaide. She said she understood it to be a fast track and expressed her gladness at knowing that her old opponents, Irvine Jones and Paddy Dean were in Adelaide, and said that she was looking forward to some more duels with them when she returned there on 9 February.

However, Taylour would have to wait for her first taste of the famous Adelaide track. The *Speedster* reporter told readers that, 'To meet Miss Taylour is to like her, and we quite realise the admiration that she compels in the hearts of Irvine Jones, Paddy Dean, and others who have competed against her'. Taylour gushed of her love for Australia praising, '...the manner the Australian agents have looked after her and her machines'. She declared, 'They couldn't do enough for me!'

She moved on to New South Wales. At the beginning of February Col Stewart won the Silver Gauntlet at Kardinia Park (the Geelong Drome) having given a dazzling display in defeating Cliff Bounds (the Victorian State champion). No one had been more surprised than Taylour when it was announced that after the 'usual custom followed in England', she would embrace the winner. As Stewart was brought before her, 'blushing like a schoolboy', Fay responded by saying, "This is rather sudden, but I suppose I must oblige you" and made a timid advance towards the rider. However, the young Victorian fled in terror, but was immediately accosted by other racers and physically compelled to submit to the inevitable. He had to be literally dragged before the officials, where he was forced to surrender to the embrace of Taylour.

The crowd, roared with delight, and Stewart rather sheepishly retired to the centre of the arena.

Fay gave the 12,000 onlookers a fine display of riding in her heat of the Gauntlet, and gained a vigorous round of applause in the Consolation Handicap, which she won in convincing style, Hec Jones having fallen after trying to pass her on the inside. The result card looked impressive from Taylour's point of view:

Consolation Handicap (for seconds and thirds in the heats of the All-Powers Handicap)
Second Heat: Miss Fay Taylour, 1. Time 1 minute 37 seconds.
Final: Miss Fay Taylour (Douglas), 5 second handicap, 1;
                  O.Warner (Cov. Eagle), 9 second handicap 2.
                  Time,1 minute 33 seconds

Castrol Silver Gauntlet One Mile, Rolling Start   (Defender, Col. Stewart, Geelong).
Second Heat: H. Jones (Rudge), 1; Fay Taylour, 2. Time, 1.30 1/5.
Semi-Final: C.   Bounds, 1 Time, 1.20 $^4/_5$
Final: Col.Stewart, Geelong (Douglas) 1;
                  C.Bounds, 2.
                  Time 1minute 26 seconds

Taylour was to reappear at Geelong on Wednesday, 13 February, to be matched with one of the local champions.

In a feature article 'Cinders in her Eye? Fay and the Racing Track - Grey Eyes Sparkle Beneath Her Safety Helmet' published in the February edition of the *Sunday Sun*, Taylour was said to have talked about 'broadsiding and leathers as equably as most girls speak about a chic little gown for a spin in a car'.

It seems that 'The cinders from the racing tack' had not 'spoiled her complexion, her grey eyes' having 'a merry twinkle, and her sense of humour' having 'a keen edge to it'. She was said to have, 'a nice flair for clothes, too, and in a brown frock, coat, and hat, she is an attractive study'.

She told *The Sun* that if she had not 'developed into a speed fiend, she says she would have taken up tennis seriously', and mentioned, '...that her travelling kit includes a perfectly good racquet'. On speedway she commented:

> I was always keen on a bit of a thrill, and I really got my first machine to take me from place to place when I was playing hockey for my county...I started riding as a novice in various competitions in 1927, and my machine was a regular old buckjumper. Riding in reliability trials for a motorcycle firm was my first real stunt, and I took part in the Southern Scott scramble.

Hundreds of riders entered in the trial, which is held on Camberley Heath, the practising ground for Army tanks. The race is over very rough ground and the most impossible hills. It's a case of all after it from the word 'Go!' and the first man home wins. I finished the morning circuit without a brake or a clutch, but that didn't worry me much.

After that I won a couple of cups, and so my name was made...I've had a few tosses, and some of them hurt a little, but when I'm racing I forget I'm a lady, and remember that it isn't the correct thing to moan about bruises.

Speeds? I really don't know to a mile. I was lapping it on the dirt in Western Australia at 56 miles per hour, and that is supposed to be very fast for a cinder track. At the Melbourne Motordrome I did 88.

The piece finished on a predictable high note, stating Fay's ability as a rider but not forgetting to emphasise her gender with a well placed feminising cliché:

Already the men riders have been betting on her chances of beating some of the well-known riders on the Sydney Speedway, but Fay Taylour tosses her brown shingled head and reminds them that in Perth on her first day on the track, her time was faster than that of any interstate rider.

She'll be wearing pink pyjamas

After racing in Melbourne Taylour gave a Saturday night exhibition ride at Sydney's Speedway Royal and was entertained at Government House.

The Royal Agricultural Showgrounds, Moore Park, Sydney, NSW (that would become the home of the Speedway 'Royale') was synonymous with Australian Speedway. It was one of the world's great speedway venues, with its fabulous spectator facilities. In its day, it was known as the Wembley of the southern hemisphere. Jack Parker believed the track to be the best speedway in the world and all the great riders in the history of the sport had ridden on it. The Royale had a narrow track but with its solid wood (later concrete) safety fence and its potential for high speeds, it was considered by some as, literally, a killer track - and indeed it did claim some notables of the sport. Many riders subsequently refused to race on the track, but there was always something fascinating about the Royale for the most skilful and adventurous racers.

The Royale was built on classic lines and was not unlike a Roman coliseum. Modern track legend, Ivan Mauger once remarked that the place made racers feel like gladiators. It was an egg-shaped circuit around $1/3$ of a mile (557 yards or 509 meters) in length. The 'sharp' end of the egg was at the southern end, the Pit turn, and the wider turn was at the northern end between the Members stand and the Bull Pens. A fast mile race might be covered in 59 to 60 seconds (about 60 mph or 97 kph). In a 1937 programme the promoters claimed that the Royale was the fastest speedway track in the world. Speedway racing was first held at the Royale in 1926 (then The Royal) and continued for 70 years. (The last of the regular weekly meetings were staged in the 1980s, but the final event was held on Saturday, 27 July, 1996. It was won by Rod McDonald in front of nearly 30,000 people.)

Many who attended meetings at the Royale will recall the famous three tier Member's stand, on the second turn, at the northern end of the arena. With its huge white clock tower, it had been a landmark from 1924 onwards. The Member's stand could seat 8,000 people and competitors knew that when the top deck of this stand was full on a Saturday night, they would get more prize money from the shared gate takings. The equally famous Suttor stand watched over the starting and finishing line. The big, open, concrete Martin and Angus stand was at the southern end of the arena, opposite the Member's stand, in between turns 3 and 4 of the circuit. It was under this stand that the continuously vibrating Pits were located. The most modern stand, Sinclair was built after the end of the Second World War, and stood between the Suttor and the Martin and Angus stands.

In a 1934 programme the 'Official Electrician' at the Royale stated that it took 25,000 Philips light globes to light up the venue for racing. The wooden safety fence, erected during the reign of Johnnie Hoskins in 1926 acted as a sounding board doubling the volume of the roar of the bikes. The Member's stand magnified the noise yet again as the echo of four bikes screaming down the constricted straights at 70 mph pulsated through its structure.

Every race at the Royale seemed to be a spectacle. There were few riders that were undaunted by the Sydney track. The average speed was 60 mph and the corners came up so fast that the riders had to rely on pure instinct to get round them. These turns were sharp and the crowd intimidating. But the circuit fascinated many good riders, as danger always seems to intrigue the courageous. Bluey Wilkinson once said it was the only track that scared him, but he loved the experience of competing on it.

Graham Warren said of the Royale that it was big, fast and quite dangerous in that the banking allowed riders to hold the throttle open the whole time. He remarked "You don't think of it when you're young, but there was no room for error with those concrete crash walls."

Looking back Ivan Mauger, perhaps the greatest speedway rider of the modern era recollected, "With those high stands so close to the track, the crowd was almost on top of you. When the stadium was packed the atmosphere was tremendous."

It was while racing in Sydney at the Royale that Fay had a bad crash and woke up in hospital. Taylour recalled the events after her accident:

> The Showgrounds Speedway which hadn't been used for racing for a long time was opened to stage a meeting while I was available. It was a third-mile oval like Adelaide, and I think I calculated I could ride it as fast. But,

unlike the smooth granite or shale of Adelaide, it had a rough cinder surface, all the rougher for not having been used.

My first race was a Handicap Heat, and the mechanic who pushed me off warned me to take it easy, saying that the firsts and seconds and fastest third would go into the final. That was all I remembered - though apparently I overtook one rider who started ahead of me and covered a couple of laps before losing control and crashing into the fence, knocking down a record chunk of it as I was told later. It was a spot notable for crashes.

When I came to in the morning I had a splitting headache, a gash on my forehead, another under my chin that had been stitched up, and I felt bruised all over. But something else was worrying me, and I beckoned to a nurse.

"Please", I groaned, "get me out of this".

"I can't", she said, "You're too sick".

She thought I meant the hospital, but it was the nightgown I wanted to get out of. It was made of wool, and was irritating me more than the bruises. And it was in that moment of agony that my lucky talisman was born, fathered, one would imagine, by some publicity expert judging from the way it was embraced by newspaper reporters. It was a pair of soft satin pyjamas, and from then on they came to every racing track with me just in case I landed in hospital again. But they proved a lucky deterrent, like the umbrella, take it with you and it won't rain. Years later, a speedway manager in Louisville, Kentucky, held up my match race till the pyjamas which had been left at my hotel were brought to the track. I was racing midgets (cars) then. The pyjamas were replaced by a nightie later on because they split when I tried to oblige a reporter by putting the top on. I had to buy the nightie because I was on the way to a race. The shop had no soft pyjamas, and I had no time to go elsewhere.

Taylour confirmed this habit in an interview published in *The Motor Cycle* (25 September, 1930):

Talking of Hospitals…I always take a pair of decent silk pyjamas in my kit to each meeting…I once crashed at an Australian track, came round in hospital, and found myself wearing the most appalling old flannel nightdress you could imagine. Ever since that I've carried pyjamas just in case – and they seem to have acted as a lucky mascot, because they haven't been called into use.

The writer seemed to be unable to refrain from making the predictable point, that appeared a necessity in most publications, to allay any doubts about Taylour's sexuality, 'Which just shows you that Fay is really very feminine!'

It seems that her recovery of consciousness in Sydney also included a pleasant surprise, although in terms of Fay's recollections the reader perhaps experiences a different reaction:

> I receive a wonderful proposal of marriage but turned it down. The challenge disappears with the proposal, and I know or feel, although I am still a virgin, that men are too attractive to be faithful to one.

Let's fall in love

The accident led to what was to be an important lesson for Taylour. Her racing was always something of a pilgrimage to find herself, a means to discover people around her and part of an effort to make human connections. This manifested itself from a normal concern to please the paying customers to developing very personal relationships. In Fay there was a deep wish for acceptance. She describes a seminal moment following competition shortly before her accident:

> In the pits after the racing an attractive young woman and three men quietly waited while I signed autographs. Then the young woman said hullo, and I saw that it was Stella, one of the Fetherstonhaughs who had watched me racing in Melbourne. She introduced me to her brother Cuthbert, and two friends, Bob and Stanley, and they insisted on taking me back with them to Clare, about a hundred miles up country, where they farmed. They had two cars, and I went in Cuthbert's, sitting in front between him and Bob. They had next-door farms, and I was to stay at Cuthbert's which was called Wyara. Stella drove with Stanley Hawker as she was staying with his family who bred pedigree sheep. Cuthbert and Bob were wheat growers.

> What a drive that was! The old open car seemed to be tied together with string, and we went at an incredible speed over soft dirt roads with a full moon that provided more light than the headlamps and cast shadows on the bumpy road, making each hole or dip look ten times the size it was. We laughed all the way as if we'd known each other for years. The staid doctor cousin in London had told these connections about me.

> "Won't it be heavenly", I said, "to wake up to the sounds of cock crowing again…it's so long since I stayed on a farm". Hens, somehow, belonged to a farm. "And I bet you have a horse I can ride"?

> "Oh yes", Cuthbert said, "you can ride my polo ponies and drive the horse and trap into the village for groceries". The village consisted of one shop, which was also the post office.

> We turned on to a narrow track and soon pulled up at the farm, stopping beside a truck.

> "Goodnight! I'll see you both tomorrow" and Bob was just getting into the truck when Cuthbert ran after him and asked me to wait a second.

What they were talking about I couldn't guess then, but it was something funny for they were both laughing. Then I heard Bob say "all right, 6am." and he drove off.

I noticed Cuthbert's profile in the moonlight. He was goodlooking. "That's where our chaperon sleeps", he said, pointing to the hut in the distance, and he was laughing.

"Isn't she rather far away", I said, "if I need help"?

"Oh no, I'm quick on my legs, I can fetch her, or better still", he added, "she can sleep in the house, though in that case you'll have to share my room".

I never found out our exact cousin relationship but I felt so contentedly at home at once, with a rapport or accord that needed no finding, that it really seemed we had the best of both friendship and family connection to our advantage.

And sure enough I woke next morning to the thrillingly homey sound of a cock crowing. And it was just under my window! It wasn't too early either. I'd had a good sleep, almost immediately Cuthbert came in with a breakfast tray.

I'd told him I liked boiled eggs, and there were two on the tray.

"Was he the father", I asked, pointing to the window.

He nodded, but when I looked out later there were no hens to be seen. There were trees around the house, and beyond them the rolling distance stretching far beyond Cuthbert's land. The house was small and compact, with a stone patio or veranda round the front path. It seemed gorgeously isolated without being the back of beyond.

I was introduced to Collie who rounded up the sheep every evening, Cuthbert has some sheep too, and then I made friends with the ponies and had a ride before lunch. The chaperon was the housekeeper, and she did the cooking. She was tickled pink with my visit.

After lunch Stella and Stanley arrived and laughingly hoped that I'd been adequately chaperoned. This suggested a theme for my cine camera, and with enormous mirth we shot a scene in which Stella acted the chaperone introducing me to Cuthbert. First was the shot of the car arriving, and then a shot of Cuthbert in the house peeping out from behind a curtain. Then Stella leading me up the garden path to the front door, and I'd been made-up to look like a gawky country lass with a silk stocking acting as a bow in my hair. Stanley did the shooting but broke up in hysterics at the final scene. And the funny thing is that he and Stella should have been the main players. They were madly in love, though I hadn't yet discovered it and within a year were married.

We were out at the back before tea just after Bob had joined us, and suddenly Stella shouted from a shed: "what's that?"?

We all ran, and found her pointing to a large pen. The cock that had awakened me was inside, and Bob was looking guiltily at Cuthbert, and Cuthbert at him. So that was what they'd been plotting before Bob drove off in the night! They'd borrowed it from the village...I said goodbye to my cousins, but only for a short time...

It was not long before Fay was back at Wyara:

Cuthbert and I were hemmed in alone by a dust storm. It was thick and red, and no one could go out. So lunch dates had to be cancelled. But so little set us laughing... Cuthbert enjoyed my company, not just because I was feminine but because I was me. He was tickled pink when he discovered that I could stand on my hands because he was expert at it. When Stella asked later: "what did you two do...", Cuthbert said: "we did handsprings, trying to see which of us could stay upright in reverse longest". Stella pretended to be shocked, but she was really as conservative as she was charming. Her sense of humour was prevalent.

Cuthbert presented Fay with a rooster as a gift.

...which of course I could not take on my racing travels. "I'll keep it till you return", he'd said, and he promised to buy the bird some wives.

"I'll come back here to recuperate if I have a crash", I told him. I expected to be busy racing till it was time to return to England.

"I'll telephone you every night after racing", he said, "to make sure you haven't crashed. But isn't there some other excuse for coming back?"

Such an accident was always a possibility on the big dirt tracks at that time and Fay kept in contact with Cuthbert. However, following the crash in Sydney, Cuthbert got no answer to his repeated phone calls. I was lying unconscious in a Sydney hospital.

Someone phoned Cuthbert to let him know where I was, and when I was told I couldn't race for a while I didn't argue. The farm seemed to be calling, the ponies, the rooster, Cuthbert, and the place itself. It would be nice to laugh with Cuthbert again. And so the threat to return if I had a crash became a reality.

I watched Cuthbert working, and together we watched his Collie as she cleverly rounded up the sheep and drove them in every evening. Then we would ride round the property closing gates. After supper Cuthbert would work the tractor by headlights because the slump had hit him badly. Working normally he would get less for a bag of wheat than it cost to produce.

He looked handsome in his working slacks and open shirt, and quite cowboy-ish when he wore the red cotton handkerchief I gave him to protect the back of his neck from the sun. I took a snapshot of him holding the rooster in his arms, for I had an ordinary camera as well as a cine. And of course the blue leather HMV gramophone was with me, so we played it at lunchtime or in the evening when he wasn't working. Sometimes we danced. Louise was our current favourite, and we spent many needles on 'Let's Do It-Let's Fall In Love' which he gave me.

We lunched on Sundays at the Hawker's sheep station where Stella spent weekends, and Cuthbert and Stanley played billiards. It was about twenty or more miles away, and I loved to pick out Cuthbert's farm from the distance as we returned - a clump of trees in the undulating land marked his small house. There were few homesteads close together, but it was nothing to drive ten or twenty miles for a game of tennis or billiards.

I'd now met Cuthbert's mother. She and Stella both liked me, and I thought they were darlings. They were happy for me to be with Cuthbert and did not consider my choice in sport the slightest bit outrageous. They were even proud of me, and they had much to be proud of in Cuthbert. He was a well known figure in the cities during Horse Show week, or on the polo fields playing polo. Typical of the name Fetherstonhaugh, he trained and even broke his own horses, and he could dance as well as he could ride. Lionel's cousin in Adelaide had told me he was a much sought-after bachelor, and for his disposition alone I could well understand it. In fact I wondered if I wasn't falling. He was sure a nice person, so thoughtful and understanding, so full of fun, and such a wonderful companion...and that song was so provocative: 'Let's Fall In Love – Why Shouldn't We Fall In Love'.

Although in her memoirs she was to say of Sydney that she 'always had bad luck' there 'either it rained' or she 'finished up a meeting in hospital', Taylour makes no mention of another crash in which she was involved during her visits to New South Wales. On a Saturday evening appearance at Wentworth Speedway, 9-year-old George Shaw suffered a fractured skull when he was struck on the head by the handlebar of Taylour's motorcycle. A wheel struck a bumpy patch, and her machine smashed through the protecting fence, the handlebar hitting the boy on the cranium. Taylour's hand was injured, and she was unable to compete in later races. This was a dramatic and one would think stressful incident, but it seems Taylour had either forgotten it or did not want to be reminded of it in later years.

Brisbane

On the evening of 27 February 1929 Speedway enthusiasts assembled at Brisbane's Central Station to welcome the arrival of an 'English motorcyclist'. According to *The Courier* of the next day they '...were surprised and pleased to see in the talented visitor a charming young woman, with a pleasant smile and a noticeable but slight accent. They had expected a more masculine type, considering the hazardous sport she had adopted, but she was decidedly feminine.'

News of Fay's efforts in Melbourne, Perth and Goulburn had gone before her and the Saturday night, Davies Park meeting with Frank Pearce was eagerly anticipated. She commented,

> I do not mind racing with men at all...They treat me as one of themselves and make me quite at home. The riders in England are very decent, and I was told before I left that they were a rather rough lot in this country. That is not true at all: if anything, I like them better than the English boys. Anyway, I have made up my mind about coming back.

Asked if she did not think the sport too strenuous for a woman, Taylour, seemingly changing her mind somewhat about this ubiquitous question, said that it was more a matter of skill.

Fay was now gaining national fame and some notoriety as a competitor and it was in Brisbane that she became widely referred to as 'the world's champion lady motorcyclist'. But the *Brisbane Standard* (28 February 1929) felt obliged to bridge the apparent disparity between being a racer and a woman by commenting on Fay's femininity:

> Although a champion on the speed tracks, Miss Taylour is essentially feminine. Her pretty blue eyes, her winning smile, and her cheerful, friendly disposition have endeared her to all those fortunate enough to have met her in the Southern States. There is a wide gap between domestic science and speedway racing, yet to be the holder of a domestic science scholarship is one of Miss Taylour's distinctions.

The day before her first appearance in Brisbane, Taylour was the 'hostess' at a tea party at Lennon's Hotel, and used the occasion as a press conference. She received her guests wearing a 'smart frock of crepe de Chine, the bodice being of figured cigar brown, while the pleated skirt was of navy blue, and in it she looked distinctly feminine, and not the least bit 'speedy''. One has to agree with the writer that navy blue and brown would not have looked at all 'speedy' – in fact it smacks more of military nurses on a winter battle front!

When the party was sitting at the round afternoon tea table, 'bright with a centre bowl of crimson roses', the hostess 'chatted freely and interestingly about motorcycling and its sensations'. Fay let it be known that she would, 'try the Davies Park track' at 7am on the following morning for the first time.

Taylour drew a record crowd in Brisbane. 'Never', said the *Brisbane Sunday Mail*, 'has Davies Park been so crowded for a speedway meeting as it was on Saturday night' for Fay's appearance.

Taylour's fastest lap on the quarter mile track averaged 44.11mph. But her motor was not as responsive as she would have liked and she was beaten by the great Vic Huxley. Brisbane was an unusual ride for Taylour in that it offered three turns instead of the regular oval. She had been able to practice on it the morning before making her competitive debut on the track, but during the evening's racing, under flood lighting, she complained of not being able to, 'remember the bends'. Although she conceded that she may have lost to Huxley even without this 'disadvantage'. But, according to Taylour, the crowd seemed 'happy'.

Vic Huxley had been Fay's hero as she had started out on the speedways, but she was to find herself dancing with him at the post event celebration at Lennon's Hotel. She told another dancing partner that she had heard the famous flyer Kingsford Smith watched the racing and she wished she could meet him. Charles Edward Kingsford Smith (Sky King Kingsford) has been called the world's greatest aviator. At the time he was the closest thing to a male sex symbol that Australia had. His record breaking flights and almost superhuman flying skills are legendary. As they glided round the dance floor her partner said "I am Kingsford Smith". He was staying at Lennon's too.

Giving welly in Wellington

The next day, at 8.45 pm, Fay said goodbye to Brisbane as the express train steamed southwest bound for Melbourne. Her stay in the 'Paris on the Yarra' would be brief but enough to make arrangements to return at a later date.

Taylour went on to New Zealand where a big welcome awaited her, including a Civic reception, and the All Blacks in Auckland. But according to her she 'slipped away' from it as fast as she could to view the race track. The next night, after riding, a doctor was called in the small hours to stitch up a finger on her right hand. In Wellington she had won two races and crashed on the third. She moved on to Auckland and other cities. General Motors had provided a white Chevrolet so she travelled by car. Fay toured alongside the Australian tennis team and as she watched them perform, they cheered her on around the tracks of New Zealand, and sometimes two or three of the team would drive with Fay, chasing the train with their comrades on board to the next city. Speedway racing had not been established long in New Zealand, but Taylour managed to record best times on a frequent basis and defeat the the country's top riders.

Admiral Byrd[37], who had just flown over the South Pole, was on the small ship that took Fay back to Wellington. The captain gave a party for them both, and she was pleasantly surprised to meet a handsome man in his thirties instead of the bearded old seafarer she had expected Byrd to be.

Fay took 'the Land of the Great White Cloud' by storm during her short stay. On her second appearance at the Western Springs Stadium, Auckland, she defeated some of the local stars, and came within $2/5$th of the record set up by Frank Pearce, setting the fastest time of the evening. Fay made a lasting impression on New Zealand as the *Wellington Evening Post* testified:

...Anyone seeing her would realise that she is far from 'ordinary'. An 'ordinary person' (as she described herself) could not retain all those feminine qualities which those who attended a function in her honour at the Grand Hotel this morning realised at once were hers, and yet compete in such a nerve-demanding sport as dirt-track racing.

A charming brunette with a wide smile and dark blue eyes, Miss Taylour captivated all who met her with refreshing manner and unassuming personality. 'No cocktails, no cigarettes' is part of her keeping fit motto, and she has a healthy freshness which many a less famous girl would envy.

Although Miss Taylour, who is a connection to Lord Riddell, won a Domestic Science scholarship before she left school, she had not a great deal to say about that...

Back beneath our radiant Southern Cross

Taylour returned to Australia in March, 1929 and competed at the Olympia Motor Speedway at Maroubra, Sydney on the 23rd, of that month.

Fay made what was to be her farewell appearance in Melbourne in mid-April. Taylour rode cautiously, swinging wide at the turns. But as the race went on she gathered pace, however it was evident that she did not want to run any risks.

In the semi-final Taylour was placed second. In the words of the *The Sporting Globe,*

> ...the little lady from the land of the Shamrock took her place in the second heat of the 'A' grade handicap. She was on virtual scratch - 5 seconds - and finished second to Mick Warner (7 seconds).

Her placing qualified Fay for the final, but she got away badly and failed to get into the picture. Nevertheless, she received a great ovation on dismounting.

In the international match against the famous interstate star and Victorian Champion, Reg West[38], Taylour took charge at the gun and gave a good display for a couple of laps. But over the last half-mile she did not appear to be going comfortably, though she was still within four lengths of West, whose time for the mile was 1minute 264/5 seconds.

Fay was due to sail for Britain the following week, but made it known that she had agreed with the management of the Melbourne Exhibition Speedway, as part of their Saturday night programme, to attack the 'B' grade lap record of 203/5 seconds, just set by Clarrie Stewart. She also said that she intended to take part in the 'A' grade handicap, and compete in a special match race.

On 17 April, 1929 Fay told *The Sporting Globe* :

> You know Australians are such wonderful 'sports' that I felt I had to appear or the public might have been disappointed. My injured finger was giving

me no end of trouble, and I could not handle my machine properly, but I know the spectators were tolerant, and I hope to do better next week.

The injury was the one sustained when she crashed in Wellington. It was badly infected, and, had she acted on the advice of her doctor she would not have taken part in competition. She had been told that if she had another fall it might mean the finger would have to be amputated. But as the *Globe* had it 'True to the traditions of the Emerald Isle—Miss Taylour is a Colleen, by the way *(Taylour altered her nationality almost as regularly as she changed tires - according to a combination of taste and expedience)* the visitor was determined to see her engagement through'. But Fay felt the need to justify herself:

> You know, you could not convince a lot of people that I had had an accident in New Zealand. Many of them might be unkind enough to say that I was pretending - that I was afraid to meet my rivals…Besides, they have billed me to appear, and I must go on. I do not like disappointing patrons. All I hope is that they don't expect too much of me.

To mark her appreciation of the hospitality extended to her during her stay in Melbourne, and with a view to stimulating still greater interest in dirt-track racing, Taylour offered to present a cup to the winner of a race on the Melbourne Exhibition Speedway. When the announcement was made on Saturday evening over the loud speakers, there was a big round of applause, and, it was said a competitor on the arena called: "Good on you, Fay you are a true sport!"

In the local press a photograph of Taylour, now being consistently referred to as coming from Ireland, and as 'the girl dirt-track motor cycle champion', appeared advertising her farewell appearance at the Melbourne Exhibition Speedway. In the background were 'Cyclone' Monkey, Maurie Bradshaw (at that point he was on his way to England with Col Stewart), Jimmy Pringle and Col Stewart.

Wizardess of Oz

A crowd of thousands arrived at the Exhibition Speedway to witness the racing, unusually at least one-third were women. Taylour, although she had been bedridden up to a few hours before the meeting suffering from influenza, told the event Manager, Frank Hunting, "Well, it's no use growling. There's work to be done, and I'd better get busy" and so saying rose to the occasion.

Taylour made a good start, finishing second to Reg Hay (the Tasmanian champion), in the third heat of the 'A' grade handicap. She was only two lengths away from Hay at the finish, and qualified for the semi-finals.

Less than 15 minutes later, astride her Douglas she made her attempt on Clarrie Stewart's record from a standing start. After winding up for a lap she got away at hurricane speed. The dexterous manner in which she took the bends astounded the crowd and fellow riders. As she turned into the final straight after a skilful and picturesque broadside, she was timed by four watches at 20 seconds, shattering the record by $3/5$ of a second. The announcement of her achievement made over the air by Mr H.J. Sullivan, was the signal for a prolonged outburst of cheering, and when Sullivan stated that Taylour would immediately attack Reg West's 'A' grade lap record of $19 4/5$ seconds, a shrill female voice from the starting point called out: "Go on Fay, show the boys how to break records!!" Taylour smiled in acknowledgement. She looked excited as she chatted with her mechanic, Les Gough, who was also a well loved rider of the era (know as 'The Richmond Flyer' and the 'Motordrome champion') who in later years would become a pioneer of Midget car racing.

Taylour kicked off to the accompaniment of rousing cheers, and in a flying start streaked along the track like an arrow in flight, and took the Aquarium bend splendidly. A little later she struck a bump which almost tossed her out of the saddle. Time keepers had their eyes glued on their watches, but as Taylour flashed over the line she had equalled West's record for the track. It was another startling feat.

Later in the evening she met Reg West in a sensational, four lap, return international match. A week previously West had been the victor. This time designated as representing England, 'the Dublin girl', lost the toss and West, recognised as one of the most renowned dirt track riders in the Commonwealth, riding a Rudge, took the inside berth. In a flying start he appeared to have the advantage. But, after just a quarter of a lap, he crashed at the southern end of the track. Taylour was clear of him, and seeing his plight, eased up. A re-run was necessary, but it was clear that the track was very uneven.

On the second start both riders got away excellently but before the completion of the first lap Taylour had a miraculous escape, narrowly avoiding a damaging crash. She developed a 'super-wobble', it was remarkable how she kept on her machine, but had to ease up in order to do so. A 'no race' was declared and it was deemed that another try at getting a result should follow, the management announcing that it would be a case of 'all in', no further mishaps being allowed.

At the third time of asking both riders combined to create a glorious battle of speed and wits. Taylour gained the upper hand almost from the start, but West tackled her with grim determination. Spectators stood up and roared themselves horse. At half way Taylour was still in command. West's goggles were covered with cinders from Fay's wake, and with the choice of being blind or battered he threw his eye gear off and set after the woman. But the visitor from overseas was never headed and ran home the winner, covering the four laps in 1 minute $22 2/5$ seconds, which bettered by $2/5$ of a second Reg Hay's best time in a competition race. This was probably, the defeat of Sig Schlam aside, Fay's greatest achievement in Australia. Although her machine was almost certainly superior to West's mount, she had ridden with controlled aggression and considerable skill.

But Taylour was not finished; she won her semi-final off 9 seconds in the 'A' grade handicap. She led from the start and finished up with plenty in hand in 1 minute 27³/₅ seconds

In the 'A' final Taylour made good use of her handicap, getting away well. With half a lap to go, Taylour got into a spectacular skid whilst in the lead, but accomplished one of the most acrobatic stunts ever witnessed on the Melbourne track, and averted what looked like a certain disaster. There was a chorus of relief as she righted her machine and careered on. Despite Reg West and Tom Maloney (both on 3 seconds), trying everything to reduce her lead, she won with consummate ease by 100 yards, in a time of 1 minute 30 seconds.

A remarkable demonstration followed, as the crowd sang: 'She likes a broadside skid, I never liked a broadside skid…but that's her weakness now!' There is no record of the melody to which these lyrics were sung, indeed it was unusual for a sporting crowd of that era to produce the type of 'choruses' that would, after World War Two become associated with soccer fans (although there was a tradition of communal singing at baseball games in the US from the earliest times). Thousands of people invaded the arena and surrounded their heroine of the night, showering congratulations and bombarding her with autograph books. In celebratory mood Fay treated many of her younger admirers to hot dogs. The result was:

'A'Grade Handicap (four laps) Final:

Fay Taylour	(Douglas)	9 second handicap, 1
Reg Maloney	(Rudge)	3 second handicap, 2
Tom Maloney	(Blackbourne)	3 second handicap, 3.

After her performance in Melbourne, Taylour was bestowed the media epithets of 'Fearless Fay' and 'Wizardess of the Track'. Australia had been wooed by Taylour and won over by a combination of press coverage and the best motorcycle technology in the world. But this mix was augmented by Fay's personality and skill. In the last analysis, the media had not really been able to explain or justify Taylour. Who she was and what she was doing had been literally characterised by those who watched and supported dirt-track; they, it seemed wanted a figure like Fay. She would have been many different things to a range of individuals and groups: speed-nun, fast woman, rebel Irish, aristocratic English – males were likely to have seen her one way, women would have interpreted her differently, while children might have developed another point of view. That entity lumped together as the 'public' loves a mysterious personality, particularly one that seems partially accessible. This is because individuals can, via the imagination, conjure up their own perspective and as such feel they have a very personal understanding of an individual who appears inscrutable to others and/or the rest of the world. How many 'stars' have fostered, adopted, habituated or had this quality conferred upon them? It is doubtful if Taylour consciously created a persona for herself in any consistent fashion, at least she may not have meant to have presented herself as a sort of Marta Hari and/or Femme Fatale but there were elements of both in the character she and the press presented to the world. However, it is likely that Fay's lack of awareness about herself, who she was, what she wanted or where she was going, helped create the 'fascination' she held for Australia in 1929.

Slamming Schlam

Whilst Taylour was re-writing dirt-track history in Australia, Sig Schlam continued to develop his style and performance on his home turf. At the same time his brother generated his own, if slightly more modest mark.

The control of the Claremont Speedway was taken over by the WA Motor Cycling Association from Speedways Ltd and some novelty events were included in the programmes. On 9 March, perhaps as an after-effect of the presence of Fay Taylour, a Ladies Race was included in the programme. This race was won by Miss Bessie Hibbert, and was reported to have 'created a lot of amusement to the habitués who were giving plenty of advice to the fair riders'.

For the Imperial Scratch Race, Schlam, Walker and Glendinning faced the starter in the final. Schlam hit Walker in the first lap, causing Walker to crash. Glendinning led all the way and won from Schlam, who was disqualified for 'cutting in'. There was a demonstration against Schlam after the race, confirming the continuing hostility towards Sig from a section of the Claremont crowd.

At a meeting of the WAMCA during the following week, the decision of the Stewards was reviewed and the disqualification removed. Schlam was therefore paid second prize money and Walker third. Schlam did not appeal against the original decision of the Stewards, the WAMCA officials had taken action on their own initiative. This would not have helped dispel the negative feelings directed towards the rider, but the point of this episode was probably that it raised interest and awareness and was therefore good for business. A tactic that has been repeated in many sports in which entertainment can ride roughshod over 'pure' competition (perhaps most notably professional wrestling, although speedway never plummeted to such levels).

On 30 March, Sig again won the Golden Helmet, this time in a dead heat with Glendinning. This was the third time he had taken the title and thereby retained possession of it. In the final meeting for the 1928/29 Speedway Season at Claremont, on 6 April, Schlam swept the board and won two trophies: the Chevrolet Special Six and the Johnnie Walker cups.

For the love of Cuthbert

It seems before it was time for her to leave Australia Fay found time to be with Cuthbert:

…one evening, before it was time for me to leave for England, he kissed me and proposed with a simple "will you marry me"? And I knew he was in love.

In the same moment I knew that I wasn't, though I loved him. My thoughts had flown to Lionel, who had not proposed and whose people hated me! Here with Cuthbert there was love all round, and a life I could fit in to…but could I? Could I make the sort of wife he deserved? Could I ignore those periodical attractions for other men which uninvitedly and inescapably turned up, the work of Nature which knows no marriage laws, the desire to go out with someone else which can only be quenched by going, quenched as quickly sometimes as an attempted kiss; a magnetic field so powerful yet so easily earthed! I wanted to feel this way about Cuthbert, it was wrong to marry without being head over heels in love, dishonest. But of course one had to love too. Perhaps the two didn't go together…they almost did with Lionel. How could I break with him, give up seeing those sympathetic grey eyes looking at me with amusement and gravity and a funny embarrassed flutter when he felt intimate. 'You belong to me', he'd written, but he shunned sentimentality, brushed it off with a shy laugh…

Cuthbert interrupted my thoughts. He'd asked such a vital question and I hadn't answered. Now he said: "there's another chap, isn't there? The one in England who races"?

I nodded.

"You wouldn't have to give up racing if you married me". His voice told me that he knew it was hopeless and that it wasn't the racing I'd been thinking of.

I knew I couldn't say yes.

"I'm sorry Cuthbert" was all I did say, and it must have sounded awfully bare. I was really sorry, but how to explain it? How to tell him he was the nicest person in the world while at the same time turning him down?

In my cabin on the ship I studied the snapshot of him, with the rooster in his arms and the cotton square around his neck. He said it would always remind him of me.

Eagerly I looked forward to the ship's call at Western Australia where mail should be awaiting me from Lionel. I'd written to his Perth office a month earlier asking them to hold any letters as I wasn't sure how long I'd be staying at Cuthbert's… there was no mail from him, and I had to wait till we reached England to know that he had really written. Not only had he written, but he'd sent me a book, and it too had disappeared. It was a volume of DH Lawrence love poems.… I should have enjoyed the voyage, but…Lionel and the picture of Cuthbert all alone saddened me.

The almost tacit, vaguely tangential affair with Cuthbert is consistent with all the other frustratingly semi-adolescent tales of untidy, indistinctly awkward encounters that Taylour describes herself as having with men. However, the apparently built-in certitude of it ending in hazy, shallow despair and the annoying insistence on her chasteness, whilst laboriously searching to develop an underlying suggestion of eroticism, tells the reader a great deal about Fay's inability to get in touch with herself as an adult or express herself as a woman. Her tale of Cuthbert's pursuit of her is the archetypal fairy story - a prepubescent, love affair; the fleeting amorousness of a boy/girl flirtation, devoid of the basic, earthiness of the truly erotic and carnal nature of unbridled and instinctive passion. The dirt-track can be understood as a parable or a redirection of that driving power of adult sexuality; the broadside perhaps embodies the very edge of things experienced in orgasm. For Taylour, it seems, the track, the symbolic metaphor, was her limit. But a metaphor can only be little more than an adjunct to allegory, it is not the 'real thing'. All human expression might be understood to be the repression of instinct. The racer is trapped in his or her experience - to that extent the 'thrill' is selfish. Although it can to some extent be shared with the crowd, all the danger and glory are *taken* by the exponent. However, it is at the moment when desire, that which compels us to take, wells up to a height where it merges with compassion, the life force that causes us to exude *giving*, that for many, might be a definition of authentic physical love.

Taylour's accounts of love, her real and/or fantasy liaisons never really moved beyond a girlish titillation. The being 'in love' that seemed to elude her might have been accessible had she been able to *give* in a fully real and adult manner, but there is little evidence that Fay was capable of giving in that way. Trapped within herself, she seemed to sustain a tragic loneliness. This was made more profound by the fact that she never really seemed fully conscious of it - Taylour repressed her isolation, suffocating it with constant movement.

Adieu or au revoir

Three days after her victory over Reg West, on Tuesday, 23 April, 1929, Fay returned to Britain. The Melbourne *Sporting Globe* (Wednesday, 24 April) cried '*Adieu! Miss Taylour's Farewell*'

> Prior to sailing for England on Tuesday, Miss Fay Taylour, the champion woman motor cyclist, wrote the following exclusive statement for The Sporting Globe:-

> There is an old saying – 'all good things come to an end' – and my sojourn in Australia is, unfortunately, about to suffer a similar fate.

> Needless to say, I am happy to return to my native land, (*apparently her 'native land' was now England*) but, nevertheless, I am full of regrets at having to leave Australia after having got to know and like you so much.

The splendid receptions which have been accorded me at the various speedways- and especially at the Melbourne Exhibition Oval on Saturday night – are keenly appreciated by me. It is a tribute to your generous sportsmanlike qualities that you should have greeted me as you have – in real 'Aussie' fashion – irrespective of whether I was successful or not.

It is very nice to know that after coming 12,000 miles I have had extended to me the hand of friendship. It is another illustration of that British tradition *(Fay seems, at this point to have decided to identify with being British)* – 'hands across the sea.' I came here a stranger in a strange land, and you made me feel just like being at home.

As a slight token of my appreciation of the Melbourne people, I am anxious to associate myself with the Melbourne Exhibition speedway, and have offered a cup for competition next season, when I feel sure the standard of racing will greatly improve.

When I meet Maurie Bradshaw and Col Stewart, two of your champions who have gone to England to try their luck, I shall do all in my power to assist them, and also take a personal interest in their welfare. I am sure that they will worthily uphold Australia's prestige on the other side.

I hope to return to Australia next year, and again ride on the Melbourne Exhibition speedway. To Messrs. Hede and Cowley, the Melbourne promoters, to Frank Hunting – the track manager and to Mr H.J. Sullivan *(the announcer)* I desire to convey my best thanks.

And now a final word of appreciation of what The Sporting Globe is doing for motor cycling in Australia…In England the sport has caught on like a bush fire and I am positive with the promise of future internationals coming to Australia next season, and your local riders improving considerably, the sport will be staged in such an attractive manner as to draw thousands of spectators.

So now let me say – not good-bye – but adieu. All being well, I hope to see you again before long.

In the same edition, *The Sporting Globe* eulogised the sudden impact of femininity on the tracks of what was still Britain's most far flung dominion:

…And now hats off to Fay Taylour, the Dublin girl *(another quick change of identity)* - the girl who has taken Australia and New Zealand by storm in the few months that she has been with us. To have defeated such riders of international fame as Sig Schlam and Frank Pearce, as well as many other noted Australians, and in addition to breaking track records, is sufficient proof that she is a champion in every sense of the word.

Her charming personality and her modesty on and off the track have made thousands of friends for her.

Success stimulates this Irish girl, who is chock full of excitement from the time she goes on to the track until she completes her task. She is sure of a warm welcome when she returns later in the year.

Only cruising

In July, 1929, Sig Schalm appeared before the Fremantle Police Court charged with speeding. Putting forth a novel plea, Sig said, "I was only cruising along, your worship. Had I been in a hurry, I would not have been caught". He was fined £2.

Creating and breaking records, beating Sig Schlam, Frank Pearce and Reg West while drawing record crowds at Brisbane had made Taylour's time in Australia a huge success, emphasised by the £1,500 in prize money she won – a lot of cash at that time.

Whilst in Australia she had, probably quite unselfconsciously, created social benefits. In 1929 the women folk of Australia were very much second class citizens compared with the male population, perhaps more so than in Britain, so Taylour's success had generated questions about the limits imagined and imposed on women. On a personal basis, it seemed as she looked back across the sea to Britain that the world was Fay Taylour's oyster.

11. And so to England

In the lounge of the cruise ship taking her back to England, Fay was 'tickled pink' to see her photo in a Melbourne newspaper alongside the other celebrities on the same ship. These included Dame Clara Butt, the world famous virtuoso singer and the writer, radical feminist and pioneer birth control campaigner, Annie Besant.

In *Cinder Siftings* in *Motor Cycle* (25 April, 1929) the writer told readers: 'A few days ago I received a radiogram from Sydney as follows:- *Returning on SS Comorin after successful trip. Open all offers bar marriage. Cheerio! Fay Taylour*'.

Fay recorded some of her experiences of the voyage which provide a sense of the time and the atmosphere of round the world travel before the 1930s.

"Fine! You've cut another second. A few more try-outs and the race is ours!"

Stanley Wootten, famed race horse owner and trainer, stabbed his stop-watch with genuine satisfaction. He might have been on Epsom Downs timing his gallops instead of on 'C' Deck of the P&O liner also taking him back to England from Australia. We were due at Tilbury in three days, and tonight after dinner the second horse race meeting would be held in the lounge. With such a trainer and his friends aboard the game had acquired quite a racecourse atmosphere, especially as the 'stakes' were won by skill, and not by the throw of a dice as on some ships.

The realistic-looking racehorses, with their different colours, are lined up at the start of the straight course which stretches the length of the lounge. They are drawn or wound to the finish, just as a fish is reeled in for landing. The jockeys do the winding. They stand in line just behind the finish facing their horses, and placed between their feet is the waist-high stick that carries the reel. The starter sees that the string between the reel and the horse is taut before the flag goes down. Women passengers are the jockeys. Men the owners. There are about six races, with the winners going into the grand stakes final.

Before Colombo I'd finished second in the final of the first races. I'd been winding with my arm as well as the wrist, and a seasoned expert romped home. She was the favourite for tonight, but now I'd learnt the knack, and Stanley Wootten was training me!

"My rival is probably cutting seconds off too" I suggested. "She's practicing on another deck".

"Don't worry", I was told, "we're keeping check". But I wasn't so confident. I'd kept my wrist loose at practice, it could seize up when others were alongside me winding for dear life, and backers and owners roaring encouragement.

When changing for dinner I was careful not to wear the flimsy dress that tended to catch in the winding pole last time. I might have been dressing for the speedway, and when I went into the lounge after dinner I could have been at the race track. Are you going to win tonight? How's your form? Shall I back you? Everybody was studying the race cards which had been printed in the Purser's office. I was entered for the third race and listed as 'Speedy' by 'Speed Queen' out of 'Dirt Track'. A race committee had been set up with stewards, starter and officials, and a tote was now taking bets for the first race. Those laying stakes were even more excited than the owners or jockeys.

I watched the first two races in case I could learn anything. And I did! The winner of the second was disqualified for 'pulling' her horse. In her excitement, while running neck and neck with the horse in the next track, she'd pulled her winding stick back thus drawing her horse over the finishing line first.

Then I found myself lined up facing my horse with the winding stick between my legs, and I was a bundle of nerves. The horses seemed a long way off, and I caught sight of Stanley Wootten giving me a good luck signal. The flag went down, there was a shout of "they're off", and I started to wind...and wind...and wind...all in tense silence. But soon the shouting started and I heard 'Come on, Speedy'. I tried to wind faster but couldn't nor could I tell where I was lying. The favourite wasn't in this race, but I could get beaten by an outsider. Cries of "Flying Fish – Flying Fish" drowned everything else. Flying Fish must be winning, but I only had a yard to go...then one foot...and then I crossed the finishing line, a clap on the back told me I'd won. Flying Fish had made a game challenge.

The favourite won the next race with poker-faced coolness, so now we'd meet for the trophy. There wasn't a split second between us, my backers had timed us both, but the tote showed she was still favourite.

"That suits us", Stanley Wootten said, "but you're going to win!

He felt I would easily outstrip my former time as I'd done each run in practice, I wasn't at all sure. The favourite had been so calm during her race that she'd probably checked her position and taken it easy to hide her real form. She could have seconds in hand: this game was her forte. She travelled with her husband and won it on every ship, so her need to win was greater than mine. My need to win was a pair of slate-blue eyes, for just as there's no thunder without lightening there's no racing for me without romance. Excitement generates it I suppose. Anyway, it had suddenly become very important to receive a well-done message through the slate-blue eyes of my trainer. I *must* win! There were plenty of younger men on board but as soon as I found one attractive, he would kill the romance by wanting to sneak to my cabin in the dead of night.

"You look as if you have St.Vitus's Dance!" Two of my table companions pointed to my gyrating wrist.

"Oh! I'm just practicing", I explained. I was winding an imaginary thread in the hope it would loosen me up to greater speed.

"Good!" They waved a bundle of pound notes and said they were going to back me again. The tote was open for the grand final and I found I had track number three, my lucky number, and wasn't the race I won also number three!

As we donned our jockey caps I heard someone shout "put another fifty on Speedy", and I wasn't sure if it encouraged or frightened me. Bets of a hundred pounds were being taken, and then the tote was closed and the race was on, and off we went winding for dear life. "Steady…steady" I was saying to myself as I did on the speedway. I couldn't crash but my wrist could seize or the stick jump for I was winding faster than I expected and the tone of those shouting for me seemed to indicate I was winning. And then suddenly the race was stopped and the stewards held an emergency meeting. The favourite had pulled her horse according to one steward but another disagreed.

The race was re-run, and thank goodness without any disqualification for a win like that would be no win at all. But I wondered if I could repeat the form I'd just shown and stand the excitement all over again. I could feel the tenseness of the onlookers, but by half way I was winding with the precision of a belt-driven motor, even to the cord piling up in the centre of the reel so that each revolution made a bigger step for the horse. The roars of "Speedy" became hysterical, and now I could see I was out in front…five more feet…four…three…two…'careful! Don't pull the stick, and I was safely over the line. I'd done it! I'd finished first, and the evening finished with champagne.

This episode is full of the adolescent fervour that Taylour habituated for nearly every activity she was involved in. An on-board game had been blown completely out of proportion and a seemingly straightforward diversionary relationship exploded into a meaningful romance. There are indications that her fellow passengers were making her the object of fun, seeing a joke in her over zealous attitude and wish to magnify herself by means of what was little more than a pointless parlour game. Taylour saw none of this. She was taken up completely by the moment and the importance she imagined the 'horse racing' to have. The fabricated figures became almost equine reality, the simple technique of the 'racing' became elevated to a high level skill, that required practice to perfect. But soon the competition became no more than a memory as the simmering of the potential love affair died down. As usual Fay looked to her next encounter.

Tilbury

In three days I'd see Lionel. London and Lionel! I'd played his records most afternoons when the rest of the ship was sleeping. I couldn't acquire the siesta habit. I didn't expect him to meet me at Tilbury as that would conflict with his office hours so I'd arranged to take the boat train to Liverpool Street. He might be there for it wasn't far from his office.

I'd left my packing till the last moment as usual, and a big quiver told me that we'd rubbed noses with Tilbury Dock. I flew up on deck and peered into the crowd below. Might Lionel be there, or perhaps one of the reporters from the motor cycle magazines?

"Don't think anyone's meeting me here", I had to admit.

" *What*"! The passenger next to me laughed and pointed to a group standing apart where a whole bunch of speedway boys were waving a banner with my name on it, and a little to one side stood Lionel and Johnnie Hoskins, and two men from the daily papers.

Moving down the deck I made waving contact and soon joined them on the dock. They had a gaily decorated truck in which I must ride to London. It was a regular circus, but not for Lionel though his grey eyes told me he was glad to see me again. "I have to dash back to the office", he said, "but phone me when all the fun is over and I'll pick you up for lunch".

As Taylour came down the gangway at Tilbury on Friday 31 May, 1929, Vic Deal, one of the Wembley Speedway League team, stepped out of the crowd to meet her. He was wearing his leathers and crash helmet, and said "Welcome to England, Fay". Like an ambassador of speed, he handed her a bouquet of red and white roses, the colours of the Speedway league, and also of Alexandra High School, Dublin, where Fay had finished her childhood education. Deal wore a breastplate of the same colours, and with his helmet similarly bedecked, looked like a crusader.

Before she had left Britain Fay had given Wills her cat (Revins) to mind during her absence. Some weeks before Taylour returned to the UK, Wills loaned the creature to the Glanfield Lawrence workshop for catching mice. But Wills retrieved the feline and took it along to Tilbury to meet its mistress cradled in his arms. Glanfield Lawrence sent a lorry for Fay, and the Wembley Speedway dispatched a motor coach/charbanc. It seems that both showed foresight – her luggage consisted of a stupendous number of separate packages!

The young men of Australia had sent her a big mail every day since she left, and some of the dirt-track magnates had sent them Fay's photo in return.

Taylour speculated, 'I suppose that got people interested'. She told of her meeting with Wills in London:

> Lionel met me. He took me to lunch in the city after first depositing my luggage at Cranley Gardens in South Kensington where again I rented a room.

Fay had avoided the glacial weather of the early part of 1929 in Britain, now, in the spring she was reunited with Lionel Wills, the man who had never been far away from her thoughts. She recalled:

> We lunched in the city near his firm's offices which was to become a frequent rendezvous…He brought me up to date with all the speedway news and gossip and then said rather sheepishly that all his thoughts of me had not prevented him from getting involved with two actresses who had parts in a popular West End Musical. His grey eyes were serious and tender.

> "Two", I laughed, adding: "there's safety in numbers".

> He explained that an ex-college friend made a foursome, and a few nights later he took me to dinner at the Hungaria to meet them.

> It was an odd meal, and they regarded me with curiosity knowing as little of my life as I knew of theirs. I tried to figure out which of the two coupled off with Lionel, and the only clue I could get was that his college friend paid greatest attention to the prettier. From the conversation it appeared that unlike me, they were welcome to Lionel's home, but I felt no pang of jealousy even remembering that he was never intimate in public. After all, other men had attracted me without changing my feelings for him. It would be natural for him to become infatuated occasionally in the same way. Our friendship was something apart, and, as before, he drove me to the tracks, and his speedway parties, which continued at Wembley did not include the actresses.

It would have been hard for Taylour not to have been disappointed by the strange treatment at the hand of Wills, but her portrayal of the encounter probably says as much about the man as Taylour's apparent naivety. There is a definite indication of a vindictive perhaps even cruel streak in Wills that Fay was not too surprised to see exposed. In different ways, both Wills and Taylour had avoided consummating their relationship, but one is struck as the story of the relationship unfolds, how hard Wills tried to avoid that commitment. His avoidance even out ran Taylour's to a point that indicates a deep anxiety on his part about opening the door to intimate interaction with Fay, maybe the most consistent female sexual figure in his life. At the same time it seems clear that Fay was anxious about what she had given up to continue waiting on Wills:

> Back in London there was a letter for me from Cuthbert. At last he'd written, I'd hoped he would write at once after I left to tell me how much

he missed me – just as I'd written a long sentimental letter on the ship after saying goodbye. I wanted to know he missed me. But why? Why rub in and prolong the pain of parting? It was illogical, thoughtless...or was it? Parting had been my choice, not his. He wanted me to stay and marry him, but Lionel was orbiting my mind, and still was. It seemed I wanted everything.

I took the letter upstairs, to my bed-sitting-room at the top of the house, and waited to open it till I was comfortably settled in a corner of the divan. It must be a long letter judging from the thickness of the envelope, but two letters fell out. One from Cuthbert, and the other from Stella, his sister, who had been disappointed that I turned him down. I read hers first. She said she was writing from the farm, Cuthbert's farm, and that she had since become engaged to Stanley Hawker. But her seemingly significant news was that two girls from Western Australia, friends of relatives, were coming to stay on the farm after she left. They would be company for Cuthbert.

I stared at the letter feeling that only now was I really saying goodbye to Cuthbert, and a conversation with a friendly Australian woman on the ship on the way home came vividly to mind. She'd met him and I told her of my visit to his farm and how sorry I was to leave him alone. Don't worry, she'd said, assuring me that no eligible bachelor in Australia is left alone for long. It's the custom, she explained, for bachelor girls to descend on such farms for long holidays. And how right she'd been! I knew I should be glad but suddenly my eagerness to read his letter had waned, I was afraid of what might be in it and almost wished as I unfolded it that it hadn't come at all. Perhaps he had only been infatuated and had recovered already, and was writing to tell me so.

But he didn't say that. He said he'd been kept busy working day and night after I left, and gave news of the farm and the horses. 'I always wear the red handkerchief you gave me', he wrote, and of that sentence I was glad. Then he mentioned his coming visitors saying Stella would have told me about them, and I knew she'd written and perhaps made Cuthbert write because she deemed it correct I should know. It was easy to read between the lines of her letter. Having turned her brother down I should not be trying to keep his affection alive. And many years later I was to know how correct this assumption was.

I read the letters through a second time and all at once felt terribly lonely. Lionel was at the theatre with his family and it was no consolation to remember that on a previous occasion he'd said he would much rather have been at a speedway with me. He'd taken me to theatre several times but not this year. He was fastidious, hated anything sentimental and loved musical comedy. We'd seen 'A Yankee At The Court Of King Arthur'[39], and he'd bought me a record of 'Thou Swell', the rather quaint number from the show which appealed to him. And one day he'd presented me with a sheet of music although I had no piano. It was a song entitled 'My Fay' which he'd composed himself, and the notes and words were filled in on the self-made music sheet in his fine artistic handscript. His apology and emotion-shunning laugh when presenting it seemed to demand that it shouldn't be taken too seriously, and I more or less threw it to one side. I'd been taking nothing very seriously except racing, with Lionel part of it. But now, with Cuthbert's letter still in my hand, I knew that I was no longer content with our special friendship. I had been unable to return Cuthbert's love for more than just friendship – surely? Or was it true in spite of all my assertions to the contrary that racing was my only love? It was the biggest challenge certainly, but such psychological reasoning had no place in my thoughts then.[40]

Fay also gave another version of events in which she indicated that after the public welcome, she and Wills had spent the time before a forthcoming Wembley event together in a country cottage which Wills had organised.

While there may have been aspects of Wills' character and maybe sexuality that Fay was either ignorant of or loathe to recognise, she understood his motivation for speedway:

Lionel was his usual mixture of shyness and sophistication and unshaken enthusiasm for dirt track racing. He'd 'fallen on his ear' as he mildly expressed it, several times since the tracks opened a month ago, and would continue to do so to the horror of his family. "I'm still te-e-e-rrified every time I go into those bends", he said.

Perhaps we all were while our fans looked upon us cool and calculated dare-devils. Certainly no ambition drove Lionel unless the challenge to overcome something difficult can be called ambition. Prize money was a lure to the boys. They needed it, but not Lionel. Lionel raced and got fun out of it.

Wembley encounters

Hoskins had taken charge of the Wembley speedway, probably the greatest of all the sport's venues at that time. Ever the doyen of the main chance, Hoskins had been the man who had stage managed Taylour's homecoming into a motorcade of riders and spectators from Wembley Stadium, home of the famous international event and eventually the World Championship. According to Fay: '..and on the way from Tilbury he told me I was to race at his next two meetings. He'd entered me for the Cinders Trophy at the second meeting…'

When Taylour told Wills about Hoskins entering her for the Cinders Trophy he replied laughingly "I know…if ever there was a promoter it's Johnnie

Hoskins", which indicates that Wills might have had a hand in the publicity around Fay's return to Britain and the connection of the same with the Wembley event. What started out looking like an act of affection for Taylour (on the part of Wills, Hoskins and speedway as a sport) quickly could be seen as a straightforward publicity stunt using Fay as a billboard. For all this, in her more sober moments Fay seemed to have a grasp on her relationship with her chosen sport and was not wholly unconscious of how it used her:

> I was now speedway property, an accepted star, and after spending a couple of nights at the house of old school friends where I'd boarded the previous year, I found myself a bed-sitting room in Cranley Gardens, South Kensington, where phone calls could be taken, and the racing bike was left at agents whose mechanics attended the speedways.

The 'Cinders Trophy' took place at the next Wembley meeting. This was a competition held regularly by stadium boss Arthur Elvin for stars of the day to lower the one lap flying start track record. The holders of the title would include American Ray Tauser[41], Max Grosskreutz[42], Jack Ormston[43], 'Smiling' Jim Kempster, and England's first speedway Test captain, George Greenwood[44]. Tauser was the first holder of the record, on 16 May, 1929 with a time of 21 seconds for a single flying lap, which represented a speed of 36.82 mph. Taylour described the contest:

> The Cinders Trophy contest was staged once a month. It was an attempt to break the existing lap record, and representatives from England, Scotland, America, Australia and New Zealand would take part. I was to represent Ireland. But I'd protested it must be a joke for I was still too aware of my limitations, and I'd never raced at Wembley which would seem cramped and strange after the bigger Australian tracks. But to Johnnie it was no joke, it was good publicity no matter how I performed. "You'll do splendidly", he said, and I think he believed it.

> "At least someone has to come last" was my conclusion.

> My first appearance at Wembley fizzled out. The bike, barely unpacked, spat and coughed and indicated that it would have to be thoroughly overhauled before the big meeting two days later.

Here Taylour is probably understating the impact of that first Wembley ride. Although she said she was glad to be back in England, with its wonderful masses of green grass, trees and flowers, Fay caused a little consternation when she shared her opinion that British tracks were not as good as Australian circuits. There were those who hoped that on a Tuesday evening at Wembley in early June, Eva Askquith, the Yorkshire girl who had only just returned from riding in Denmark, would put Taylour in her place. Fay explained that Hoskins had arranged for her, '...to race against Eva Askquith, the girl who had been racing on the tracks up north and whom I had not yet met.'

Facing Eva

Taylour described her closest female rival:

She was a butcher's daughter from Yorkshire, a quiet unassuming girl whose riding skill was far superior to the small batch of women riders who raced among themselves…It was important to me to defeat her since I held the internationally bestowed title of Women Champion or Queen of the Speedways, and so the race assumed enormous significance.

Eva, by that time had added to her experience of northern tracks with a stint in Copenhagen, where dirt tracking was booming. In the event Askquith beat Taylour 2-0. This seemed to relieve Fay of her informal title of 'women's world champion dirt-track rider', but Taylour blamed 'water on the plugs owing to the wet track, resulting in her mount running on one cylinder most of the time'. She also pointed to the fact that she had never raced at Wembley and there had been no time to re-acclimatise to the relatively small track. But the fact remained that Askquith won more or less how she liked at 34.5 mph. Whatever the reasons or excuses, Taylour had been beaten by another woman and this would certainly have been a blow to her credibility. But she put on a brave face:

At least I'd had a feel of the track, and the fans a glimpse of my style, and I spent most of the next two days in the workshop watching the engine being tuned. It had better go well on Thursday!

On the morning of 6 June, *The Motor Cycle* gave a glowing report of Fay's abilities. But Fay seems to have had some doubts:

I was unsure that I could live up to such fine words, and the report added that I would be pitting my strength that night against top male opposition in the contest for the lap record.

The Cinders Trophy

Taylour's recollections of probably her biggest race to date on a British circuit were as follows:

As I drove into the arena and looked up at the stands all round where people were scrambling for seats, I thought of my first visit to Wembley. I had come then to watch the great Rodeo show, and I was so thrilled and impressed that when I went back to Ireland I wanted to ride a wild-looking bull in the fields. Little did I then think that I'd be riding in the same arena on a bucking motorcycle!

Lionel left me at the pit entrance and scurried off to make sure of his usual seats in the grand stand opposite the starting line. "Join us between races", he called. He made Wembley and the Crystal Palace occasions for a large party with a big meal after the racing for which he unpretentiously paid the bill. Speedway promoters, reporters, riders, mechanics and their girl friends were in the party. It made no difference to Lionel whether they were school drop-outs or university folk, they were all his friends. But his cousin who had a soft spot for him and access to his disapproving family, did not crusade to lessen the dissent. On the contrary she used the parties as an amusing conversation piece, not that a meal in the stadium restaurants could be described as 'rough', the adjective used then for a wild get-together.

The drive to the stadium earlier, in Lionel's long Rolls Royce Tourer of 1907 vintage, had been wild. The open car was packed, and as we rounded Marble Arch and drove down the Edgware Road, Jimmie Taylor, an upcoming speedway rider, stood up in the back and led a lusty male chorus in 'Shut The Door They're Coming Through The Window'. The last line, sung with great emphasis, 'My God They're Coming Through The Floor', could indicate bombs today and bring the police running!

"Are you ready to take a few laps"?

The warm-up laps preceding the programme were already under way. Practice days had been eliminated at most of these tracks where greyhound racing and other events took place, so I was more than ready to test the bike and feel the track. The surface could differ from night to night according to the weather and the amount of watering it had had. The mechanics pushed me off and I knew at once the bike was going well – too well for those tight turns before I slithered to earth and taught myself a little of what I could or couldn't do. Lionel was back in the pits and had seen the over-slide, so had many of the spectators who came early to watch these laps. But I didn't intend to do it again, not if I could possibly help it though the track was tricky.

"You seem to forget that I'm just as terrified watching", Lionel said as I went out again to beat that over-slide.

Then racing started and I ran in the third event, a heat race, and won it. Next time out I only managed to finish third, but the big event was still to come, the attempts on the lap record, which would take place after the interval. I stayed in the pits instead of going to the stand because, as always I had that tense and urgent feeling of having to work myself up for the Pit Marshal's call: "You're On Next". I still felt I hadn't a chance but I was going to do my damnedest. Wally Killminster, the New Zealand champion, wished me luck, adding "if I fail". He was making the attempt too, and he smilingly reminded me that I had defeated him in New Zealand a few months back. But Wally had done a lot of racing since, and he was one of the most popular boys around.

The big rake pulled in having smoothed out some of the ruts, and the contest began. Near the starting line was the Cinders Trophy, the cup that would be presented to the breaker of the record, if it was broken. It was shining and handsome, but I looked away. If only wishing could make it so!

"You're on next"! The tenseness cracked, and I was suddenly very busy with my helmet, goggles and face mask as my bike was wheeled from the infield. Then I was astride, and the mechanics from Glandfield Lawrence, where so many of us had our racing engines tuned, pushed me off on the starting lap. I would be timed when I crossed the line again so I opened out on the back stretch and took the bottom corner at an angle that would give me the greatest speed over the start.

The Cinders Trophy took place just two days after Taylour had been soundly beaten by Askquith, on Thursday, 6 June. This competition involved riders representing their nations with the object of breaking the Wembley lap record, attempts at which had been a feature of the Wembley entertainment in front of around 25,000 people, Taylour was not feeling physically at her best, but her engine was functioning well. Representing Ireland, Fay's riding was excellent, showing a marked improvement on the previous season, although as might have been expected after her experience of the big Australian tracks, her style was very cramped on the tighter bends at Wembley. After one or two attempts at riding close, Fay had wisely given up the white line idea in favour of the outside. Near the end of the straight she would cut out for a few yards only, and then, opening out flat (or nearly so) would go full-bore for the bend round the outside. Although fast and spectacular, Fay never once lost her focus: at all times her riding was well controlled and appeared absolutely safe. Although the manner in which she turned the bends showed that she was fearless, it was obvious to a close observer that she was using her brains as well. In the end she dramatically seduced the Wembley crowd by winning the Cinders Trophy, defeating the English, Scottish, American, New Zealand and Australian riders. According to Taylour, the competition was little more than a stunt to draw the crowds. She still felt inadequate and inexperienced and the track seemed strange and tricky. She said later: "Was I scared when I found I had to represent England in international match races against their top men!" (Notice she wrote almost unselfconsciously about representing England rather than showing affinity to Ireland).

But Fay defeated the Wembley circuit itself, taking the track's flying-lap record with a time of 20.8 seconds, averaging 37.18mph, and bettering the great American Ray Tauser's time (he had skidded badly during the event). The excitement of the crowd knew no bounds when the announcement came: for the first time in the history of the sport, a woman had won the one-lap record! Taylour was to recall that she was more surprised than pleased when she circled the track with the trophy. The next morning newspapers reported 'Woman breaks Wembley Track Record'. According to *The Motor Cycle* (13 June) 'it would have been quite understandable (and even permissible in a woman) if her success had gone to her head (which might have resulted in another $1/2$ mph, or on the other hand, something very much the reverse). But it didn't.'

Taylour's record time was to endure longer than Fay's career on two wheels. It took the efforts of the famous Australian international Max Grosskreutz to beat her time, but he managed to shaved off no more than a mere 0.4 seconds. Fay recollected her feelings after her victory:

The cup was mine! And it could seem that it did go to my head, for after it was presented I was pushed off with it to do a slow lap of honour but was unable with one hand to control my racing steed, which objected to being reined in. Half way round it kicked me off, and there I sat on the track to everyone's amusement with the trophy still in my arms.

Although in an international triangular match race that followed, after beating H. Whitfield (Eangland) at 34.76 mph, Brew McQueen (Scotland) got the better of Taylour in the final heat, defeating her by 40 yards at 35.83 mph, she had returned to the British track scene with the world as her witness.

Askquith revisited

Late in June, Taylour and Askquith met again. Fay told the story:

"You'll have no trouble", my friends assured me, and I won the first heat all right. It was a best-of-three-heats match. But then trouble did arrive and I lost the second heat when the motor spat and coughed and limped home second.

Probably dirt in the carburettor, and I stood by fervently praying they'd clear it up.

"Good Luck", Lionel said as I followed Eva to the starting line for the decisive heat. He had come down to the pits to see if he could help, and looked worried.

In match race fashion we would be pushed off to a slow lap around the track until within ten yards of the start, then riding together we would accelerate into a 'flying start' across the line. But now for this third heat my bike played dead. It was pushed and pushed but refused to fire, and finally I dismounted and it was pushed infield near the starter who said he'd put on another race while it was fixed.

"It should be all right now", the mechanics said as once more we were called to the line. But a test lap had been denied and I was nervy and anxious.

Johnnie Hoskins was standing beside the starter. "Listen", he said, putting his hand on my steering damper, "We're running late so this has to be it – we cannot give you another start". To Eva he said, "keep going".

I felt forsaken, desolate and helpless. Eva was such a sport that I doubt she would have kept going if she saw I wasn't moving, but a draw was no use to me, a win was vital.

The mechanics got the signal and started pushing…and yes! The engine fired, but not properly. But I was able to keep going on the slow preliminary lap and prayed that it would pick up when we opened out just before the starting line. A burst of full throttle was perhaps all that was needed.

Then the moment came and I gave it the gun, but oh no! it was silent and almost jerked to a stop…then it fired and jerked forward and I twisted the acceleration…it coughed, then fired, then spat as if it hated me but kept on trying.

Eva's bike meanwhile had purred off smoothly and smartly. She was approaching the first bend, and I was barely across the starting line. My mechanics were on the grass to my left…I might just as well join them, but why, oh why couldn't the engine pick up. "Come on, Duggie, come on", I prayed and limped on. But now I wouldn't have a chance. Eva was too far ahead, I couldn't make up such leeway in just four laps, for that was the length of each heat and now the engine's efforts to keep alive were weakening. And then, with a compulsive jerk and a final retching cough that could mean it was giving up the ghost, I found myself shooting forward under full power, the twin cylinders firing properly, evenly and with such a healthy crackle that they seemed to be laughing at the idea they'd ever been sick. "Come on", that exasperating bike seemed to say, "I'm in fine fettle, give me my head!"

Give it its head! I gave it the works, and to pay it out I turned everything on there and then in the middle of that first turn flinging it fiercely into a broadside. If I couldn't win I could at least have the fun of the ride. Every lap is fun without competition. I could go mad. What difference now if I over-slid? Eva wasn't in sight. I had the track to myself.

Streamlined over the tank with my left leg trailing to the rear so that my knee seemed to be touching the ground, I slanted into the next turn riding wide and fast, and the Duggie and I were still in one piece as I straightened up and crossed the line to complete the first lap. Then, hungrily, I ate up the next bend, and as I entered the back stretch I saw my opponent racing out of the turn ahead, too far ahead to excite optimism or steady my pace. But when I passed the starter for the second time and swept around the fist bend I saw that Eva was now entering the turn ahead, not leaving it. I'd diminished the distance so considerably in one lap that maybe…yes *maybe* I could catch up…and win! And suddenly my ride became very serious, but with less than two laps to go I would have to keep up the same pace or I wouldn't have a chance.

Comfortably ahead, Eva raced stolidly on, riding the track in her own inimitable way. Her style and mine could not have made a greater contrast. She was a white line rider, riding close to the white line on the inside of the bends. She sat more upright on the bike, and instead of trailing her inside leg in a straight line to the rear she held it upright with knee bent so that her heel rather than her toes touched the ground when necessary. She was away ahead in that respect because a couple of years later the leg-trailing style disappeared and all the boys became white line riders.

As I passed the starter again I took the signal for the last lap and threw the Duggie into the first turn even harder than before. My sliding back wheel behaved perfectly, and there on the back stretch, for the gobbling if I was lucky, was my opponent. She would reach the bend first, the last bend, but if I kept up that speed and didn't overslide or develop a wobble I could catch her on the turn...or could I? She'd just looked back. If she quickened her pace it'd be touch and go.

Once more my back wheel stood by me as I heeled over into the turn. Half way round, at the apex of my swing, she was still following the curving white line. She was still ahead as she left the bend, but now she was picking up speed while I was on full engine revolutions...and catching her! Then my front wheel drew level with her back. In a flash I was past, and the finishing line was still ahead! Only just, but I'd made it! Eva's handshake made me like her, and Lionel's "Well done!" made me glow.

Fay won the encounter 2-1, she was back with a vengeance!

12. Wheels on Fire

Taylour's racing career had been energised by the news of her exploits and achievements filtering through from Australia. She was now more widely accepted as a racer and very much in demand. Taylour was also a much more adept rider after her experience on a range of surfaces, track lengths and against some of the best speedway men on the face of the planet. The *South Wales Echo* (Saturday, 1 June) called Fay, 'One of the stars at the Wembley Speedway' and reported that she had 'a programme of engagements, including a week in Denmark, awaiting her.' The Echo carried on the tradition of patronising eulogies regarding Taylour's womanly credentials, so not much had changed in that respect:

> Fay is certainly attractive, and in no way manish…it is astonishing that a delicately nurtured woman should have become a queen of the motor track. She admits most women could not do it. She told me how she hurt her knee in one race and how she gashed her finger in another and had to have it stitched. She is to visit Cardiff White City Speedway in the near future

In July 1929 Taylour made what was reported as her first visit on speedway business to the West Country and was described as a 'very world famous person' having broken the Wembley track record on two occasions: it being considered 'rather astounding to find a girl lowering records'. She was booked to ride at Exeter in a Match Race, and probably to attempt the lap record as well as giving an exhibition of her skill at broadsiding. She would not appear in Scratch or Handicap races.

Exeter genesis

The Exeter track had only been in existence for a few months. Following the introduction of Speedway to Britain, Exeter born Leonard Glanfield decided to open a track at the County Ground and work started in January, 1929. Together with Mr F. Cottey and Mr Henley they formed a company known as Southern Speedways Ltd and secured a five year lease at £300 per annum.

The County Ground Stadium had been built in 1898 and in 1929 it looked very much as it does today, the present Grandstand having been completed in 1921 replacing a wooden structure that had been burnt down in 1918.

The first racing was scheduled for Saturday, 9 March, but a week earlier there was a demonstration of the sport following a Rugby match by the first two riders ever to race the circuit; Freddie Hore[45] and Bert ('Baby Cyclone') Spencer.

Hore, a former Exonian who had gone to Australia, learnt to ride 'down under' and then returned when the sport started up in Britain. Spencer was at the time, a 16-year-old Aussie.

The first meeting went ahead with 11,000 spectators looking on. Admission prices that opening night were 2/- and 3/- (two and three shillings, or 10p and 15p in today's currency) for the Grandstand and 1/- or 1/6 (one shilling or one and sixpence, 5p and 7.5p) for the Ground.

Les Dallimore won the first race in 88.0 seconds and he went on to win the final, while Ron Johnson was victorious in the Golden Helmet. Also included that day was the famous Australian, Frank Arthur. The crowd went away thrilled after the meeting and were eager for more. Exeter Speedway had become a reality.

Meetings were held every Wednesday and Saturday. The Easter weekend of the track's initial year saw racing on both Saturday and Monday, with a combined total of some 19,000 fans turning out, such was the interest of the sport. Star attractions to the Devon circuit that year included Lloyd 'Sprouts' Elder and Lionel Van Pragg who began speedway racing in 1926. He skippered Wembley in 1931 but started his working life as a typewriter mechanic. He was known to be one of the best engineers in speedway, having a wonderfully equipped private workshop

According to Fay her summer visit to Devon was not, as advertised, her first. She recorded that she had previously met Nora Barber, from Coventry and beaten Phyllis Cookson of Bideford on the track. At the same track on 18 May two local women, Miss Manley of Honiton and Phyllis Cook had a close race, but on the last bend, Phyllis, on a Coventry-Eagle, clipped her opponent's back wheel and fell. However she remounted and finished the race.

On 29 May, 1929 the first team racing got off the ground as the Exeter City Speedway team defeated Bristol 17-12 over 3 heats (points were awarded 4-3-2-1) after drawing 17-17 the evening before at Bristol's Knowle Park. A week later Exeter beat a Harringay Select side 13-8. Riders for Exeter included Barker, Buckland, Fleeman[46] and Swift.

The big attraction that year took place on Tuesday, 25 June when the first Great Speedway Revel was staged. It included all the top stars of that era and an amazing crowd of between 15,000 and 16,000 turned up: an estimated 3,000 had to be turned away. The legendary Frank Arthur won the Express and Echo Gold Cup on his Peashooter.

Matching Buggie

Unfortunately, on Saturday, 16 July, Fay was unable to show her true form at Exeter. Her machine had given her trouble while practicing earlier in the afternoon but happily a Miss Hull, an aspiring local rider, made her similar Douglas available.

Prior to the meeting Taylour was allowed a few laps to accustom herself to the different machine. In spite of the original intention, Fay had been programmed to ride a match race series against the popular Buggie Fleeman, and he won the first leg fairly easily. The second race proved more interesting due to the number of incidents it encompassed. This race was rerun no less than four times when Taylour had engine trouble and then took a couple of falls while in the lead. One of these crashes took place directly in front of Fleeman who 'gallantly and with a great effort threw himself from his machine to avoid running over the fallen lady'. The crowd were not slow to show their approval, and Fay shook him by the hand in gratitude and relief. At the last attempt Taylour went all out from the start, setting such a pace that Buggie could not close the gap. In the decider Fay again streaked away but on the third lap Fleeman overtook her. Alas, as he reached the finish line his front tyre burst. He went into an uncontrollable wobble, and came down heavily after being thrown over the handlebars. Fleeman was carried from the track but fortunately had only been winded.

It was at Exeter, on Wednesday, 2 October, 1929, that Dorothy Bunt from Delabole in Cornwall made her first public appearance matched against Taylour. Although Dorothy was given half a lap start, she was good enough to hold on to it, even though her very much more experienced opponent made a great race of it. Miss Bunt's trainer, Nick Drake was quick to celebrate the victory with his pupil.

Towards the end of the year the Exeter crowds started to dwindle and Wednesday, 9 October saw the last meeting held under the Leonard Glanfield Southern Speedways Banner. Two days later came the news that Southern Speedways were giving up control of Exeter Speedway. Salvation came from Crystal Palace promoters Fred Mockford and Cecil Smith and they did much to breathe new life into the venue.

Turning point

Taylour, recalled thinking of Wills and his social circle towards the last part of the British speedway season of 1929:

> The actresses would be having supper with them after the show, and their friendship was probably encouraged. Any acquaintance who had nothing to do with speedway would be encouraged. Lionel was his mother's favourite and she was pressuring him to stop racing. I was still the unspeakable wench whom her son insisted on speaking about, and at this moment he was probably having great fun telling them all that we'd be racing together at Coventry this weekend.

A major turning point in Fay's life came when she and her long term companion and mentor Lionel Wills visited the Coventry track. She recalled the events leading up to what was to be a crucial moment:

> We drove up from London on the morning of racing, having an early lunch on the way, and arrived at Coventry in time for a practice before the meeting started. It was a lovely track with well-shaped turns and a smooth shale surface, and I won two races against a local rider quite easily but Lionel was not to have such luck.

It was a daylight meeting and as I wasn't racing again, I changed in the track office and emerged in time to see him start in a semi-final of the handicap race. He started third but soon drew level with the man ahead. Then down the back stretch they raced to catch up with the leader, into the pit bend. Next moment the three machines tangled in a heavy crash with Lionel in the middle. My heart was in my mouth as I headed for the scene. The race had been stopped and ambulance men were packing one rider into the ambulance: he was obviously in great pain. *(The rider down was Lionel Wills)*

"Broken a darned arm I think", he said, and asked me to follow him to the hospital. The other two riders were all right.

After an hour's wait he was delivered to me all tied up in splints having refused to stay overnight.

"Mother'll have a thousand fits", he said, "if she hears I've crashed and can't go home". Then added, "she'll have fits anyway, but if I'm on the spot I can at least try to referee her thoughts".

It was an awful ninety-mile drive. The fine day had clouded over and before we'd covered twenty miles, it was raining bucketfuls. I was driving and could hardly see where I was going; the windshield wiper was sticking, and every movement of the car hurt Lionel. He was bruised all over and felt as if every rib was bashed in. But I was happy. I was happy because at last I would have the chance of meeting his mother. She would want to hear about the accident and have the Coventry doctor's report. I had a reason now for meeting her face to face, and let her see that I wasn't the coarse beer-drinking girl she'd been led to believe.

We arrived about 9pm and Lionel was hustled upstairs. One of his brothers showed me into the front study and asked me to wait as his mother would want to hear some details. I was offered a drink but refused, and then found myself alone as all the noise of our entry died away. It was a tall house and I pictured everyone in Lionel's bedroom up at the top. They would be fussing over him and asking questions, and I was glad that his mother would be able to see that he wasn't seriously hurt before coming down to talk to me.

I didn't mind waiting, nor did I mind how long I might have to wait because at last I would be able to speak to her. I tidied my hair in the mirror over the mantelpiece. I was wearing a neat brown tailor-made suit that matched my hair, a suit that reporters seemed to like, and I'd been able to wash at the hospital in Coventry, so I felt I was looking my best.

Then at last I heard a step on the stair and braced myself for the moment for which I'd waited so long. Then a hand was on the door knob and I couldn't hold back a sudden surge of excitement as I faced the opening door.

But it wasn't her. It was the brother. "Mother told me to thank you for driving Lionel home", he said, "and if you are out of pocket…"

Out of pocket! I waited for no more. It wasn't the insult that made me dive for the door. It was the disappointment, the overwhelming disappointment that after all I wouldn't see her. When that big hall door closed behind me I felt miserable.

It must have been three weeks before I heard his voice on the phone.

"I'm back at the office. How about lunch at Pims"?

He sounded tentative. Perhaps he wondered why I hadn't answered his letters, he'd written twice, and when I sat down opposite him in the city restaurant he looked at me questioningly with that tender concerned look in his grey eyes which I felt was reserved especially for me.

"I believe they gave you a bad time that night"? He was referring to my visit to this home after the accident, and I wondered if for the first time it occurred to him that I might get hurt.

I laughed. "They wanted to pay me off! I should have demanded the price of a new bike".

"You can have mine", and pointing to the sling on his arm added: "the war is over, I lost".

"What? You're not going to race any more"?

He nodded. "Not worth the continual strife, and now perhaps they'll stop reminding me that I'm the future head of the firm". He smiled wryly. "But how I loathe sitting in an office".

So his mother had won! The accident was the bomb blast that ended his family war, but he was still consorting with the enemy, if he couldn't race he'd watch. Yet the news depressed me. It felt like a victory over me too, and the glamour of racing suddenly lacked lustre because it was time to book a passage for the coming Australian season and I did nothing. Summer became Autumn.

Then November arrived, and, without allowing myself to put facts on the table and say forget Lionel, I acted as if I had done so.

Wills had always refused to get involved in quarrels. His accident signalled the end of his racing career and he started work in his father's offices in the City, the business that one day he would control. The mummy's boy had become the mummy's man!

Without the attentions of Wills, Fay found racing did not have the same appeal for her. He still saw her, but the relationship was never to be the same: Mrs Wills' attitude seems to have extinguished any notion of romantic permanence.

Once more - the Antipodes

Perhaps Taylour's most notable win of 1929 after the Cinders Trophy was at the Crystal Palace. She beat A.R. Frogley in a mile match race. Taylour had a 5 second start, but she scarcely needed this advantage as she covered the first circuit only $2/5$ of a second outside the record, and won easily at 36.22 mph. But for Fay it was hard to see a way forward in the context of British speedway. In many ways she had broken the mould and was merely repeating the point she had been making since breaking into the sport. Newspapers were finding it hard to say anything novel about her and even they were seemingly bored with constantly extolling Taylour's femininity. For Taylour Australia was a much more attractive milieu in terms of racing. It was a young, exciting land and a place where her pioneering spirit could push at new boundaries. However, it was also the place where she had experienced most glory and adulation and where she was the undisputed 'woman champion'. The emerging competition for this title in Britain had yet to reach Australia.

Casting her mind back to the last days of the 1920s Taylour wrote:

It was still 1929 when I reached Australia for my second visit...first I raced at Perth, and this time I was beaten. I was matched against the veteran ace, Jimmie (*Charlie*) Datson, and hadn't a chance after hitting a big bump going into the first turn. My recovery from what seemed like a certain crash pleased the fans almost as much as if I'd won. Jimmy had coached me in England. It would have been kinder to beat him than Schlam.

Fay returned to Australia and New Zealand with a number of English riders, several of whom, like Roger Frogley, Arthur Atkinson[47] and Jack Ormston would become immortals of speedway.

Making her farewell appearance at the Claremont Speedway on a late November Saturday night, Taylour delighted the crowd with her fine riding. Based on the criterion of the number of races won during the evening, she was not successful, but she rode with a noticeable zest and keenness, and figured in the most sensational 'save' seen during the whole programme. For the first quarter lap against Charlie Datson she rode shoulder to shoulder, but thereafter Charlie scurried to the front. Attempting to catch up to her former teacher, Taylour got into a terrific slide at the grandstand corner. To the watching crowd it seemed that a crash was imminent. From within the miniature cloud of cinders Fay rode on, seemingly unperturbed, but she failed to gain ground on Datson and had to follow him to the post from a distance of several lengths. In the handicap event she also performed creditably.

Sig Schlam had been scheduled to ride in the scratch event but he had to pull out because of trouble with his magneto. It seemed the Schlam family were in for an unlucky evening all round as in the second heat of the scratch event Syd Parsons and Cyril Schlam were the outstanding riders but it was Parsons who won by two lengths after an electrifying contest.

Len Stewart, Taylour and Harry Lewis were the starters in the third heat. Len Stewart was in fine fettle and completed the three laps in 1 minute 16^2/$_5$ seconds. He won easily, with Lewis and Fay chasing him home in that order.

The final was a thriller. Datson drew the inside position, Cyril Schlam the outside, and Stewart the middle berth. Datson sped to the front at the start. At 'Fowlhouse Corner' he had the advantage of Schlam and Stewart. Datson then crashed, Stewart hopped to the front, and Schlam lost ground in avoiding the fallen rider. Schlam dashed after the flying Stewart and just failed to beat him to the post.

In order to establish a time which Eva Askquith might later attempt to lower (Askquith was expected to appear at the track within the following few months) Taylour completed three laps in 1 minute 18 seconds

The Royale road

Fay recalled her arrival in Adelaide:

This was to be my first racing appearance at Adelaide. At last I would be able to sample this city's fast Speedway Royale and meet Lionel's cousins! The Adelaide track looked smooth in comparison. It was a light shale surface and might prove slick, but a practice run made me understand Lionel's enthusiasm. And a meeting with his cousins left me equally thrilled. They were prominent in social life and immediately threw a party for me at their lovely home, also arranging to come and see me race. What friendliness compared with his relatives at home!

On Saturday at the end of November the Adelaide Speedway Royale staged 22 events. To give Taylour, and the other star riders taking part the best possible conditions, a portion of the sand was raked near to the outer fence, thus improving the possibility of achieving faster times. Thirty-two riders were selected to contest the four lap, 'A' grade handicap event. There were eight heats played out in front of more than 16,000 people.

However, Wills was still on Fay's mind: 'There were two letters from him in the pocket of my racing jacket as I drove to the speedway on Saturday. My thoughts, however, were churning over on the evening ahead. Eagerness to put up a good show was mixed with the usual doubts and fears...'

In the eighth heat Taylour faced Norm Mitchell, Alby Frost, and Ben Jones. She took them all by surprise by dashing away, making full use of her liberal handicap and gaining a lead about 100 yards on Jones when the race had really only just begun. Her riding ability was immediately apparent at the 'pit end' corner. She took this in one continual slide, which was fast and exceptionally clean. Norm Mitchell had a quarter lap to make up, but although he caught and passed the other pair, he was 80 yards in arrears as Taylour sped home in a time of 1 minute 36^3/$_5$ (making the heat the third fastest of the meeting). She had cornered splendidly; although at first travelling somewhat wide for an extra safe ride and never, at any stage of the race did she appear likely to be overtaken.

In the first semi-final, which was easily the most thrilling and entertaining event of the evening, Rass Lee went out as pacemaker, closely followed by George Marques, Arnold Hansen, and Alby Taylor. In the third lap Hansen was in front of Marques, with Lee still riding beautifully to maintain his leading position. At the last turn Lee and Hansen were neck and neck, both showing ability above the average to keep their machines up at the pace they were travelling. Hansen defeated Lee by less than a wheel, after the latter had skidded and then ridden on the grass at the turn into the straight. The winner cut the time down to 1 minute 34^3/$_5$, showing that the speedway was drying and becoming faster.

Jack Rau and Keith Litchfield provided another mega-tussle in the second semi-final. Rau beat his opponent by three lengths, with Bob Medwell pulling out. Charlie Gray gained the honours in the third from Allan Edgecombe. Hanson encountered trouble with his petrol pipe and slowed up. Gray, soon after the start, got himself into a winning position. He made a time of 1 minute 35^1/$_5$, beating Edgecombe by 60 yards.

Taylour then shaded the performances of all those who had succeeded her in the heats. She was up against Clem and Norm Mitchell and Eddy Moreland. Moreland had a 4 seconds start, one second less than Taylour, who went off at a remarkable pace and was 100 yards ahead of the nearest of her pursuers when entering the back straight. Clem and Norm Mitchell lost a few yards through skidding, but Clem would have had to have equalled Frank Duckett's[48] track record time to have overtaken Taylour. In the event, Fay was astonished with her time: 1 minute 33^4/$_5$ was the fastest time by a heat winner at Speedway Royale that season and she came home with a handsome 65 yards to spare.

In the final Taylour was once more smartly into action, pulling away from the off. Jack Rau (4 second) and Charlie Gray and Arnold Hansen (each 1 second) found the chase too severe to hope for success. Gray was 100 yards away in second when Taylour crossed the line. The time (1 minute 36^1/$_5$) was a little slower than her semi-final, but onlookers were given the impression she could have gone faster had she been more closely challenged.

In her heat, semi-final, and final Taylour had never allowed her pursuers to get within striking distance. In each instance the 'pick up' was smart, and she won her races in the opening furlong, smashing around the southern bend like a speeding bullet.

Two mile match races were also decided the same evening. Taylour raced Charlie Gray who made a request that the usual toss for positions be dispensed with. Fay started from the inside and led for the first lap, but in the second, although tightly contested, Gray managed to dash through on the inside and secured a slight advantage of about five yards, which he maintained to the end.

Dick Wise[49] and Alby Taylor met once more in the second match race. They had encountered each other on the previous Saturday, but had both struck trouble with their machines. This time Wise led from the off, but the race was stopped when Alby Taylor's machine slackened speed. Eventually both speedsters put up a real fight that Wise eventually won by 20 yards in 64 $^2/_5$ seconds. This was his best ride since his return from England a fortnight before.

Eighth Heat.
Miss Fay Taylour, Eng. ($3^1/_2$ Douglas), 5s.: Norm Mitchell ($3^1/_2$ Norton), 5s.: Alby Frost ($3^1/_2$ BSA.), 2s.; Ben Jones ($3^1/_2$ Rudge), 3s. Won by 80 yds. Time, 1min.$36^3/_5$.

First Semi-final. Arnold Hansen, Rass Lee, Alby Taylor, George Marques. Won by a wheel. Time, 1 min. $34^3/_5$.

Second Semi-final. Jack Rau, Keith Litchfield, Bob Medwell, Ted Gage. Won by 8 yds. Time, 1 min.$38^1/_5$.

Third Semi-final. Charlie Gray, Allan Edgecombe, Jack Hanson Harry Butler. Won by 60 yds. Time, 1 min. $35^1/_5$.

Fourth Semi-final. Miss Fay Taylour (Eng), Norm Mitchell, Clem Mitchell, Eddy Moreland. Won by 65 yds. Time, 1 min. $33^4/_5$. Track-winning record time for season.
Final.Miss Fay Taylour, Charlie Gray, Arnold Hansen, Jack Rau. Won by 100 yds. Time, 1 min. $36^1/_5$.
MATCH RACES. £15 and £5
No.1. Dick Wise ($3^1/_2$ AJS) d Alby Taylor ($3^1/_2$ AJS) by 20 yds. in 1 min. $4^2/_5$.
No. 2 Charlie Gray ($3^1/_2$ Douglas) d Miss Fay Taylour by 5 yds. in 1 min. 8.

A reflection of Taylour's performance was published in *The Motorcycle* (23 January, 1930)

A letter to hand from an Australian reader who says 'After having seen Fay Taylour in action, I wonder at the dismal speeds recorded at your third mile track. The 48.9 mph at Leicester Super is a crawl which the worst 'B' grade rider can do at the Speedway Royale, Adelaide. At Fay's first appearance we were a bit doubtful as to her ability, but this was quickly dispelled, for she rode magnificently and won her heat (four laps, standing start, $1^1/_2$ miles) at 49.8 mph, the semi-final at 51.2 mph, and the final at 50 mph. Her time of 1minute $33^4/_5$ (51.2 mph) is the best four-lap standing start time in a race this season. Also in a three-lap (rolling start) match race with Charlie Gray, she was beaten by five yards in a time of 1 minute 8 seconds (52.9 mph)'.

After the racing at the Royale a party had been arranged in Taylour's honour, but an official was obliged to excuse her absence by explaining that 'the poor child is like a crushed flower'. The party goers were highly amused having earlier in the day seen the same 'crushed flower' roaring home to victory on the cinders!

Although Fay felt tired and worn out, another official insisted on taking her to a theatre that evening. She was so exhausted that she fell asleep in the middle of the show.

But she was to look back on the whole occasion with satisfaction:

> ...after surviving two heat races, I won the senior handicap event in the fastest time for the season. Gard Motors, who serviced my Douglas were delighted and brought out an original advertisement in which the first letters of my name shared the 'F' and 'T' of Fastest Time.

The large advertisement lodged in the Adelaide press read:

ALL BEFORE THEM!

WORLD'S WONDER LADY
AND
THE WORLD'S FASTEST MOTOR CYCLE

FAY AND HER DOUGLAS!

FAY   TAYLOUR
FASTEST   TIME
FOR THE SEASON 1.33 $^4/_5$

DOUGLAS WON - A GRADE HANDICAP, ONE MATCH RACE, AND FIVE HEATS!

DOUGLAS SECOND – A GRADE HANDICAP, MATCH RACE AND SIX HEATS!

SEE DOUGLAS MOTOR CYCLES AT THE AGENTS
GARD BROS.
GOUGHER-STREET

Fay's performance at the Royale was hailed as an unqualified success and the meeting as undoubtedly the best of the season. It was thought that Taylour 'fully justified her title of Champion Lady Rider'.

Wayville ways

One of Taylour's best match races in South Australia took place at the Wayville track, Adelaide. Fay intelligently tried to work Charlie Gray down on to the grass, but Gray accepted her bluff and refused to drop back, ultimately winning by about three lengths. Both motors were good, and with Gray squaring his machine on to the track every few yards and Fay riding as steady as a rock, the crowd appreciated the contest.

At a reception attended by Taylour after the meeting, she stated that she was: "…very pleased to have the opportunity of racing on the Wayville track", which she said was the best she had met, and went on to state that "the local riders and officials were amongst the greatest sports that could be found."

Push-off

Before what might be called speedway's modern era, the skill of the 'Pusher Off' or 'pusher' was very much a part of the sport. Len Silver in *The Vital Cogs (p29-30)* in *The Speedway Annual* (1969) eloquently described the role:

> There can be any number of these men up to the number usually varying according to the wishes of the promoter, or the quality of the men available. Like the rakers, they must be strong and preferably fairly tall, for their main task is to push the rider and his machine in order to get the engine started. This apparently simple task needs much more skill than one would at first think. Most young men who start this job without any previous experience find that they usually stop pushing much too soon. The common mistake is to stop pushing when he hears the engine start to splutter into life. The experienced pusher will know that it is at this time when most effort is required. Another part of his job is to actually push the machine from the rider's pits position to the pits' gate and then out on to the track in readiness for the rider to mount. If the Pit Marshal is chasing them, some quite chaotic conditions can sometimes prevail as two or more pushers try to get their respective machines through the same space at the same time!

In *The Speedster* (5 December) '*Speedway Spasms*' asked the light hearted although slightly risqué question: 'Vic Sandford gained the honour this week. Who will be Fay's pusher-off next Saturday?' This was followed up by a more serious point involving an 'A' Grade Handicap (one and a third miles) at the Royale.

> It should be pointed out that the time made by Fay in the semi-final of the Handicap was not, as has been stated and published in various, papers, the fastest time for the Handicap. That honour goes to Norm Mitchell.

The remarkably fast time done by Fay in the semi-final has caused a considerable amount of comment. The times for the races are kept by four gentlemen, whose integrity is beyond question, wielding timepieces which are known to be correct. Although it is easy enough for a skilled spectator to judge the time in which a race is run with a reasonable degree of accuracy, there is a wonderful amount of conceit in the man who will disagree with watches, having only his own mental judgment as a basis of comparison.

It seems that confusion and controversy followed Taylour. The piece continued seemingly trying to pour oil on troubled waters:

There was no ill-feeling between Foale and Taylor arising out of the stewards' action, as Foale lent Taylor his machine (which it might be noted really belongs to Vic Bognor) for the re-run.

In the same publication *Hawk Eye*, apparently showing further interest in the covering of Taylour's rear, commented: 'After Jack Goodale secured a pusher's job last Saturday, you would have thought they would have let him push Fay Taylour off!'

Also in that edition of *The Speedster*, some sensitivity seems to have been shown to the presence of a member of the fair sex in the pits:

For the first time in the history of Speedway the stewards have found it necessary to call before them for an explanation, a person who was apparently guilty of using bad language in the pits. It is considered that a practice night is just as important as an actual race night insofar as the maintenance of due decorum is concerned.

For all this, just as in the previous year, Australia seemed enamoured of Taylour: the more she raced, the more in demand she became. Fay remembered:

On Saturday we were back in Adelaide for my second racing appearance. I can remember going like a scalded cat but dreading that plunge into the first turn. An action photo taken when I was racing or practicing on the track came to light recently and shows the speed and terrific sliding angle at which we took the bends.

Next to a third of a page advert proclaiming, 'Speedway Royale – Super Program – Final Appearance of Fay Taylour, The World's Wonder Woman', *The Mail* (Saturday, 7 December, 1929) told the tale of the racing at the Speedway Royale that same day. 'The ground had echoed to the cheers of thousands of spectators when Taylour, riding with more daring and greater brilliance than a week earlier, led Keith Litchfield, South Australian champion, home in the match race, broadsiding as skilfully as any of the speedmen. She had 50 yards to spare after a thrilling race'.

Applause had marked Fay's entrance to the arena. After winning the toss, Litchfield gave his opponent the inside running. From a good start she shot ahead almost immediately, establishing a 10 yard lead which quickly became a

50 yard break. Her elegant powersliding was loudly cheered. As the race progressed Taylour went farther away and had one-third of a lap to spare when the post was passed.

Litchfield, who had recently returned from Britain, was overwhelmed by Taylour's superb riding. She did not make one mistake on the turns, and sped up the straights with great aplomb; she was never really troubled by her opponent and her time was a great improvement on that of the previous Saturday, cutting three seconds off of her best and bettering the season's four-lap ($1^1/_3$ mile) record

Taylour won her heat of the 'A' grade handicap, off 3 seconds, in the smart time of 1minute 34 seconds, her winning margin being 100 yards. In the semi-final she improved on her previous best time winning from Charlie Gray by 80 yards.

In the final, she and Jack Chapman got away badly, but unlike Chapman, she failed to make up much leeway, eventually finishing third, when Bertelsmeier pulled out.

Over the loud speaker Fay thanked patrons for the reception accorded her in Adelaide. She said she hoped to come again as she had made many friends.

MATCH RACES
Fay Taylour, England ($3^1/_2$ Douglas) d Keith Litchfield ($3^1/_2$ Douglas) by 50 yards. Time, 1.5

A GRADE HANDICAP
Heats
Eighth- Fay Taylour, 3 secs ($3^1/_2$ Douglas). Vic Benish. 2 secs. ($3^1/_2$ Harley). Won by 150 yards. Time, 1.34.
Semi-finals – Fourth - Fay Taylour d Charlie Gray by 80 yards. Time. $1.33^3/_5$.

FINAL. - Jack Chapman d H. Butler by 15 yards. Fay Taylour was third, and Con Bertelsmeier pulled out. Time. $1.30^1/_5$.

Flying

In Adelaide *The Mail* of 7 December asked South Australia: 'Can An Aeroplane Land at Moana? To-morrow afternoon, December 8th, Pilot Mollison[50] will endeavour to land a 'Junker' at Moana to see if the grounds are suitable. Miss Fay Taylour, the famous Speedway Racer, and the American Consul, Mr T.C. Wasson, will be passengers from Parafield. *Come and see them Land!'*

Jim Mollison, one of directors of the Eyre Peninsula Airways, left Parafield at 2.30 pm bound for Moana. The directors of the company were considering introducing a regular service to Kangaroo Island, and making Moana a stopping place on the way. The trip was to test the landing grounds. While the directors of Lake Beach Estate had secured suitable grounds for a future aerodrome, these were not yet available to them. In the meantime temporary grounds were used. It was envisaged that a regular service operating on Sundays and holidays would be initiated.

The undulating country and the Onkaparinga River, together with the beautiful coastal views would afford magnificent panoramas for passengers for a fare of 10/- and £1, according to the trip.

Mollison was known throughout the State as a skilled pilot. He was, at that point, contemplating a flight round Australia. Taylour said of him:

> Poor Jim ('the playboy of the skies'). He did have a name for fast living, but then don't all flyers? But I was glad I'd refused his invitation *(to his quarters)* although black-sheep labellers make me rebellious.

Apart from Taylour and the Consul to South Australia, Mr. H. Krantz, chairman of Eyre Peninsula Airways, Miss Eunice Culley, daughter of the managing director of Lake Beach Estate, and two principals from the Majestic Theatre also made the test flight. Fay expanded on the event:

> A big dinner in my honour took place two nights before the racing, and I found that the guest on my right was Jim Mollison, a crack flyer who was soon to make a record flight to England and marry Amy Johnson.
>
> "Take care", someone laughed when we were introduced, "he's also renowned for women".
>
> I agreed to fly as a passenger with him the following Sunday in some advertising stunt, but declined an invitation to his bachelor quarters after the dinner although, or perhaps because I liked him. Instead, I let the American vice-Consul and his rich friend who was in the diamond business, take me for a drive. The vice-Consul, Thomas Wasson, who was residing in the hotel where I stayed, had been to the dinner. He had the longest eyelashes I've every seen on a man, and they intrigued me, and after the two men had taken me out several times I began to wish, fun as the trio was, that the diamond merchant would get lost. As if reading my thoughts, one of them jokingly suggested that two might be better company than three.
>
> "Of course!" I joked back, "now I'll expect only one of you to ask me out tomorrow".
>
> I may have said something else to hide that I liked the American, or else the American concluded that no girl could possibly prefer his company to that of a diamond merchant who was also a bachelor. In any case I got the most pathetic note from him accusing me of heartlessness, and saying he was going away; and I was never able to put it right because I'd left the

city before he returned. Years later I read in a newspaper that he'd been killed in Palestine - with the UN Forces I think. Perhaps he liked me more than I thought, and I was doing precisely what he did, not crediting myself with the ability to attract him. Was my early home life, which allowed me to grow up…with the unruffled belief that I was not attractive, except in a friendly hail-fellow sort of way, not so advantageous after all? Would it have been better to have had the assurances that would give me conceit? Was I not losing out by being unaware that I had what it takes? What it takes, that's to say, to capture a man on a pedestal, for the man who attracted me was on a pedestal. And what of those who wanted to capture me? Was I not reversely depriving them of a pedestal instead of realising that their interest in me was telling me that I did have what it takes, and that such interest marked them for distinction? Did my lack of vanity affect my relations with Lionel?

For the present, at any rate, I was happy with the very special relationship with Lionel

As they say in my own humble, easterly London dockland home - sort that lot out!

Injury in Melbourne

As she stepped off the Adelaide Express in Melbourne on a Friday night she was welcomed by Frank Hunting, track manager of the Melbourne Exhibition Speedways, Fred Tott (president), A.C. Wilson (secretary), on behalf of the Auto Cycle Union of Victoria; A.L. Nicholls, R.R. Van Senden (Vacuum Oil Co.), H.I. Jones (Raleigh Motor Cycle Club), and 'other well-known motor cycle identities', Fay asserted, "Yes, I'm jolly glad to be back in good old Australia once more".

Discussing dirt-track racing in Britain, Taylour said that the sport was booming more than ever. In many places it had supplanted the 'tin hare', while many people connected with 'mechanical coursing' had included dirt-track racing in their programmes and made it one of the features (one can only guess at how greyhound track owners would have taken these comments).

Taylour said that the Australians had made a name for themselves in dirt-track, and were easily the world's best on the speedways. She was booked for the Melbourne Exhibition Oval, with carnivals in Sydney, Brisbane and New Zealand to follow.

On Saturday, 14 December, the promoters of the dirt-track motorcycling carnivals at the Melbourne Exhibition Speedway were unlucky in terms of the weather for their huge international meeting. The programme was easily the biggest Exhibition Speedways had organised, and so a record crowd was expected. Nevertheless, about 5,000 enthusiasts braved the elements, which, in the circumstances, was an excellent attendance.

Chief interest at the meeting centred on Taylour. Pitted against Victoria's best, she had proved herself an accomplished exponent of dirt-track racing, the fact that she shared the one lap record of $19^4/_5$ seconds with Reg Lewis was sufficient testimony to her skill.

Keen interest also attached to the first appearance of the British rider Clem Cort[51]. He had been given no opportunity for training rides, and so was racing under a great disadvantage. In the circumstances Cort did exceptionally well to win his heats of the handicap and scratch races.

The Final of the fast and furious scratch race was to prove the most sensational contest of the season. The best four riders on the track qualified; Con Cantwell (Norton) earned the right to contest the final by a brilliant win in the first heat. His time of 1 minute $21^1/_5$ seconds was the fastest time of the evening. Cantwell thereby won the Fay Taylour Tankard, a silver trophy presented to the rider making the fastest time for the night.

The second heat was won by Taylour who handled her Douglas machine with power and grace, to dispose of Hec Jones (Rex Acme) in 1 minute 25 seconds. The third heat went to Reg West (Rudge), who was clocked at 1 minute 22 seconds. The fourth and last heat was won by Clem Cort, who, like Taylour, rode a Douglas, in 1 minute $23^2/_5$ seconds. At first glance Cort's effort hardly seems outstanding, but it was really a splendid feat given he'd had only one previous ride on the track.

The crowd expected something out of the ordinary in the final, and they were not disappointed. The quartet provided a thrilling five minutes. From a flying start Reg West took the initiative and the crowd was on its feet as he daringly took the Aquarium bend at speed. With West in the lead and thrilling the crowd, Fay tackled the Rudge rider. West, though, threw caution to the wind and broadsided spectacularly at the far bend. How he recovered from that big skid was a revelation, and it sent the spectators wild with excitement.

Undeterred, West continued his wild charge, but he had too much pace to negotiate the turn into the straight, and though he threw himself into another broadside, he was unable to recover and crashed. That was the signal for another outburst from the fans and it increased in volume as Con. Cantwell, striking West's machine, also came down causing a re-start as one lap had not been completed.

Both West and Cantwell were badly shaken, but they lined up again bravely. Sensing another great struggle, the Melbourne faithful stood hushed until the gun signalled the start. On this occasion, greatly to the liking of the gathered multitude, Taylour flashed out and established a lead. But her haste was to no avail, for she made the same error in the same place as West did in the first essay, and she fell heavily. West was following her at a fast pace, and in avoiding her was forced off the track and again fell heavily.

But for West's courageous action Taylour might have been seriously injured. As it was, she sustained an injury to her arm, and she was unable to take her place in the field at the third start. West had a noticeable limp, but that did not prevent him from starting.

On this occasion West, streaking off at the gun, soon made a determined break, which he increased to 15 lengths at the finish. The winner received a wonderful cheer from the thrilled onlookers. His time was 1 minute $21^4/_5$ seconds. Clem Cort again rode well to finish in second place ahead of Cantwell.

Prior to the final of the scratch race, Taylour made an attempt to break the one lap flying start record of $19^4/_5$ seconds, held jointly by herself and Reg West, but she just failed taking 20 seconds for the distance. The track was heavy after the rain, so her ride was a good one.

Speedway fans were informed that at the Speedway Royal in Sydney on the Saturday night, Billy Lamont, who had returned from Britain after two years, was to make his reappearance. Taylour would be on the same programme. Billy was a real swashbuckling racer: a risk taker of the first ilk, but gifted with a great feel for speed and uncanny track sense.

As the Speedway Royal was close to the Royale in terms of size and shape, it was assumed that Taylour would match her Adelaide performances in Sydney. Lamont was the idol of the Royal's first season and he had made a reputation for himself in the UK. He demonstrated both his aggression and skill on his own New South Wales ground, but Taylour was not disgraced, and could boast in the future that she had brought the best out of one of the most adventurous of all the great Australian Test riders.

Advertisement in a Sydney newspaper for Fay's match with Billy Lamont

Half machine

According to Taylour, dirt-track racing was totally different to any other riding because more than half the success of a rider was due to their machine. For Fay, no matter how good a rider was, if the front wheel of their bike could not be perfectly controlled, they were bound to come off. She also considered that speed and acceleration were major features to be considered for really safe riding. She insisted that if one went into a corner fast, and threw the machine into a slide, the acceleration pulled you out without difficulty. If the acceleration was not good, she asserted, "…you'll probably end up against the fence".

For Fay, dirt-track racing was not dangerous, providing a rider had the requisite features on their machine and rode with thought. Typical of her own attitude to racing, Taylour designed a face mask in January, 1930. It looked a bit like 'gimp' headgear, but could be effective. It caused something of a stir at the time, but decades later variations on the theme were common on the speedways.

Fay was at the very peak of her powers as a racer in 1929. She was now much more than a novelty act; she was a major contender and a real threat in every race in which she competed. There were those who were prepared to accept a woman as an 'attraction', a curiosity, but it was quite another thing for a female to be considered on equal terms to men. By now Taylour was making a mockery of the handicaps she was given and so was an obvious symbol of female demands for parity with their male counterparts - and not only with regard to the dirt-track.

13. Haere Mai Wahine Wehi[52]

On Taylour's return to New Zealand, a function in her honour was held at the Grand Hotel, Wellington. It was, in part, a press launch of her intended track campaign in the country. When asked how she took up motorcycling she replied:

> Oh, that's what every one wants to know…Well I had a motorcycle and I thought I'd like to race, and I did, and then when I saw dirt-track racing it appealed to me immensely. I tried it and I fell off and then I tried it again and again, until I got better at it. After my first three appearances, other tracks asked me to compete; I suppose they saw I was steady and yet made good times, and so I got known, and have competed on sixteen tracks in England, Scotland, and Ireland. I got a job with a big firm, but when I first started I found the expense very heavy. When I said I was going out to Australia, everyone threw up their hands in horror, and said 'They won't allow women on the tracks out there; you can't go without a manager or a mechanic,' and so on. However, I took all I had made in England and borrowed £250 and went, and the Australians gave me a marvellous reception.

She went on to give her views on athletics for women in Britain and New Zealand:

> They are keen on athletics at home, but not in the same way as they are out here. Candidly, I think it is because of the papers. They are not sporting. True, they publish results of hockey matches…I think I'm going to like Wellington, and I think it is perfectly wonderful of so many people to come and meet me as early as eleven o'clock in the morning.

A number of well-known people in the local sporting world were present at the Grand's 'do', as well as the representatives of various sports bodies in the city. Fay also received a musical welcome and a posy of flowers. She thanked everyone for their good wishes, and after refreshments had been served, and some time spent in conversation, the guest of honour was whisked away to be photographed, in full riding regalia, including a little tan and black velvet hound mascot, (perhaps in deference to her father's notorious and brutal allies in the attempt to crush Ireland's struggle for freedom).

After competing in Wellington, Taylour was due to return to England in time for the opening of the 1930 speedway season. In response to the normal questions about her intentions, she remarked, "But if I ever get married - say, when I'm 26 or so - I'll give up racing!" (she was of course just a few weeks away from her 26th birthday).

Taylour's intention to ride on the Western Springs track, Auckland, on the evening of Wednesday 12 February was announced the week before as the coming of a 'lady who has ridden on almost every British and Australian track'. She was also said to be, '…considered so good now that she starts from scratch with the pick of Aussie riders…Some lady, this!'

Western Springs

On her appearance at Western Springs, Fay captivated the crowd by her daring riding to the extent that a subsequent Saturday appearance drew ten thousand spectators. During the final days of February in 'The City of Sails' a huge crowd turned up at Auckland speedway. *Programme and Speedway News* (Saturday, 22 February, 1930) told the story:

> At last the enterprise of those responsible for Western Springs broadsiding has met with well-deserved reward. Struggling so frequently against weather conditions, it must have, at times, been heart breaking, but their perseverance was well rewarded on Wednesday night, when an attendance of between 11,000 and 12,000 greeted the opening event. Apparently, Auckland has now developed the broadsiding instinct and the future can be looked forward to with confidence. Probably curiosity was a large factor in the wonderfully increased attendance, a desire to see Miss Taylour being a great factor. Just to see a lady ride was the feeling of many thousands, but that the lady could ride such fine races and put up such splendid times more than surprised the curious. To her presence, the management may give credit for the attendance, and certainly she produced the goods. Her times would compare more than favourably with the men stars, and she may be ranked as a classy rider.

> Her appearance to-night should be more than interesting, whilst her task will be even more strenuous than was the case on Wednesday evening, as she proposes to make an attempt on existing records.

Fay and friend at Western Springs

Unfortunately, owing to many minor machine accidents, delays occurred during the evening, but these are matters over which the management have no control. These are inevitable and, though at times a little tantalising, patrons realise this and are fairly patient.

These comments on Fay's racing on the Western Springs track were given under the headline 'Wednesday's Meeting. Another Great Success. Miss Taylour's First Appearance. Arthur Mann's Return'.

Despite the necessity, due to stress of weather, of postponing last Saturday's meeting until Wednesday of this week, though it may have affected the attendance to some degree - as postponed meetings usually do - the huge crowd was a great tribute to Miss Fay Taylour. It was the first occasion on which a lady rider has graced an Auckland track[53], but, judging by the reception given to the fearless little lady, the time is not far distant when quite a few of the gentler sex will follow in her footsteps. It was amply demonstrated that to be a broadsider is not unladylike, and the fear of this has perhaps been the bogey that has kept many girls from taking part in meetings at Western Springs. The sport is a healthy one, with just that spice of risk which makes it attractive, and this is probably the main reason that caused it to appeal to Miss Taylour.

What a typical Auckland reception the immense crowd gave this wonderful rider. Her appearance caused such an outburst of cheering that surely meant, for her, half the battle of winning. And she deserved it all, for rarely has such pluck and determination been shown in a contest. It required a man's courage to tackle the job and Miss Taylour tackled it courageously. There was no sign of fear or hesitancy when bends had to be rounded in big broadsides. The lady drove her machine into them with almost abandon, and not on any one occasion did she look like parting company with her cycle. The stretch out of the home straight was evidently somewhat rocky as quite a number of spills took place in this particular area, but Miss Taylour was able to safely negotiate the rough seas without mishap. It was a wonderful exposition of broadsiding and fearlessness and Miss Taylour is deserving of the heartiest congratulations on her deserved success. To-night she proposes to make an attempt to reduce the lap record of the track, and it can be left to imagination the wild reception with which such news would be received by the fans.

Miss Fay Taylour certainly deserved all the good things that had been said of her prior to the fine exposition of broadsiding this intrepid little lady gave on Wednesday night. Many thousands attended because of the novelty, but they soon realised that Miss Taylour was not simply a show rider, but that she knew all the intricacies of the sport. There was no more attractive riding at the meeting than hers. Her time compared more than favourably with that of other stars who have been acclaimed, and that is the whole crux of her success. The wonderful reception tendered on her first appearance, must leave a lasting impression of the sportsmanship of Aucklanders.

SPECIAL MATCH RACE, 3 LAPS.
Miss Fay Taylour v. Bill Herbert.
First Heat: W. Herbert (Royal Enfield) 1; Miss Fay Taylour (Douglas) 2.

This was a wonderfully exciting race. The crowd grew almost frantic as Taylour jumped away from Herbert from a rolling start and maintained a length lead in the first lap. Going into the bend out of the straight 'at a strong bat', Fay found the going a bit rough, allowing Herbert to gain a slight advantage, but when she was able to accelerate hard and regain the lead the applause was almost frantic. Taylour passed the post on the final lap about a foot in front of her opponent, but by some error the white instead of the chequered flag was shown and the two whirled on for another round, Herbert just gaining the judge's verdict.

The second heat was more exciting than the first. With the advantage of the inside running, Herbert gained a slight lead, but on reaching the home stretch the two racers were going wheel to wheel, with the crowd yelling themselves hoarse. Both riders were taking huge chances piling into the bends, and broadsiding with amazing balance and poise, particularly given the pace they were hitting. Over the final two laps there was not more than the length of a wheel separating the two machines, with Herbert in front and looking like a winner until he reached the last straight into which he made a wide turn. Seeing a good run on the inside, Taylour just pipped him on the post by not much more than a tyre's width in a time of 68 seconds.

After two such fine heats the resultant final promised much, but, with his usual bad luck, Herbert fell after leaving the home stretch on the second round. His opponent had a slight lead and it was in a rush to wrest this away that Bill came a cropper when in the midst of deep powerslide.

In love with New Zealand

On Taylour's next appearance at the Western Springs Stadium she came within two-fifths of a second of the lap record set by Frank Pearce, defeating two of Auckland's top riders, Alf Mattson (the New Zealand champion, who in the 1932-33 season would ride for Coventry) and Jack Garmston.

In winning two match races against Auckland's brace of best riders' the *Speedway News* (1 March) extolled,

> …this daughter of Erin covered herself with glory. And what a cheer went up when she shot away from Alf Mattson (who later on won the Chevrolet Cup) in her Chevrolet Cup heat, and then the 'oh's' of sympathy to be heard as her machine pulled up after leaving the bend and coming along the straight with the chain dangling from it, were indeed expressions of sympathy at her bad luck. For barring this, or some other accident, there is not doubt that Miss Taylour would have won.

At the same meeting Fay made presentations to Jack Garmson and Alf Mattson, and when the question was broadcast as to whether she should make a return visit to the track the crowd replied in a deafening round of cheers.

As a finale Miss Taylour took the seat of a side-car and circled the track. There was a rush of girls and boys to the safety fence, calling along with the adults on the terraces, "Good luck Fay".

At Monica Park Speedway, Christchurch, Fay knocked four-fifths of a second off the lap record and made the best speed of the night for the four laps at Dunedin, where she also broke the lap record and defeated the Dunedin champion, Young.

In early April Taylour told the world:

I am so much in love with New Zealand and its people that I have actually cancelled my steamer reservations five different times...Speedway fans may think that the continual reiteration that this is my final appearance is a 'gag' on the part of promoters to secure attendances, but this is not so. My failing is that I can't make up my mind to leave New Zealand.

When I first came to New Zealand, it was on the understanding that it was for a six weeks engagement only. On coming to Christchurch for the first time, five of these weeks were up and only one week remained; that meant only one appearance here. It was advertised that this was my one and only appearance - and this was true.

The fact is that when I came down here I had fallen in love with New Zealand so much that I couldn't bear going away. Another factor to play a prominent part in my lengthened stay in New Zealand was the fact that just prior to the expiration of the six-weeks contract the speedway to which I was under contract in Adelaide had closed down, all the star riders having gone to England. When I heard that, I decided to extend my tour of New Zealand to a further week anyway.

In fact Taylour's proposed appearance in Adelaide had been advertised in 1930. It seems that things may not have been quite as Fay described them.

TOMORROW NIGHT

SPEEDWAY ROYALE

FINAL APPEARANCE OF

FAY TAYLOUR

THE WORLD'S WONDER GIRL!

Taylour chose to ride at the local Christchurch speedway in March because she claimed to like the track so much. That was to have been her final appearance in New Zealand. Efforts were made to reserve a passage to Australia but according to Fay,

> ...the local speedway wished me to extend my contract. After riding here...Auckland wanted me, and here I was, still wavering between going home through America or Australia.

There was to have been one appearance only in Auckland, but, having had bad luck with her motorcycles, she was asked to follow up her initial appearance with a ride the following Saturday to make up for the disappointment the public felt. To keep faith with the New Zealand speedway fans, Taylour cancelled her berth on the Australia bound 'Niagara'. The engagement for the following Saturday was fulfilled, and a berth booked on the Ulimaroa, which was to leave the following Friday. But early in the week, just before departure for Wellington, a telegram was received from Christchurch, expressing surprise that Taylour was still in New Zealand. The telegram asked if she would be free to stay on in New Zealand. Fay remarked:

> I take it they thought I would never be leaving New Zealand...When I received the telegram I was conversing with a friend in the street, and there and then the toss of a coin decided. The result is I am here once more, and I have again had to turn down a berth, this time on the Ulimaroa, and I am now booked to sail for Australia by the Maunganui next Tuesday.

Taylour noted the development of the sport in the country, 'New Zealand boys have made quicker progress at the game, when compared with riders I have seen in other parts of the world'.

At this point Taylour revealed that she had been made an offer from an English promoter to race at Madrid and Barcelona, but confessed that she was also keen to ride in South Africa, South America and China, 'The great difficulty is that I am unable to split myself into half a dozen pieces and send each to a country in which I should like to race.'

It is likely that Taylour was a little 'split' in terms of her personality and this is perhaps why she changed plans on the spur of any given moment. It seems all that had to be done was demonstrate a want for her to be around and she would be, although she was well aware that she was more of a draw in New Zealand at that time than she would have been in out-of-season Australia. In effect she milked the New Zealand cow before she moved on. For all this, Fay's Antipodian Odyssey proved immensely successful and she came back to London with a considerable amount of prize money.

14. The Empire Strikes Back

Fay described her return to Britain in 1930:

Hugh, a young naval officer on the ship, partnered me for dancing and sports. "You must come down to Gosport for a dance some time", he said before we reached Tilbury. He was fair and very handsome, and I'd enjoyed his company without the involvement that makes parting a sober affair. He was attached to aircraft carriers and was now on his way to a training course at Gosport near Portsmouth.

Tilbury again! But this time no one met me as the P&O liner docked.

I wanted to hear Lionel's surprised voice when I said hullo on the phone... I'd written saying that I...would like him to give a message to the motor cycle tuning shop that had looked after his bike as well as mine. But the real reason for writing was to tell him I was having a wonderful time, even hinting that I might say 'yes' and settle down out there...

The season was already under way, and once more I was raring to go, but before phoning Johnnie Hoskins I would ring Lionel. It was only eleven o'clock and if he said 'meet me for lunch' as he always did, I'd have time to wash and change. I was back in the same room at Cranley Gardens, and felt grubby after hanging around Tilbury.

"Mr Lionel please", I said to the switchboard girl.

"Just a moment! She put me through to his office and his typist said hullo. "Is Mr Lionel in?" I asked.

"Oh that's Miss Taylour" she recognised me, "when did you get back to England?"

"This morning". I hoped Lionel was in another room so that my surprise wouldn't be spoilt, and I asked again if he was in.

"Oh haven't you heard?", she said, "He left for Australia last month and this morning we had a cable to say he was married."

"Well that's that", I said limply, "I'll phone when he gets back".

When he gets back! I dug into my suitcase, anything to stop thinking. At least he wouldn't have been racing any more...as if that weren't sufficient amputation. He had been part of the racing. It had been racing and Lionel, and yet what had I expected? Hadn't I decided and known it would be different now...how could it be the same after leaving his home that Sunday night Who had he married anyway...

I opened the case with my racing leathers, and the smell of alcohol fuel, that exciting and familiar scent, more stirring than the perfume from my favourite dance frock, sent me to the telephone again. I could race better perhaps without the feeling that I must finish 'in one piece' for that supper party. I phoned Wembley Stadium. Johnnie Hoskins wasn't there but they gave me another number.

"Johnnie"

"How are you"?

"Bless me if it ain't the Irish gal. Where are you"?

"Back in England, and I want to ride…"

"Oh girlie", his animated voice had suddenly lost its punch, "haven't you heard"?

"Heard what"? Even if Lionel's typist hadn't used the same words a few minutes earlier, 'haven't you heard', I felt they meant bad news. "I've been on a ship for weeks". I added, "just disembarked".

"Oh then you don't know. Women are banned from racing".

"BANNED…what…ME?"

"I'm sorry Girlie, I'm really sorry but you're just too late. We wanted headlines and you weren't around. In fact Lionel said he thought you'd married and settled abroad and we'd heard nothing of you for so long…"

"But Johnnie, I'm here now, and I want to race"…

It was no use. No amount of pleading could alter the fact that the publicity gained had to be honoured. They'd staged a women's race, and one competitor fell off on the ramp before even reaching the track, she'd broken a collar bone and that fitted in perfectly with the prepared announcement that was to follow: WOMEN BANNED FROM SPEEDWAY RACING.

"Too bad it cuts you out too, I'm really sorry I can't book you". Johnnie's tone was final, and he added: "would you like some passes for my next meeting?".

Passes to watch! "No thanks", I said, and the mental image of sitting up there in the stands as a spectator made further words impossible. They'd used me to get headlines, and now I was banned for the same reason.

Taylor found the proposed gift 'galling' and all the more so in that she knew that Hoskins was implicated in the decision to outlaw her and her sex from the tracks. "He had been in on the ruse!" she reflected bitterly.

The ban was to last for a full half century. It had been imposed after Jessie Hole (later Jessie Ennis), a renowned trials rider, had tried in cooperation with Hoskins, to get proper ladies' races established. The women's race staged the previous year had been primarily to promote speedway and held for what Fay saw as almost purely publicity reasons. The press had used the, by then well-worn theme: 'are women capable of racing on speedways?' Taylour had applied to enter but claimed her request had been refused, being told it was a 'special race'[56]. She asserted that the event had been organised by one of the promoters who had refused her a trial when she had first tried to get into speedway racing. There was almost certainly some truth in the accusation that females were used as a gimmick by promoters in the very early days of speedway. Like many sports, speedway was an entertainment, and deployed well trodden means to pull the public through the turnstiles. In its time the sport has called on fair ground and circus-like tactics to do what it had to do to survive, and this meant attracting spectators by almost 'any means necessary'. This would not have been a surprise to Taylour, who had ridden on the wave of novelty to break into dirt-track racing in the first place.

The ban was premised on the events at Wembley on the evening of Thursday, 15 May, 1930. This was to be Jessie Hole's big chance to take part in a special race for women riders at Wembley's Empire Stadium. The *Glasgow Evening News* carried a picture of Jessie and her opponents, Mrs. Billie Smith and Sunny Somerset, claiming, incorrectly, that it was the first time that such a contest had been staged at Wembley. Matches between women had been staged at Wembley in 1929 and apart from Fay, Eva Askquith had taken on Art Warren and Geoff Taylor there and Sunny Somerset also had raced at Wembley.

The contest was billed in *Speedway News* as a *Novel Match Race* and, significantly, what happened does not appear to have been reported by the magazine. Jessie recalled leading the parade of women riders at the start of the event. "The stadium was packed. I was in front of the other two and going quite fast. I didn't actually see what happened because they were all behind me, but I was told later that one of the boys cut across in front of Billie, she shut off and went over her handlebars, breaking a collar-bone".

Some commentators have written that a ban was imposed on females riding the speedways when a woman was injured at Wimbledon soon after the Wembley incident. But according to Jessie, 'They announced over the loudspeakers that the women's race would not now take place, and at the end of the meeting they announced that the accident had been reported to the ruling body for speedway in the country, the ACU which had ruled that women were to be banned from ever again taking part in dirt-track racing in England.' The immediacy of this decision seems to indicate there had been a deal of 'prior consideration' of the situation.

Prohibition, incentives and personality cults

According to Tom Morgan[54], writing in the *Speedway Gazette* in 1947 the ban might have been the result of the whole thing becoming embarrassing for men. Morgan conjectured that male riders, not enjoying the idea of having a woman beating them and yet, because of their 'chivalry the men wanted the girls to win, but, on the other hand, no man could allow his reputation to be damaged by being beaten by a woman.' For Morgan,

> The women could rarely put up a good show, and all too frequently, they would fall for no reason at all. Even if only for that, no man rider wanted to ride behind a woman.

> After the novelty had worn off the crowd did not want to pay to see women riders. The quality of riding wasn't worth it; if speedway racing was going anywhere it had to throw off the circus stuff, and women riders had no place in the League, anyway.

Other explanations have speculated that the banning of women was connected to the fears that male riders might have had about women 'swamping' the sport and so diminishing the 'pool' of prize money available to them. But there is little if any evidence of this being the case. There were relatively very few women riders, certainly only two or three of any note and the best of them, the likes of Fay Taylour and Eva Askquith, were never better than able, 'competitive' racers. Their presence was only likely to enhance the earnings of individual riders as it provided interest by way of what many 1920s male writers saw as 'added glamour'.

It would seem that the motivation behind the ban was more complicated than any of the conventional or 'common sense' explanations that have been offered over the years. It was a product of the times for sure, but there are some considerations that are perennial in a society wherein the profit motive is all pervasive. For example, it is probably true that the nature of Smith's injury, which meant that the St John Ambulance men attending her were obliged to cut her clothes away on the track, was felt to be improper. To expose a woman to thousands of spectators in this way would be seen as vulgar and in the worst possible taste. Probably more importantly, speedway was coming to a point where it did not need women: if women were not needed it begged the question 'why have them?' In short, for the ACU and the promoters, females were literally more trouble than they were worth. Before anything else speedway was a business and considerations about profit and loss took priority over every thing else. The comprehensive banning of women made the news, and that alone might have swayed a number of people involved. Many entrepreneurs in the sport believed that the dirt-track was a passing phenomenon: this is evidenced by the consistent lack of investment in the infrastructure of the sport, even in its golden age. Women's involvement was probably regarded as a means to a swift buck, so their preclusion from the sport would have been wrought out of a similar sentiment, allied to the motto 'any publicity is good publicity'. At the same time, any future female involvement were the ban to be reversed, would add novelty value. The subject continued to be 'live' for many years to come, so there may well be a lot in this notion of using women's involvement to keep speedway in the news. Soon after the ban was imposed it was announced that newcomer Gladys Thornhill, a sixteen year old, had been granted an ACU licence and had signed on for the Sheffield management! Clem Beckett and 'Skid' Skinner were loaning her machines and giving her tuition. So it seemed that the female riders were still not totally barred by the sport's governing body and could be used as and when it was seen as profitable. Indeed, the ban provided a potential opportunity for another 'publicity coup' if and when the abolition of women from the tracks was repealed or ignored. For all this, the official line was that the ban covered all tracks and as such Fay was out.

The banning of women from the speedways of Britain was not only a sign of the sexist times, but it was also a 'win/win' situation for the business: any analysis that leaves that consideration out is partial. Taylour was the first to recognise this. For her the whole affair was a scam by the promoters. She corroborated Jessie Hole's feelings on the Wembley affair:

> The promoters, finding their crowds dwindling, and searching for ways to get extra publicity, decided to stage a women's race and then announce a ban on women riders…They'd put women on the tracks to get publicity. Now they were banning them for the same purpose.

Connected to all this was the need to change the face of speedway riding to 'correct' what was becoming an economic imbalance from the perspective of those who financed the sport. In those days, with the riders taking the bends in that streamlined slide, the left leg trailing in line with the bike to the back wheel, bodies pushed forward over the longer wheel-based machines, speedway racing had a dynamic aesthetic never before seen by a mass audience. Some rode 'wide', some in the middle of the track. Only one or two dug their way around the inside with bent knee. Match racing between top riders was a draw-card feature. As Taylour put it, the fans appreciated 'personalities not pot winners'. They turned up to marvel at solo demonstrations by a favourite ace.

> …it was personalities who drew the crowds, different styles of riding, different bikes, frequent crashes as newcomers went into the bends faster than they knew, and the thrilling novelty.

The dirt-track had had been a thrilling and novel experience for riders and spectators alike. Taylour was convinced that the paying customers appreciated her style of riding more than the fact that she was a woman, but as much as anything else, the prohibition on women was part of the promoters attack on the speedway cult of the individual. Big stars cost big money, but there were not enough track celebrities to go round. This meant that those who sponsored speedway were played off against each other in a bidding war, the only outcome of which was to make a few riders very rich and the eventual 'species suicide' of the promoters. Taylour was part of this personality cult of speedway that would be vastly watered down with the coming of team racing. Indeed, one of the agitators of the coup against rider personality, Johnnie Hoskins, had by the late 1930s, made himself one of the largest personalities in the sport. Even today there is not and probably never will be a figure that has loomed so large over the speedways of the world.

Not unnaturally, there are other versions of what provoked women's rejection from dirt-track racing. Hoskins, always swift to show the leaders of the sport to be doing 'the right thing' in the face of those further up the food chain, had it that:

> Five lady riders had been booked in at the Empire Stadium to boost the publicity and the attendance. Among them was a married woman competitor (Billie Smith) who fainted on the line in front of a huge crowd. That was too much for the strict disciplinarian Arthur Elvin[55], the Wembley Impresario, managing director of supreme authority and knight to be (in 1946) ordered "Get them out of here. All of them. I never want to see women racing here again. I'll bring in legislation to have them stopped," he thundered. He did all that he threatened.

'Can do' Fay

Taylour had been on her way back from Australia at the time the ban was imposed, however some writers have claimed that she was on the starting line 'calmly' powdering her nose. But according to Fay she 'was never calm on the starting line and seldom if ever indulged in that old-fashioned custom of powdering one's nose'. Later in life she was to analyse her feelings immediately before the start of a race. Throwing the bike into an all-out power-slide called for a high level of strength and skill to keep from over-sliding and to stay on when she hit the bumps. She saw herself pushed to the limits of her power racing against a man who 'might only be using half his muscle power'. However, at the same time Taylour saw herself as having 'the art, the skill and the sensitivity that such loose-surfaced racing required, perhaps more sensitivity being a woman!' Fay was racing as fast and even faster than many top grade men but she was, for the most part, the only a woman to regularly compete against male riders. For all this, she made it clear:

> 'Only' is no inferior admission. Women are prettier than men, and we are proud to have daintier muscles! But the task ahead of the starting line thus held more trepidation for me, although one Englishman confided that he was 'terrified' each time he hit the turns *(this was probably Wills)*. Perhaps a woman's sensitivity and intuition helped me, together with the challenging doubt I could do it.

The motivation of 'proving' that she could 'do it' was a recurring theme in Fay's life. She undoubtedly experienced fear when she opened the throttle but, as she said, "I opened it all the same because it was such a challenge and so fascinating". And the crowds appreciated the fact that she threw her bike into the bends with equal gusto to any man.

In the 1970s a woman took part in a Midlands challenge match but the authorities acted quickly to prevent a repetition. In the 1980s, Dick Bracher, manager of the Speedway Control Board said: "We don't think girls should take part and neither do the promoters. It is a dangerous sport and though fatalities are rare, I don't think any of us would forgive ourselves if a girl rider was killed."

But the likes of Fay Taylour and Eva Askquith were the equal of most of the men and other women competed against the males for years. The prohibition of female riders was never really adequately justified because it had no moral or ethical rationale. Fay pointed out the illogical nature of the ban a few years after it was imposed: "It just isn't fair" she protested. "Nobody minds a woman driving a car - so why complain about our riding a motor bike?" But the ban was a political and economic expedient just as any eventual rise of female involvement in speedway will doubtless be powered by a similar profit motive.

A last ride

Taylour was permitted a last meeting. It took place at Southampton and pitted her against the only woman it was felt had the qualities to match Fay: Eva Asquith. The two had raced before and each time produced intriguing battles of style and temperament. The track felt strange to Taylour though she had raced on it before:

> I persuaded my father and stepmother to come and watch as Lymington was quite close and they'd never seen dirt track racing before. I stayed with them for the weekend, arranging for the bike to go direct from London, and so we drove to the track together. But before we got there I had misgivings. It would have been better not to take them. It could make Dordy more worried for me in the future, though he'd never admit it if he felt nervous, and the stepmother would scoff about the other riders.

> My own nerves were in high gear as usual as I headed for the pits after finding them seats. To confirm my Wembley win, and make Dordy proud of me now he was here, was a must. But would the bike play up again? And what was the track like? I'd never raced here before, and practise had not been permitted, but it looked good, larger than Wembley and with well-shaped bends just asking to be eaten up in an all-out powerslide. As long as it wasn't full of hidden bumps! Eva had raced here before: she'd know where the bumps were. It was a cinder track, and cinders could get rough…but they could also give a better grip…

> "Can I have your autograph"? Two excited girls stopped me and I signed their books.

> "Are you going to win tonight"?

> "I'm going to do my best", I told them, and they scurried on. The stands were filling rapidly and I was pushing through jostling crowds. Warming up laps had already begun and the peculiar smell of racing fuel hung in the

night air, tantalising my senses as catnip would a cat. The crack of straight-through exhausts, as exciting as that heady smell made me hurry, and when I reached the pits I was raring to go. The bike was there, and the mechanics ready to push me off for the warming up laps. "You'll have no trouble tonight", they assured me.

"You can go out with the next batch". The pit marshal beckoned me to line up, and that next moment I was getting a feel of the track and the bike. Both felt good though it wasn't possible to take the bends at racing speed, and I felt confident as I chatted to Eva and a reporter while waiting to race. I found that Eva also liked horses, and rode to hounds in the north.

Then we were called, and the result was published in the Southampton Echo of July 24th 1930:

'A special match race was arranged between Miss Fay Taylour, the young rider who has been much in the lime light lately, and Miss Eva Asquith. It was Miss Taylour's first appearance at Southampton, but Miss Asquith has raced here before.

Only two of the three heats were necessary as Miss Taylour won both quite easily. Although not unduly pressed she gave a good display of riding. Her time in both heats was 80²/₅ seconds.'

The fastest time of the night, recorded in the final of the scratch race for male champions, was 76²/₅. So I ought to have been satisfied, but each lap had given me a better feel of the track, and the men's record stood at less than one second a lap faster (72 secs), so I begged to go out again. I might never return to Southampton and I felt sure I could now equal or beat that record. How proud Dordy would be!

The *Southampton Echo* recorded that Fay failed in her attempt to beat the track best, but still managed to get her name in the record books: '...in a special attempt to set up a ladies record for the track she returned the excellent time of 75⁴/₅ seconds.'

Taylour asked for another crack at the circuit record, but as she recalled, the request was refused, and she mused that perhaps her father '...was happier to have me sitting in the stand beside him for the rest of the racing. The stepmother was chatty and expressed surprise at the number of well-dressed people in the stands around her, but speedway racing had quite a following in upper circles.'

Press cuttings record that Taylour had defeated Askquith easily. She had also, in establishing the female best for the Southampton circuit, come within 3 seconds of Vic Huxley's existing record for the track. Fay's last ride in Britain had been the fastest time of the meeting. Taylour was sad that she was disallowed from making a second attempt at the overall record for the

Southampton track, particularly as the meeting had provided the first and last opportunity for her father to see her ride.

Between time

In July Taylour was in Ulster, a guest of Miss A. Dorman, of Keady, a 'chum' for years, both having attended Alexandra College, Dublin, together. She was among the many visitors at the Armagh Archery and Lawn Tennis Club tournament. Partnered by J. Love (Keady), playing on No. 2 court, Fay demonstrated that her tennis talents had not rusted. They won their match, 6-2, 6-3. Of speedway she remarked, 'I'm, terribly keen. My people don't care a lot for it, but I love it.'

Fay, at this time, was almost in a state of shock. Her future had been taken away and she was more or less directionless. For three years the dirt-track had given her a purpose, if only from day to day. Now with no racing and no Wills, she was left in a state of limbo and she hung on to any possibility of returning to the speedway fold. She made public that she was greatly disappointed that the track in Belfast had closed down, but she said her one wish was that a good track should be laid in Ireland, and hoped that she might be able to facilitate this at some point. Her preclusion from the dirt-track had done little to alienate her from motorcycle competition - Taylour reportedly covered the Isle of Man T.T. course in nothing short of record time.

Whilst in Ireland Taylour made the news as something of a good Samaritan. It seems on a Tuesday evening a motor cyclist was returning from Keady when his engine developed trouble. Having spent considerable time in endeavouring to detect the cause, he had practically given up in despair when a young lady came on the scene and at once offered her services, which were readily accepted. After a few preliminary questions, the woman discovered that the problem was with the carburettor, which she dismantled and overhauled. In a few moments the repaired carburettor was fitted.

It seems that the motorcyclist marvelled at the mechanical knowledge displayed and was suitably surprised when informed that the young woman was none other than Miss Fay Taylour.

Change

In retrospect, Taylour felt that 1930 was a point at which she was ready for change and the move from two to four wheels seemed logical. But she found that speedway and car racing were poles apart. For a start, car racing was a rich man's game. Factories, with rare exceptions, did not race though they built fast streamlined cars for those with the cash.

The ban, together with the arrival of team racing and the league structure seemed to sap the last vestige of Fay's enthusiasm for British dirt-track racing. She was generally disappointed with the way the sport was organised. In an interview with Patric in *The Motor Cycle* (25 September, 1930) she complained;

> I am afraid I was disappointed on my return…The boys are just as wonderful as ever they were, but somehow racing has become too much like professional football and I cannot work up any enthusiasm for the League business.

Taylour highlighted some of the challenges facing the individual rider on the speedway:

> Getting 'filled up' by a rider in front is thoroughly unpleasant, even if you are wearing a face mask; that you often have the impression that somebody else's motor is roaring along beside you, when there's nobody else there at all; that in a slide a lot of your attention must be centred in keeping your front wheel steady; and that when you are sliding you make the back wheel act as a rudder – if you want to go to the left you slide the spinning back wheel further out to the right…

Taylour was keen to keep an involvement in the sport. According to Patric 'Her ambition at present is to return to her native country and organise a third-of-a-mile track in Northern Ireland'.

Fay certainly had ideas about what such a circuit might look like and insisted '…the third-of-a-mile is about the minimum size for really useful speed.'

Whether it was a lack of energy to fight the ban or that she felt exposed by the demise of handicap racing and the rise of the face-to-face, wheel to wheel confrontations of team racing, part of Fay wanted to give up dirt-track racing in the light of what she seemed to take as a personal rejection. She indicated that she found racing not altogether 'dignified', but she found its fascination too strong. "It's a great game", she said and wanted to show, and have it recorded, that she was the best woman in the sport. She was of the opinion that apart from Eva Askquith, the few women some promoters had occasionally used were too slow to interest spectators. Leaving speedway meant a decline from the celebrity status she had only recently established, but to which she had grown addicted.

Not long after the ban was imposed a club of around fifty women motor-cyclists was formed in London. One of their first aims was to meet with the speedway promoters to discuss their claims to race at meetings. A number of women motorcyclists had been agitating for the inclusion of women's races at the meetings held in London. So strong was the agitation from some quarters that a company controlling a number of tracks were reconsidering their decision not to hold women's races.

Art Pechar, the United States champion, who was in London for a series of races at the time the ban was imposed, said:

> I certainly do not approve of women taking part in dirt track racing. It demands too much strength and nerve. The risk of crashing is too great,

even with the most experienced riders…I have been racing in America for nine years, and I think I can claim to be an old hand at the game, but I should hate to think that any woman was going to feel as I feel at this moment after crashing last night at forty miles an hour. And forty miles an hour is not the highest sporting speed—sixty miles is usual in America.

The quarter-mile circular tracks which you have over here make steering very hard. In America the tracks are at least half a mile in length, which gives us a chance of getting up speed on the straight. For a man steering a motor-cycle at high speed on a circular course the strain on the arms alone is terrible, I cannot imagine a woman's arms standing the strain. I think if women attempt dirt track racing, the speed they will attain will be so low as to take away the sporting atmosphere.

For all this, Taylour had become a skilful rider, with the judgement and courage that many experienced males might have envied and her name had became a familiar one in households throughout the United Kingdom. In *The Motor Cycle* (25 September, 1930) in an interview with Patric, Fay explained the intricacies of dirt-track riding:

"This salt cellar" said Miss Taylour "is the starting line, and these two knives show you where the finishing straight begins and end.

"Now the third-of-a-mile lap goes round – whoosh-like this…" the prong of a fork inscribed a magnificent arc in the receptive tablecloth, so that the proprietor of the restaurant gasped with apprehension.

But Fay was well wound-up, and soon a salt-spoon that was Sig Schlam was chasing a sugar-tongs Charlie Datson round a soup-plate turn, only missing oversliding into a serviette safety-fence by a crumb's breath.

But as soon as the chat got on to more personal issues Fay did her best to sidestep.

 I would put a question about Miss Fay Taylour; the answer would start to come, only to be abruptly side-tracked in a breezy torrent of words tinged with the faintest of Irish brogues, and soon we would be in the throes of another salt-cellar speedway meeting.

This story demonstrates Taylour's obsession with the track; it seemed to be a compensation for her seeming inability to sustain any meaningful relationship with others. Her difficulty here is well illustrated in her writing concerning her relationship with Cuthbert and Lionel Wills. She needed racing as it was a reliable means of acquiring the adoration she seemed to crave. The speedway might have banned her from that outlet, but such was her appetite she would find sustenance elsewhere.

15. Conclusion

With the ban in place, Fay looked to the continent for help, guidance and solace. She had made a number of previous visits to Germany and now that she had lost faith in Britain and Ireland to rise to her needs, decided to go to Oberhausen. There she raced with her Douglas on the 14 mile dirt-track, defeating the local champion Herr Muller. A few years later, in the first years of the Nazi regime, she competed in a hastily organised event the 'Frauen Speedway Weltmeisterschaft', (The Womens Speedway World Championship) the roots and outcome of which have become blurred in the mists of time and the fog of war.

It was said by some that Taylour would use 'favours' to get rides from the various stadium owners after speedway's prohibition of women riders. Whilst there is no evidence of this, there were certainly some reports of her continuing activity in Britain after the spring of 1930. For example, in *The Auto* (1 August, 1930) 'Broadside Breezes' reported that Taylour, in establishing a ladies' track record at Southampton, was only $3/5$ th of a second slower than Geoff Taylor's attempt of the previous April (which had been beaten by other riders in the interim). The writer went on to say '…it has been suggested that these two riders might fix up a match'.

Long after the ban Taylour was still attempting to get back into motorcycle sport. In *Motor Cycling* (3 June, 1932) she showed she was still incensed at the prevailing attitudes, but also there is a sense of understandable bitterness in the light of her own treatment:

I am absolutely seething about this ladies' event at Brooklands on June 11th, and I would much appreciate it if you will express my views in your journal.

Early this year I was informed by a friend that there would be a ladies' race at Brooklands, and that he could produce a fast mount for me if I would compete. I told him that I had not ridden a motorcycle for over a year and that I should be afraid to open the throttle! Nevertheless, since it is always the thing which frightens one which is so attractive, I promised I would enter, and from that moment looked forward to the event.

When I saw an 'open ladies' race' announced I rang him up to make further arrangements. But I knew at once by his tone when he said, "Oh, haven't you heard the conditions?" that it was a wash-out. A complete and absolute wash-out - comparable to the publicity-stunt ladies' races which have been staged once or twice on the dirt tracks to attract the crowds. And I'm told that on one of those occasions the spectators shouted "Get off and walk."

It will be much the same at Brooklands, I imagine. The race is, no doubt, being staged as an extra attraction, but the organizers are apparently so frightened of us falling off and hurting ourselves, that they are making it impossible for us to go really fast by forbidding us to ride racing machines.

Not only are we to ride standard petrol motors, but we must leave the mudguards, registration plates and kick-starters on, so that the wind can also do its most to resist us. Incidentally, I should have thought it safer to remove these fittings. And then we must not get tired, I suppose - so we are given only two laps! It is a pity they did not go a little farther and instruct us to ride in pretty frocks and straw hats. There would be some point in it all then - and there could be a beauty parade afterwards, with prizes given to the riders who had kept tidiest over certain speeds. But, as it is, it will be a farce.

The daily Press will, no doubt give the event a certain amount of publicity beforehand. We shall see photos of women tuning-up their engines for the great race. People will go to watch it because they are curious to see how women can handle racing machines - whether they will have the nerve to go fast and, if so, whether they can stick on.

And what will the result be? 'Fastest lady rider wins at 70 mph!'

Who wants to see a race at that speed, when all the other races are being won in the region of 100 mph? Certainly not one of the people I've spoken to on the subject. And what will it look like? Too silly for words!

Perhaps the organizers think that, as few women could probably obtain racing machines, they will get more entries and a more even race if standard mounts are the rule. But, then, it is a handicap event. The real reason, I imagine, for limiting us to standard machines is because, as I said before, they are afraid of a crash. But actually I very much question whether such models are suitable for the track at all: proper racing machines would be safer.

Motorcycling may not be a very ladylike sport, but on the rare occasions of a race being included in the programme for women, why not give them a chance of showing what they might do? A standard machine may do 90 mph on the track, and the woman rider may not have the nerve to open the throttle above 80 mph: but, on the other hand, she might!

Many years later Taylour was still trying to make a motorcycle come back.

Passage to India

Apart from the years of the Second World War, Fay never left motor sport. Not long after speedway outlawed women from taking part, she left Britain for a protracted stay in India. She had initially meant just to stop over on her way to Australia, hoping to find a place on the dirt-tracks there, but Fay became distracted by an alternative life-style and this led to a change of direction. She looked back on how her 'passage to India' came about:

I wrote to a school friend who had given me an open invitation to stay with her in India, where she was married to a British army officer, and suggested I would visit her on my way to Australia. After visiting her I could still catch half the racing season 'down under'. But I made no racing contracts ahead. To be free to wander without being pinned down was for me the spice of life. And I arranged that the bike would be put on a ship direct for Australia after I cabled from India. That cable never went.

By December I was on the way, and when I heard that the P&O liner would call at Malta I sent a cable to Hugh, the naval officer who had been such fun on my last voyage. He was now attached to the aircraft carrier 'Eagle' at Malta, and no sooner had we anchored off-shore when a naval sloop dashed alongside with a busy whoop, whoop, and there was Hugh all smiles.

"I'm taking you to lunch on the *Eagle*", he laughed, "the Navy's kidnapping you", and the next moment I was in the fast motor boat heading for shore.

"You simply must meet my wife", he said, "she's singing carols and couldn't come with me".

"Your *wife?*"

"Yes, I got married the other day, and she's dying to meet you...she's great fun...you'll get on like a house on fire."

We did. In fact when they took me back to the ship just before sailing she decided that I really had to be kidnapped, and with only ten minutes to go she started grabbing all my clothes from the cupboard and drawers and threw them into my trunk and suitcases, or into Hugh's arms, and Hugh threw the lot into the sloop.

"Quick! Your ticket and passport, have you got them"?

I dashed to the Purser's office, and while I was there the ship's whistle gave three blasts and I thought we were moving with all my belongings now off the ship. But three minutes later I was in the little naval vessel staring at the passenger liner and trying to realise it was sailing without me.

"You can catch the next ship", Hugh said, "the P&O calls here every two weeks. Besides, you couldn't choose a better moment to visit Malta if you tried."

In British jargon, the Fleet was in. It was all around us, resting peacefully but gaily on the sunny blue water, battleships, destroyers, aircraft carriers, submarines, and myriads of smaller craft. And the next two weeks would include Christmas and New Year, and all the special festivities hosted by His Majesty's Navy.

Hugh was living ashore with his wife at the Imperial Hotel and I stayed with them there. The two weeks were so packed with parties and other events that there was no time for reflection or anticipation. There were lunches, dinners, dances, cocktail parties aboard ships and on shore. If I needed a reminder later I would only have to look at the blue chiffon evening dress put into retirement after the dance on Hugh's aircraft carrier. The 'mountain slide', a feature of such dances, had ripped it from top to bottom.

There were horse races too, and someone arranged for me to give a demonstration of speedway broadsiding on the loose-surfaced course during the races. The fastest local motorcycle was borrowed, and the left footrest removed so that I could heel over into the turns in the characteristic dirt track powerslide. The course was similar to a speedway, two straights and two sweeping turns.

Practice for a demonstration like that was unnecessary and so I rode on the track in the middle of the meeting and after being introduced set off full bore down the straight. The loose surface was smooth and the bends wide, perfect I thought for a daring exhibition. I could now show my friends what I'd been trying to demonstrate on paper, and I approached the first turn on full throttle. No need to cut out on a beautiful track like this!

It was time to throw the bike into her slide, and exultingly, almost savagely, I heeled inwards to allow the back wheel to slide out and start skidding. But it wouldn't slide!. It just wouldn't slide. Instead, it bucked, reared and twisted, as none of the horses had done, and off I came. The beautiful surface was made of wood chips, and I'd just learnt that wood chips don't like dirt track riders. I didn't like them at that moment! To ride around the turns without skidding would be slow and colourless. It was as if they'd snatched a delicious morsel from me just as I was about to partake.

But I wasn't really hungering for racing. I was seeking another atmosphere, and had found it. I was seeking new friends and had found them too. I made friends easily, and maybe I was a little crazy because wherever we went we seemed to be laughing. I took nothing seriously and made fun of everything. But when the masked ball at the Malta Club ended, the gayest event of all, I felt a little sad. In a day or two I would be sailing on.

"Why must you leave so soon for another part of the world just as I'm getting to know you." one of my partners said. "I want to see more of you".

I wanted to see more of him too, but Sheelagh my friend in India was waiting for me. I'd cabled that I was arriving by the next ship, and this would be another new adventure.

Four wheel drive

Arriving two weeks late in the colonial subcontinent and then extending her stay scuppered any Australian ambitions, but her time in India included her first serious challenge on four wheels. She entered the 1931 Calcutta to Ranchi Run (291 miles) driving a Chevrolet and broke the record for the event. Her performance so impressed the previous holder of the record that he gave her an introduction which resulted in a machine for her first race at Brooklands late in 1931 with the Le Mans Talbot. Again she was victorious against a field of the top women drivers. This was followed by her first Road Race, the classic Leinster Trophy in Ireland: Fay was the only female entrant (she was to win this event in 1934 in a German-made Adler). She then won her first Hill Circuit Trophy at the famous Shelsley Walsh in Worcestershire and the Class Cup at Craigantlet Hill Circuit (Ulster). At Donington, Fay won the Women's race and then competed on the famous Mountain Circuit at Brooklands with an Alfa-Romeo. This was the first time that women were allowed to take part and she lapped the tricky circuit, which demanded hard breaking and slick gear changing faster than any British driver. It is interesting to note that she was driving a borrowed car and had been unable take the vehicle out for a practice run. In 1939 she drove one of Freddie Dixon's record-breaking Rileys in the South African Grand Prix but was one of six drivers who failed to finish.

Fay in her car racing years

In the war years, Taylour's political views led to internment, imprisonment and deportation. Following the War, her connections with the Moselyites branded her an 'undesirable' and despite a massive effort to get back into motor sport it became clear she was a social and sporting pariah in Britain. With no recourse in Ireland, she went to the USA where she found work promoting the sale of Jaguar and MG cars. But the hankering for speed was still there and, back in the UK again, she took up racing smaller cars, notably the Cooper-JAP. In Sweden's International race at Skarpuak airport in 1952, Taylour made the fastest lap and was the first and only woman to race there at that time.

However, as the years passed, her ability to race competitively diminished and she placed all her hopes in attempting to generate and sell her life story. She made many attempts, generating a mass of memoirs (much of this enriched with melodramatic embellishments), film scripts and romanticised, fictional versions of her biography with a view to producing a novel based on her experiences. The energy that went into this was apparently total. Gradually falling into obscurity in her adopted American home, she faced the twin prospects of poverty and anonymity. Fay survived on a sparse income from a variety of informal employment, such as baby sitting and house keeping, whilst watching the files of the rejection letters she kept grow to horrifying proportions.

Fay had some intimate relationships in later life, but never married or had children. She finally came back to live out the remainder of her life in Britain.

The art of motorcycle maintenance

For all her glories as a driver, it is likely that she was a relatively better rider. In spite of his reservations regarding women's participation in motor sport, Johnnie Hoskins was quoted in *Speedway Star* (3 February, 2001) paying homage to her skills:

> Fay had personality and winning ways. We called her the lass with the blue Irish eyes and she was the equal of any but the very top most performers in any branch of motorcycle or car racing.

Taylour's comparative ability was probably reflected in her tastes. Late in April 1947, Fred Mockford, then the speedway manager at New Cross, introduced Fay Taylour to the fans at the Thursday night's racing. For many her name meant nothing. She was in London taking a holiday from Ireland and she felt the need to taste the atmosphere of the track once more. Breaking the official ban, she made for the pits. Taylour knew quite well that she was contravening rules and regulations. It seems the riders were 'hiding' her until she had watched Ron Johnson race, no mean feat given the presence of ACU Stewards and Fred Mockford. Apparently she had quite a long talk with Ron afterwards and, back in the track club house, she expressed surprise that he was still beating the youngsters. She said,

I though I'd lost all my love for speedway racing when they banned women from taking part in the sport…but although I've done a lot of motor and midget car racing in South Africa, this is my first love and will always be my greatest.

She said she had been in South Africa since 1939. This of course was not true as she spent the War years interned in Holloway Prison and on the Isle of Man before being deported to Ireland.

She intimated that her greatest ambition was to ride again on the speedway, and she was amazed to see that some of the men with whom she used to race were riding better now than ever. "If only I could persuade Mr. Fred Mockford to let me ride I should be happy," she said. "I was the first woman rider in this country and was under contract to the New Cross manager when he was at the Crystal Palace in 1929. I wish he would arrange an 'Old Crocks' race, with old bikes and old riders like myself. What a thrill it would give me to race again…" As she spoke her right hand twisted in the motion of opening and closing the throttle.

Just a few weeks later, under a photograph of Fay mounted on a track-bike, with Jack Cooley and Malcolm Craven (who had been nominated as challenger to Jack Parker of Belle Vue for the match race championship) the *Weekly Sporting Review* (10 May, 1947), informed the world that, 'Fay Taylour, speedway's Queen of the Cinders, hopes to return to the saddle. Frank Arnold, West Ham's team manager, has invited her to take part in a trial and the public may later see her give demonstration rides. The ban on women riders still keeps her from competing against men.'

It certainly seemed that Fay had been a model for other women. After the Second World War, during which females had been given (by necessity) access to many previously male dominated areas of life, an expectation for parity between the sexes on a wider scale was expected by women. This seemed to include the dirt-track as reported in 'Star Man's Diary' in *The Star* (Friday 11 October, 1946):

> Hundreds of women from all parts of the country are writing to speedway promoters asking how they can become speedway riders. Harold ('Tiger') Stevenson, the former rider who is to train riders during the winter has had many applications from women. The West Ham manager, Arthur Atkinson, has replied to scores of letters informing women that they are barred on the speedways.

At West Ham in 1947, Fay took a trial run on a track bike loaned by Arthur Atkinson – she had not ridden for more than a dozen years, but had hardly lost her skills, despite riding a much faster machine. My grandfather, who had been Fay's pusher on the day she smashed the lap record at Lea Bridge in the late 1920s, watched her ride and told me it could have been 20 years earlier. In fact he claimed she looked a better rider those two decades later.

But attitudes had not really changed. Bobbie Cox, in the *London Speedway Reporter* (21 January, 1947) started his article with the statement; '...leave speedway to the men. Women are not tough enough.' He went on:

Every day my post-bag contains one or more letters from girls wishing to know how they can become speedway riders. My advice to them is to forget it. Speedway racing is a really tough game that should be left entirely to men. There is no soft grass or mud to break a fall - just plain hard cinders. There are no brakes on machines to prevent a crash, and the average speed for racing is 50 mph.

You may quite likely say that you know all this . . . that women have been riders, and have also beaten the men. Yes, I know - but the sport is still not for women. Their place is on the other side of the safety-fence. Anyhow, the ACU have put the bar up to women, and it is not likely to be lifted.

The women riders who did gate-crash into the sport in 1928 were used, more or less, for their publicity value to speedway. The way they put their hearts and souls into the sport, however, shook most people.

Face-powder gave way to cinder dust, and their perfume was the smell of petrol. The fans loved them for their daring.

'Women as speedway riders are not wanted. They cause too much trouble, and men don't like racing against them,' was the reason given.

According to Cox, Taylour was something of an exception: 'At the age of 24 most girls settle down to a quiet married life. Fay had other ideas. Having 'the strength of Sampson in her wrists' and being one of England's top motor-racing drivers *(which of course she was not at the time when she took up motorcycle sport)* she was able to adapt to the demands of the dirt-track'.

Many years after her glory days on the speedways of the world, Fay kept abreast of affairs on the track and guarded her reputation vociferously, forcing doyens of the connected media to sit up and listen or - as Cyril May was obliged to do in *Speedway Star* (3 November, 1973) - do what they were told.

Fay Taylour - An Apology

Miss Taylour was the acknowledged 'Speedway Queen' when women were permitted to race on dirt track speedways. As I pointed out in my article on her which appeared in this magazine in January 1960 she was, to quote: 'The greatest of all girl speedway riders and the real champion of her own sex.' Her records were also detailed.

Miss Taylour's speedway achievements were many. At one time she held the men's lap record at Wembley. She journeyed to Australia alone soon after taking up the sport and was the first rider, man or woman, to challenge the Australians on their own tracks. Two of her successes were, the defeat of the late Sig Schlam at Claremont and the Victoria Champion Reg West at the Exhibition track, where she clocked fastest racing times and equalled and broke track records. In New Zealand she gained the lap record at Christchurch and at Dunedin and also defeated Auckland's top men riders, Alf Mattson and Jack Garmston.

Her hard luck in experiencing engine trouble and spills in races she lost to Eva Askquith were recorded in the Askquith story, but a reminder from old fans shows that the last race between the two girls at Southampton in 1930 was not recorded. Fay Taylour, as the Southampton newspapers reported, won that best-of-three rounds match race 'quite easily' in two straight heats of $80^2/_5$ seconds, and then, although it was her first appearance at that track, set up a ladies' 'four-lap record' in the excellent time of $76^4/_5$, all but equalling the fastest time of $76^2/_5$ seconds made by the winner of 'The Golden Gauntlet Scratch Race'.

For all this speedway's relationship with women has not really changed since 1930. I have seen young women riding in junior grass track meetings and performing as well as the boys. But what do the females do when the boys reach 16 and many switch to Speedway? At the moment some drift away from motorcycle sport all together, while others are recruited to the ranks of other two wheeled contests that have begun to find a place for *everyone*. But many are doomed to be spectators for the rest of their lives, replicating a former age and outmoded beliefs. In short it is a retarded attitude with regard to women, but also to men, who have higher expectations of life than the sexually segregated model of society promoted by speedway.

When Fay first rode in Australia the crowds and riders called her 'Fearless Fay' and one glance at the records she notched, on both two and four wheels, show she was indeed worthy of the name. It might be about time to recognise her and the contribution she made by making speedway a truly modern sport and doing much more to open the tracks to women.

The Last Word

Although seemingly often distracted in some areas, Fay was often brutally single minded. Amongst the copious collection of material she kept relating to her life, I found a press cutting recording the death of Sig Schlam on Monday, 3 November, 1930. Although her racing relationship with Schlam did much to define her as a rider of quality, she made no mention of this in her memoirs. The only sign of any acknowledgement of Schlam were a few words in the cutting that Taylour had heavily underlined in blue ink:

> *One of the few defeats that he experienced was at the hands of Miss Fay Taylour, the English woman champion, on his home track at Claremont.*

Sig left a wife and two children at the start of the great depression that would blight the 1930s. This attitude seemed unfortunately typical of Fay's thoughts and feelings for others. But my long relationship with Taylour, through her own memories, press reports, family stories and what others have told me, collectively demonstrate that life had made her what she was. She was never a victim, but she existed at a particular time and navigated her way on a certain type of social sea that left indelible marks and deep scars – to that extent her biography is a cautionary tale as much as it is an inspirational story.

In her final years Fay lived a quiet and relatively isolated life in a cottage in Dorset, trying to write a book covering her extraordinary career as rider and driver. The pages of this book have called on much of the material she generated at that time. Fay died on 2nd August, 1983 in Weymouth, Dorset in southwest England. In many ways, her motorcycling career was just the start of the adventure that was her life. It was to offer her other glories, but probably also a great deal more than that the sum of those splendid moments in terms of pain and confusion. That is, as they say, another story that I one day hope to tell. For now, we can see Fay Taylour as an individual who struggled to find who she was as a person and her potential as a woman. She often fell in the pursuit of these goals and undoubtedly got badly hurt many times over, and she also injured others in the process. I don't think she ever fully gained the knowledge she desired, but her race was certainly one worth watching and you and I who stand together in the stands of these pages are hopefully the better for it.

Fay Taylour

Appendix:
Fay Taylour - Major Achievements

5 April 1904	Francis Helen Taylour born	Birr, King's County (Co Offaly), Southern Ireland
Autumn 1919	Enters Alexandra College Dublin	Won scholarship in Housecraft
Autumn 1922	Arrives in Berkshire, England	
February 1927	North London Cycle Club	First competitive motorcycle event
5 March 1927	Southern Scott scramble	Venus (Ladies) Trophy and Class Cup – 350cc
7 May 1927	Camberley Meeting	Unlimited cc Trophy, Runner up in 350cc event
Summer 1927	Gained employment with Rudge Whitworth Ltd	Rode as a member of the official Rudge trials team
1927-28 meetings	*Club races:* one grass track, one sand and two cross country races	Four Premier Awards, Three fastest times
	Hill Climbs: Leeds and Camberley	Two Cups
	Demonstration Climb - Hepolite Scar	Only woman to climb the 'Rodeo' Course
	Alms Hill (club meeting)	Only rider (man or woman) to climb the hill
	Trials National Alan and Travers Trophy	Gold Medals
	Colmore, Cotswold and Trophy Trials.	Victory, Silver Medals
	Bemrose Trial, the Wood Green M.C.Ladies' Trial	Bronze Medals
	ACU Six Days Trial	Gold Medal
May 1928	Southern Scott scramble	Cup and Team Award
9 June 1928	Crystal Palace	First speedway competition
August 1928	Taylour v A.R. Frogley in a mile match at Crystal Palace.	First major speedway
27 August 1928	Albion Greyhound arena, Salford	Rides in front of 20,000 spectators
4 September 1928	Cleveland Park Speedway, Middlesbrough	Defeated Eva Askquith
6 October 1928	Windsor Park, Belfast	Races for the first time in Ireland
October 1928	International Six Day Trial	Takes part with Lionel Wills
January 1929	Arrives in Australia	First British rider to compete on the speedways of Australia

5 January 1929	First Race in Australia at Perth	Defeated Frank Brown in a match race
26 January 1929	Taylour v Sig Schlam on his home track	Beat West Australian Champion. Equalled claremont track record
February 1929	Crashes competing in Sydney Wentworth Speedway	Hospitalised Crashed, fractures a 9 year old's skull. Injures her hand
Early March 1929	Arrives in New Zealand	Raced in Wellington and Auckland. Defeated some of the local stars, within 2/5th sec of Frank Pearce' record
23 March 1929	Competed at Olympia Motor Speedway at Maroubra, Sydney	
20 April 1929	Taylour v Victorian Champion Reg West in Melbourne	Defeated West in International Match Race and in winning handicap. Held track record for a year.
23 April 1929	Leaves Australia	
31 May 1929	Arrives in Britain	
4 June 1929	Taylour v Eva Askquith	Defeated 2-0 At Wembley
6 June 1929	Cinders Trophy	Wins the trophy at Wembley
27 June 1929	Taylour v Askwith, Wembley	Wins 2-1
November 1929	First appearance in Adelaide	Broke season's 4-lap record Wins big handicap event
End February 1930	Western Springs Stadium, Auckland, New Zealand	Defeated New Zealand champion Mattson and beat Fastest lap of the meeting
March 1930	Monica Park Speedway, Christchurch, New Zealand Dunedin, New Zealand	Knocked four-fifths of a second off of the lap record Best speed of the night for the four laps. Broke lap record. Beat Dunedin champion Young.
April 1930	Leaves New Zealand Arrives in Australia Leaves Australia	
15 May 1930	Women's Meeting at Wembley	Women banned from riding the speedways
June 1930	Arrives in Britain	
End of July 1930	Final ride at Southampton	Defeated Eva Askquith 2-0; Set women's record for the track. Fastest time of the meeting.
Summer 1930	Oberhausen, Germany	Beat local champion Muller Fastest time of the meeting on 14 mile dirt-track circuit

Bibliography

Allsports Weekly
Auto-motor Journal
Belfast News-Letter
Hoskins Weekly and The Westrailian Broadsider Motor Cycling and Wireless
Motor Cycle
Motor Cycling
Opposite Lock
Programme and Speedway News
Speedway Mail
Speedway News
Speedway Reporter
Speedway Star
The Auto
The Bath and West Evening Chronicle
The Brisbane Courier
The Brisbane Standard
The Brisbane Sunday Mail
The Courier
The Daily Chronicle
The Daily Dispatch
The Daily Express
The Daily Guardian – Sydney
The Daily Mirror
The Daily News
The Daily News Perth WA
The Daily Sketch
The Evening Chronicle
The Evening News
The Exeter Glanfield Lawrence Gazette
The Jockey
The Leeds Mercury
The Leicester Mercury
The Mail
The Mail – Adelaide
The Manchester Evening Chronicle
The Manchester Evening News
The Melbourne Sporting Globe
The Melbourne Sun
The News of the World
The North Eastern Gazette
The Register News-Pictorial
The South Wales Echo
The Speedster - SA
The Speeway Gazzett
The Sporting Chronicle
The Sporting Globe

The Star
The Sun
The Sydney Herald
The Sunday Pictorial
The Sussex Daily News
The Ulster Gazette
The Wellington Evening Post
The Wolverhampton Express and Star
Vintage Speedway Magazine
Weekly Sporting Review

Brian Belton (2003) *Bluey Wilkinson* – Gloucestershire: Tempus
Brian Belton (2002) *Hammering Round* – Gloucestershire: Tempus
Tony Lethbridge (1989) *The Story of Exeter Speedway (Non-League Years 1929-1945)* -
    Exeter: Ali-kat Publications
Silver, L. (1969) *The Vital Cogs* (p29-30) in *The Speedway Annual* Compiled by Silver,
    L. and Douglas, P.: London - Pelham Books
WIMCA (1980) *Women's International* (Booklet written to commemorate Women's
    International Motorcycle Association Pearl Jubilee) - Micham:Francis Popley

Notes

1.   According to her death certificate Frances Helen 'Fay' Taylour, was born 5/4/1904, died third quarter 1983 in the Registration district of Weymouth: source General Register Office index for 5th April. The GRO index only shows the quarter in which the death occurred although it gives the date of birth. The US Social Security Death Index also lists Frances Taylour as being born on 5th April, 1904 and lists the death as August 1983 in Europe. This indicates that she had taken out American citizenship during her time in Hollywood.

2.   Fay's (immediate) family tree

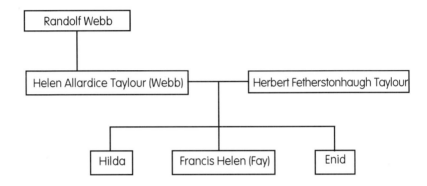

3.   Billy Lamont first saw light in Newcastle, New South Wales. Darling of the crowds from the day he started in the sport at Rutherford, (near Maitland) in his home state on an AJS in 1924, he was arguably the greatest of all the dirt-track riders of the early period in terms of pure 'thrill factor'. 'Cyclone Billy', a winner of the News of the World belt at Crystal Palace, was famous for his 'neck or nothing' style that made him the sensation of the first English season of speedway and of practically every country where speedway had gained a foothold. During his career he broke almost all Australian records and won many of the most prestigious titles. He came to England with International Speedways and held several track records that included an impressive performance at Stamford Bridge. When in action he was one of the most exciting of riders to watch, invariably smashing into the bends at full throttle. Although his worldwide activities interrupted Billy Lamont's English career, he rode for Wimbledon and Clapton League teams before joining Wembley in 1935, transferring to Nottingham in 1937. His best international match performance was in the second Test of 1932 for Australia, when his partnership with Dickey Case was unbeaten.

      A leg trailer and the original 'fence rider', a man who rode inches off the fence lap after lap and who could only ride with the throttle wide open, he didn't know what it meant to shut off! It has been said that Billy would often knock the programmes out of the spectator's hands if they were too close to the fence. Billy, whose proper name was not Billy but Wilfred, had his first initial 'W' mistaken for William (hence Bill and Billy) when listed in the programmes as W. Lamont. The name Billy stuck.

After serving his apprenticeship on NSW tracks Bill ended up in Brisbane, Queensland and, in 1928 he was a member of the original party of Australian riders to go to Britain under the guidance of A.J. Hunting. Others that went with him were Frank Arthur, Vic Huxley, Frank Pearce, Charlie Spinks, Dicky Smythe, Hillary Buchanan and Ben Unwin. During the seasons he rode in England he competed on 27 different tracks and was publicly voted the most popular rider in Speedway in 1929.

4.   Elder started racing in the USA and rapidly attained prominence on the big American tracks, securing many trophies and records. He came to England in 1928, with Johnnie Hoskins and his Australian riders. Sprouts was not just a star rider but a spectacular leg-trailer and he became one of the best known speedway names competing in England. He rode as a freelance before League racing was established, but turned out for West Ham, White City and Stamford Bridge later. Elder eventually joined the board of management at West Ham, but he still maintained his freelance approach to racing. On his retirement he became a Californian Highway Patrolman in 1935.

5.   Australia's Keith McKay is remembered for his participation in the first speedway meeting held in Britain at High Beech. He had travelled to Britain primarily to find a venue at which to stage speedway meetings himself. He was one of the people from whom Jack Hill-Bailey sought advice during his planning of the initial High Beech fixture.

   In 1927 McKay travelled from Sydney to Adelaide to find a site at which to stage a speedway meeting. In early February of that year he met with the Motor Sporting Club, and then approached the Royal Agricultural Society expressing his interest in using their Wayville Showground and became the organizer and manager of the first speedway meeting to be staged on the Wayville Showground (called the Speedway Royal) on 26 February, 1927. The Adelaide Advertiser reported: 'South Australians saw for the first time up-to-date motor cycle racing on a suitable banked track ....'

   McKay crashed while racing on the Sydney Showground on 22 December, 1928 and passed away nearly six weeks later.

6.   Many years later Bishop would ride for and manage West Ham Speedway. Bishop learnt the broadside at Lea Bridge but he first came to prominence in 1930, as the star of the High Beach side, and was almost unconquerable on his own track. He was one of the few men to defeat Vic Huxley in that year. From High Beach he went to Southampton, Clapton and Harringay. West Ham was to be Phil Bishop's last club. His eagerness was often his undoing: he had over four hundred crashes and escaped few League campaigns without injury. At the end of the 1936 season Phil fell and broke his leg. He lost his life in a motor accident, together with several West Ham riders, when travelling in Belgium in 1970. It was the most tragic of events, often called 'Speedway's Munich'.

7.   In 1978 Wolves Speedway celebrated its Golden Jubilee. When speedway began in the town, in a meeting organised by the Wolverhampton Dirt Track Motor Cycle Club, the big attraction was a match race between Sprouts Elder, legendary Californian, and Ivor Creek, holder of the Glasgow Golden Gauntlet. Unfortunately, Elder's machine failed to start and the crowd were left disappointed

8.   As can be seen F.R (Reg) Pointer had a good day in the solo event. He was amongst the most prominent English riders in the early period of speedway. He went on to ride for International Speedways and was a popular figure at Wimbledon and White City where he had good successes in handicap events. Pointer started out riding an Ariel but took up the Rudge Special later.

9.   Australian Frank Pearce took the World record for a 2 ¾ hp machine in November 1928, and was three times the winner of the Golden Helmet. Pearce probably had more experience of dirt-track racing than any other rider before 1930. After coming to England he met with a run of bad luck. Many times he was on the verge of a brilliant win, only to drop out as the result of mechanical problems with his bike, often involving broken chains.

10.   Hilary Buchanan was an Australian who came to the UK in 1928. He became popular at Wimbledon, White City, Harringay and other International Speedways tracks after acclimatising well to the small British circuits.

11.   Australian Ben Unwin was known for the extreme angles he attained in the bends. He won the Silver Wings at Harringay in August 1928 riding a Peashooter. He returned to Australia for the 1928-9 season.

12.   Noel Johnson was known as 'The Baby' because of his diminutive stature. The small Australian often drove recklessly into the bends but won a Golden Helmet on single-geared Peashooter

13.   Frank Arthur was born in Lismore, New South Wales. He started racing at an early age, but he had to wait until 1927 for success. It was in that year that he surprised everyone by winning the Golden Helmet in Australia when competing with some of the best-known riders. Arthur came to England and carried off many top trophies, including the Golden Helmet, which at one point he had won more than any other man.

14.   Gear Ratio Chart. Most riders carried this with them. Gearing was often adjusted higher or lower during the meeting to suit track conditions.

Rear Sprocket	Clutch	Engine	Crank Shaft	Gear Ratio
58	44	20	17	7.5
58	44	19	17	7.6
58	44	20	16	7.9
58	44	19	17	7.9
57	44	20	15	8.36
58	44	19	16	8.4
60	44	21	15	8.4
59	44	18	17	8.48
57	44	21	14	8.5
58	44	20	15	8.5
59	44	19	16	8.54
59	44	20	15	8.65
58	44	21	14	8.68
57	44	19	15	8.8
60	44	20	15	8.8
58	44	17	17	8.83
59	44	21	14	8.83
58	44	18	16	8.86
58	44	19	15	8.95
59	44	17	17	8.98
57	44	20	14	8.9
60	44	21	14	9.0
59	44	18	16	9.0
58	44	20	14	9.1
59	44	19	15	9.11
60	44	19	15	9.3
59	44	20	14	9.3
59	44	17	16	9.38
57	44	19	14	9.4

15.   If the ruling body of speedway at that time had not have been distracted by the TT racing Fay may never have been allowed to enter competition in the first place, by the time the members of the ACU got back to the mainland Taylour had established her capabilities.

16.   It is very likely that this is a mistake or the sum of handicaps Taylour received during an entire meeting

17.   Dean would become Australian Champion, but first started riding in the mid-1920s. He performed at most of the better-known tracks in Australia and in September 1927 broke the track record at the Speedway Royal, Sydney. He then came to the UK to ride for Dirt-Track Speedways Ltd and was to become one of the most popular riders at the West Ham track, winning many of the big handicaps and trophy races. He made the headlines when he broke the record for the Crystal Palace track. Dean had beaten the lean, flamboyant, larger than life, Sprouts Elder into second place in the Handicap, the great American Champion, possibly the biggest draw of his day, had lost a lot of time at the start. However, Elder made up for his misfortune by taking the main event of the day, the track Championship, winning the Golden Gauntlet.

18.   Pechar was known as, the 'American Crack'. He was born in Tarry Town, New York in 1901 and started racing at the age of 18. In 1926 he entered 27 races and won 23 of them. A year later, just before leaving for Britain, he held the American three and ten mile National dirt-track Championships on a half-mile track. The first time he appeared in England he broke both the Greenford and Stamford Bridge track records in a single day. During his short stay in England he rode with great success on most tracks and was well supported at Stamford Bridge

19.   Alec Jackson was a product of the north of England. He was appointed speedway manager at West Ham in 1931 and in 1932 he would become manager of Wembley Speedway. He was certainly the finest speedway manager that team ever knew, and arguably the finest in the history of the sport. This was recognised when he was given managerial control of the England test side.

20.   Byers was riding motorcycles in his native Sunderland at the age of 14, but learnt his profession at Middlesbrough in 1929. Later he rode for Newcastle and was a leading member of the Leeds team in 1931. Gordon reached his peak when he joined Wembley in 1932, where he began a high-scoring partnership with Ginger Lees; at the age of 19 he won the club's Championship and became England's youngest Test rider. Byers was to be picked for England again over the next two years. A leg injury and eye trouble caused by cinder dust set him back. Although he came back in 1936 he was forced to retire a year later.

21.   At the peak of his powers Kempster captained the British Speedway Team which competed against Australia. A 'Silver Sash' winner, Kempster skippered Wimbledon and won a Gold Helmet defeating Frank Arthur and Vic Huxley.

22.   Cliff Parkinson was a regular member of English test team. He started his racing at Middlesbrough and came to Wembley in 1930. He was also to ride with Clapton and Harringay before joining Hackney Wick in 1936. He spent most of his time as a mechanic assisting his brother Ronnie but returned to Wembley at the close of that season

23.   Fred Fearnley was a motorcycle dealer from Openshaw, famous for his track skills, who, in 1933, would take over the great Custom House track, home of the Speedway Hammers in East London under the auspices of West Ham (1933) Ltd. Stanley Greening joined Fearnley in 1934 and as a team they co-promoted the side. By the early fifties, then known as 'Major' Fearnley, he was the Speedway Control Board manager.

24.   Col Stewart would ride for Australian in the first ever test mach

25.   Australian Arthur Simcock was the first Team Manager of the Wolverhampton Speedway side (nicknamed the 'Wasps') when it entered league speedway for the first time ever in 1950. The promotion opted for the team to begin racing in the third division of the National League.

26.   Bert 'Baby Cyclone' Spencer was one of the most popular Australian riders with both spectators and fellow competitors. His career, which saw him race in Australia, Great Britain, the United States of America, and on the Continent, spanned four decades. Bert had no previous big track or road racing experience before making his debut at Davies Park on Thursday night, 15 September, 1927. The 19-year-old from the Brisbane suburb of Red Hill equipped himself well on his AJS. Over the next six months the young man continued to show promise on the tracks in and around Brisbane, although he was not always lucky in terms of the performance of his machines.

    Bert Spencer's life changed forever when an unexpected opportunity came his way during July,1928 and he travelled to take on the British speedways.

27.   The King's or Queen's prize is, as the name implies, the reigning Sovereign's prize for rifle shooting and was instituted at Bisley in the UK in 1860 by Queen Victoria. The prize she gave was then £250, nearly enough to buy a house. Each Australian State holds its own Queen's Prize as its annual Championship Prize Shoot.

28.   Claremont was to become an Australian citadel of speedway. The track is, and was then, a pair of long straights with two long turns known respectively as the 'Pits 'and 'Fowlhouse' bends. In 1927, Fowlhouse was referred to as the 'Poultry Yard' bend. Two and a half laps of the track were said to equal one mile. The cinder track was used from 1927 to 1936 with a break from the 1930 to 1932 season when Speedway moved to the WACA ground in East Perth.

    In 1936, the cinders track was removed and replaced with a hard packed clay and sand combination surface, with modified bends to facilitate higher speeds. That year, it was announced that, 'Owing to the big changes effected to the track, since racing was held here previously, former records have become obsolete'. On 19 December,1936 the three lap rolling start record was set by a visiting English rider, Wal Morton at 1 minute $14^4/_5$ seconds, probably mounted on a Rudge Special Speedway machine (with a JAP 500 cc Long Stroke engine running on alcohol). His average speed was $57^1/_2$ miles per hour.

    In 1977, the W.A. three lap record was held by Dud McKeon at 1 minute $7^2/_5$ seconds. The world record at Claremont was held by an English test rider, Doug Wyer, at 1 minute 4.3 seconds.

29.   Following early success with Sheffield, White City (Manchester), Leeds and the English Test team, Frank Charles disappeared from the limelight. Then in 1933, when a Belle Vue reserve, he won the Wembley Championship and broke the track record. He was transferred to Wembley in 1935 where he was almost unbeatable and won the League Riders Championship. He made the best score of the 1936 Test series and became the only rider to go through eighteen test heats undefeated. Charles, who would later die in a glider accident, was a wonderful rider but had a bad habit of looking back over his shoulder.

30.   Tommy Benstead was the first to suggest safety fences after the initial meetings at Maitland.

31.   As his moniker suggests, Charlie 'Daredevil' Spinks was one of the most audacious riders of the early days of speedway. In his first days in Britain, Spinks would break the lap record at Harringay (19.7 seconds) and win both the Silver Wheel and Silver Wings titles.

   Spinks had a spectacular and some said reckless way of broadsiding, which made him extremely popular at most big track meetings before 1930. In 1929 he would ride in 40 races, winning 18 (45%) and won the 'Home' Star Championship at Wimbledon on Monday 21 October, making him the first British Star Rider.

32.   Geoffrey Buzz Hibberd was born in Sydney and was an electrician by trade. Buzz at around six feet, was one of the tallest riders of his period. Hibberd came over to England from Australia in 1928 as a mechanic, but rode at West Ham showing himself to be a racer of great ability, winning the Golden Gauntlet in Glasgow and gaining good successes in handicap racing. He further illustrated his pedigree by defeating Frank Pearce and Dicky Smythe in match races.

   Hibberd died whilst wintering in Australia in 1929. His machine had seized solid and a fraction of a second later he was struck from behind by another rider and killed instantly.

33.   One of the best-known Vintage BSAs, whose forward-sloping engine started something of a trend in the design of big singles for several years.

34.   Scientific abbreviation for 'containing oxygen'

35.   Len Stewart was Bluey Wilkinson's mechanic when the Australian won the World Championship in 1938. On the night prior to this all-important meeting, Wilkinson crashed while racing at New Cross. He badly damaged a shoulder and, as he was in great pain on World Final night, had to rely heavily on the person who was on hand to help him in the pits - Len. Wilkinson was very aware of the contribution Stewart made to his success on that occasion as he thanked him over the public address system during the presentation ceremony.

   Stewart was one of the crowd favourites in his home State of Western Australia just a short while after starting out on the speedways. His spectacular performances at the Claremont Showground thrilled the fans. He was such a keen racer that he also competed in sidecar events. Stewart didn't confine his racing to the speedway track - in 1927 he was in the starting line-up for the famous Isle of Man Senior TT race.

   Stewart, riding a Norton, was in the first race witnessed by the 5,000 who were present at the opening meeting of the Wayville track in Adelaide

36.   Eric Langton, one of the world's greatest all round motorcyclists, this Yorkshireman, born in 1907, was a star almost from his first ride on the speedway. After captaining Leeds in 1929, he joined Belle Vue, leading the club to an unbroken run of success from 1934. He went on to be a top scorer of the thirties. In partnership with Jack Parker he won many matches. He secured the British Championship in 1932 and won the League Riders' Championship in the same year and was the runner-up in 1934. His second place in the 1936 World Championship was probably the most glorious, and the worst moment of his speedway career, having initially tied for first place.

   Langton rode Speedway all over the world, from England to Argentina, New Zealand and Australia between 1928 and 1947, when he retired at 40 years of age. He was married in 1934, the same year as he skippered the English Speedway Test Team on their Australian Tour, (a feat he repeated in 1935). In 1932, Eric had ridden a full season in New Zealand, taking two machines fitted with JAP engines with him from England.

The frames on these motorcycles were custom-made and were virtually a style prototype of the dirt track motorcycle used in contemporary speedway contests.

At the conclusion of the racing season in New Zealand, Langton returned to Melbourne and was asked to ride against a visiting American rider, Cordy Milne, who would be the Champion of the United States in 1934, 1935, 1947 and 1948 and finish third in the 1937 World Champion when his brother Jack took the title. Cordy, riding a JAP-Martin machine had been unbeaten in Australia. Langton defeated him in a match race.

In 1957, Langton moved from England to Applecross, Western Australia with his family and became a founding member of the Vintage Motor Cycle Club of W.A. with a great interest in Veteran machines.

37.   Evelyn Byrd was a famous aviator with the United States Navy. His success as a transatlantic naval aviator led him to be involved in Antarctic expeditions. In 1926 Byrd left the Navy to go on a privately sponsored expedition to the Arctic. Along with Floyd Bennett he reached the North Pole on 9 May,1926. They were both awarded medals of honour when they returned. It was the first flight over the North Pole.

38.   In 1930 Reg West would win an Australian Championship at the Melbourne Exhibition track (he held the Australian 2 mile Solo Championship in 1930).

39.   The Rogers and Hart musical 'A Yankee At The Court Of King Arthur' was staged at Daly's Theatre in London's Leicester Square (now the 9 screen, 2,475 seat Warner Cinema) in 1929, running for just 43 performances starting on 10 October.

40.   In her own writings Fay placed the stay with Cuthbert as taking place at the end of 1929 prior to her arrival back in the UK in May 1930. Like many personal reminiscences of the type, her memoirs include inconsistencies relative to other sources, but this section is particularly prone to contradiction. Firstly it cites her hospitalisation in Sydney following her racing accident which happened in February 1929. Secondly it precludes Taylour's successful and high profile (relative to her earlier visit to the country) two month 1930 stay in New Zealand, depicting her returning directly to Britain from Australia. These anomalies have motivated me to place Taylour's relationship with Cuthbert as starting prior to February 1929 and reaching its conclusion after her return to the UK in that year.

The apparent incongruities in this part of Taylour's writings might have been due to simple confusion, writing-up the events more than a quarter of a century after they took place, but it may also be a consequence of her efforts to accentuate or exaggerate her personal chronicle with an eye to breaking in to something akin to romantic fiction. She was ambitious to publish and at points had aspirations to create a film script based on her life. The most awkward aspect of her writing style was her propensity to place particular scenarios in a sequence that appears to be an effort to emphasise drama rather than adhere to any logical or chronological order! For all this, the episode of her life involving Cuthbert is the only part of Taylour's writings that has been relocated to fit actual events and as such represents a minimal intrusion into Fay's version of events.

41.   Tauser won the Star National Speedway Championship whilst with Wimbledon in 1931.

42.   Australian hard man, Max (Maximillian Octavius) Grosskreutz was the son of a Queensland farmer. He first took to the track at Brisbane and won the Australian Championship in 1928. After a year with Lea Bridge, he joined Belle Vue in 1930. He had a superlative Test record, riding in all 42 matches until mid-1936, when he suffered his only serious accident. Max retired at the end of that year with easily the highest ever score of all the internationals (Australians or Englishmen). He went on to become

a member of the Australian selection committee and manager of Norwich. He alwaysrode with a characteristic, sweeping style. He was an exceptionally clever technician, and popularised the short-wheelbase machine.

43. Jack Ormston was North countryman who started his racing career at Middlesbrough in 1929. He rose to captain Wembley and in 1930 won the London championship and was 2nd in the League rider's charts. He rode for England in 1930 and 1931 and twice in 1932. He won league honours with Wembley three times and the National Cup twice. He was also part of the sides that won the London Cup twice. He retired in 1933 but came back to assist Birmingham in 1934 before joining Harringay.

44. George Greenwood had a glorious partnership with Harry Whitfield riding for Wembley in that club's best years. A Yorkshireman, George was winning Championships in the north at just 17 years of age. He joined Wembley in 1929. In 1931 he rose from his sick bed to win all his races in Wembley's most difficult Cup match of that term. Attached to Nottingham in 1933, he returned to Wembley in 1934, but sustained an arm injury. Again in Nottingham's colours he won the Provincial League Riders' Championship in 1936 and came back to Wembley in 1937. After a spell with Hackney Wick, he took on the responsibility of captaincy at Nottingham.

45. In 1929 at the County Ground Stadium, Exeter held its first meeting of Motorcycle Speedway and became the home of the Exeter 'Falcons' Speedway Club. Freddie Hore and Bert Spencer became the first two riders to try the track during a demonstration on 2 March 1929.

46. Richard 'Buggie' Fleeman rode for Exeter Riders in 1929. He passed away in 1995.

47. Atkinson had learnt to ride a motorcycle at the age of thirteen. He had competed in grass-track and rough riding races before taking to the cinders at Blackpool in 1928. The next year he was Yorkshire Champion, and captain of Leeds. Arthur won the West Australian title that winter, then joined Wembley in 1930, but a crash, after which he was unconscious for three weeks, began a run of bad luck. He gradually regained his form on joining West Ham in 1932, after a short time with York. Atkinson became a Test rider in 1936, making two Australian tours. In the latter part of his career he took up farming.

Arthur Atkinson was in the finest form of his career during 1939. He was selected for the Test series, turning out for England four times. In the first test he clocked up an 18-point maximum and in the third match he was his country's highest scorer, making a dozen points. He was to make double figures in the other two tests, averaging 12.75 for the series, just short of top scorer Bill Kitchen.

In the World Championship Atkinson was amongst the leading qualifiers, holding 6 bonus points for Wembley, just two less than 'Cowboy' Cordy Milne and one short of the estimable Kitchen, Lamoreaux and Langton. Although Milne was a clear favourite, there were many who reckoned that Atkinson's form during the year could take him to the title. However, there was to be no Final in 1939.

48. In 1927 the second event on the programme organized at the Wayville track was the contest for the Silver Gauntlet. The trophy was a brown leather gauntlet bearing a silver inscription. The winner would receive five pounds per week until he was defeated. The programme finished with two heats and a final of a match race contest. Frank Duckett was the winner of the Final defeating Frank Mitchell.

Frank Duckett's name appears on the Australian Championship winners' list. It was at the Wayville venue he recorded his victory in February of 1929. He defeated Paddy Dean and Tommy Benstead in the Final. Duckett also finished in third place in the Australian

Championship staged in January of 1931 at the Melbourne Motordrome. He also made the trip to Britain to compete during the early years of speedway. At the conclusion of the 1929 British season, AJ Hunting put together a team of riders to tour South America which included Max Grosskreutz, Frank Duckett and Buzz Hibberd.

49.   Dick Wise was born in 1909 in Adelaide. He had a lot of misfortune early in his career but in 1930 became a test rider. However in 1931 he broke a leg and the following year a collar bone and another broken leg. He was hurt on visits to Denmark and was injured once more in Buenos Aires in 1934. Wise was with Plymouth in 1934 and was captain of Norwich in 1937.

50.   James Allan 'Jim' Mollison was a famous pioneer airplane pilot. Born on the 19 April, 1905 in Glasgow, Mollison was to set many records during the rapid development of aviation in the 1930s.

       During one of his flights, he was matched with the equally famous pilot Amy Johnson, whom he proposed to only 8 hours after meeting her, and while still in the air. Johnson accepted; they married on July of 1932, and she went off to break her husband's England to South Africa record. They were dubbed the flying sweethearts by the press and public.

       The Mollisons' marriage became strained by the effects of being rivals for the same aviation records, and also because Jim had a drinking problem, and they were divorced in 1938.

       Jim Mollison later settled in London and ran a public house. He died on October 30, 1959.

51.   Clem Cort was an English rider who started his racing career as a young man. Unlike some of his contemporaries he was not superstitious, often riding in green whilst at White City. He won the *News of the World* Belt and was one of a group of racers that went to Cairo to compete during the British winter of 1928-9.

52.   Maori - Welcome! Come! Woman to be held in awe.

53.   This is incorrect as Taylour had ridden in Western Springs the previous season, although during a much more low profile tour.

54.   Tom Morgan was the Sports Editor of *The People* and one of the few writers in Fleet Street to take an active interest in speedway racing. Morgan was one of a tiny band of journalists who could claim specialist knowledge of the sport. It is unfortunately true that the experienced speedway journalists in Britain, in the immediate post World War 2 period, could be counted on the fingers of one hand. Morgan had been identified with the sport since its birth in the UK. It was hoped that his article would explain to many of the 'girls' who had written to Speedway Gazette shortly after World War Two why there was 'little hope of women's speedway racing being revived'.

55.   Born 5 July, 1899 in Norwich, Arthur Elvin left school aged fourteen and tried numerous jobs before joining the Royal Flying Corps during World War 1. He was later shot down over France and spent two years as a prisoner of war.

       His association with Wembley started in 1924, working as an assistant in a tobacco kiosk at the British Empire Exhibition. After its closure, he made his fortune by buying up and clearing out the derelict pavilions one by one, and selling off the scrap materials. When the stadium went into liquidation, Elvin quickly raised sufficient backing to buy up the complex, becoming managing director of Wembley Stadiums Ltd in 1927. His next move was to persuade the board to build a multi-purpose indoor sports arena to complement the main stadium. The result was the Empire Pool and Sports Arena, later known simply as Wembley Arena, which opened its doors in 1934.

Having promoted new sports such as greyhound racing and speedway in the stadium, Elvin introduced ice hockey to a wider British public and within a couple of years, two further large arenas were constructed in the London area, at Harringay and Earls Court. All three of the London arenas were capable of seating eight thousand spectators.

Arthur Elvin was made a Member of the British Empire in 1945 and received his knighthood from King George VI in 1947. He died at sea, on a cruise to South Africa, on 4 February 1957

56.   Fay might have been confusing this with a later race planned to take place at Brooklands in 1932 (see p194) as she was in Australia at the time the Wembley Women's Event of 1930 was organised.